THE BODILY NATURE

OF CONSCIOUSNESS

The Bodily Nature of Consciousness

✦ SARTRE AND
CONTEMPORARY
PHILOSOPHY OF MIND

KATHLEEN WIDER

Cornell University Press   ITHACA AND LONDON

First published 1997 by Cornell University Press.

Printed in the United States of America

Cornell University Press strives to utilize environmentally responsible suppliers and materials to the fullest extent possible in the publishing of its books. Such materials include vegetable-based, low-VOC inks and acid-free papers that are also either recycled, totally chlorine-free, or partly composed of nonwood fibers.

Cloth printing   10 9 8 7 6 5 4 3 2 1
Paperback printing   10 9 8 7 6 5 4 3 2 1

Library of Congress Cataloging-in-Publication Data

Wider, Kathleen Virginia, 1944–
    The bodily nature of consciousness : Sartre and contemporary
philosophy of mind / Kathleen Wider.
        p.   cm.
    Includes bibliographical references and index.
    ISBN 0-8014-3395-9 (cloth : alk. paper).—ISBN 0-8014-8502-9 (pbk. : alk. paper)
    1. Sartre, Jean Paul, 1905–1980. L'Etre et le néant. 2. Sartre, Jean
Paul, 1905–1980—Contributions in philosophy of consciousness.
3. Consciousness. I. Title.
B2430.S33E8384   1997
126'.092—dc21

                                                              97-16989

FOR PATRICIA AND CHARLES,

intellectual companions of my youth

Contents

Acknowledgments

I first began to think about Sartre's analysis of consciousness in light of recent work on consciousness by analytic philosophers during a National Endowment for the Humanities Summer Seminar I attended in 1985. It was given by Sydney Shoemaker, and the topic was self-consciousness and self-reference. I thank the members of that seminar for both stimulating and refining my thinking about the relationship between phenomenologically based accounts of consciousness and the accounts given by analytic philosophers of mind. I am especially grateful to Natika Newton for the numerous conversations both during the course of that seminar as well as in the years since. She has always provided me with rich material for thought as well as encouragement and useful challenges.

Over the last several years, I have presented papers at the Sartre Society of North America meetings as well as at the Sartre Circle meetings held in conjunction with the meetings of the Eastern division of the American Philosophical Association. I thank the members of the Sartre Society for their interest and support of my work and for their extremely helpful critical responses to it. My special thanks go to Phyllis Morris, who as one of the founders of the Sartre Society and as organizer of the Sartre Circle helped provide me with a forum for my work. Her own work as well as her thoughtful response to mine have been invaluable to me.

In addition I am grateful to my students, both those in the independent study class on consciousness I offered in the summer of 1994 and those in my philosophy of mind and existentialism classes. Their questions and comments contributed to my ongoing attempts to rethink and clarify my understanding of various philosophers' views on consciousness and my response to those views.

An earlier version of Chapter 3 titled "The Failure of Self-Consciousness in Sartre's *Being and Nothingness*" appeared in *Dialogue: Canadian Philosophical Review* 32 (1993): 737–56. This article will be reprinted in the Garland Series on Sartre. An earlier version of Chapter 4 titled "Sartre and the Long-Distance Truck Driver" also appeared in the *Journal of the British Society for Phenomenology* 24 (October 1993): 232–49. I thank the editors of these two journals for their permission to reprint this material.

I also thank my editors at Cornell University Press—Alison Shonkwiler, Carol Betsch, and Nancy J. Malone—for keeping me informed at each stage of the review and editing process, for giving helpful suggestions for improving the manuscript, and for their quick replies to my numerous questions. I am grateful to the readers of the manuscript for their evaluations of the initial version. The final version is stronger because of their advice. Finally, my thanks go to my family and friends, especially Joseph Catalano and Lori Wider, whose encouragement kept me going during the years needed to complete this project.

K. V. W.

THE BODILY NATURE

OF CONSCIOUSNESS

Introduction

The last decade has brought a tremendous resurgence of interest in the nature of consciousness. Philosophers, psychologists, and neuroscientists are attempting, in various ways, to understand consciousness: its nature, its importance, its foundation in neuronal activity. During this same decade there has been a revival of interest in the philosophy of Jean-Paul Sartre. That revival has focused primarily on the political and ethical philosophy of the later Sartre. The goal of this book is to bring together the renewed interest in the nature of consciousness and the revival of interest in Sartrean philosophy. By examining Sartre's analysis of consciousness in *Being and Nothingness* in light of the present work on consciousness, I intend to show both the value of his study of human consciousness and its inherent flaws. In particular I am interested in exploring the meaning and use Sartre makes of his fundamental claim about consciousness: that all consciousness is, by its very nature, self-consciousness. The belief in the reflexivity of consciousness is one whose history reaches back at least as far as Descartes. It is a belief that for centuries has seemed self-evident to the vast majority of philosophers. In *Being and Nothingness*, Sartre has shown with a great deal of subtlety, wit, and detail the power and consequences of such a belief. Sartre's claim that all consciousness is self-consciousness is central to his entire analysis of being. Indeed, I argue that it is *the* foundational claim in *Being and Nothingness*, the one that grounds all the other major claims Sartre defends in the work.

I

This belief in the reflexivity of consciousness has, however, come under attack in recent years. The ongoing findings of experimental psychologists and neuroscientists have been used, with greater and greater frequency, by philosophers of mind, especially in the analytic tradition, to undermine this most basic of claims about the nature of consciousness. D. M. Armstrong, for example, in his now classic discussion of consciousness in *The Nature of Mind* distinguishes perceptual from introspective consciousness and argues it is possible to have the one without the other. More recently philosophers such as Fred Dretske and Stephen L. White have argued that consciousness does not always involve self-consciousness. Perhaps the best-known philosophic opponents of the Cartesian belief in the reflexivity of consciousness are Patricia Churchland and Paul Churchland.[1] The debate over the truth or falsity of this claim about the human mind and its access to itself continues to be intense among analytic philosophers as well as among scientists. The debate, however, proceeds with seemingly little awareness of the extensive study of consciousness engaged in by Continental philosophers during the first half of the century. John Searle, for example, says: "We ought to allow ourselves to be struck by the implications of the fact that at any point in a man's conscious life he knows without observation the answer to the question, 'What are you now doing?' Many philosophers have noted this fact but none, to my knowledge, have explored its implications for Intentionality."[2] The analysis Sartre offers in *Being and Nothingness* of the reflexivity of consciousness belies Searle's claim.

I offer in this work an exploration of Sartre's use and defense of the claim that all consciousness is self-consciousness, arguing that serious problems exist with Sartre's defense of his central thesis. But I go on to try and save Sartre's claim by taking very seriously Sartre's belief that it is the body which is the subject of consciousness. Appealing to the work of those analytic philosophers of mind who remember that it is the body which is the subject of consciousness, as well as utilizing the work of empirical psychology and neuroscience, I contend that exploring what it means to say that it is the body which is conscious will reveal ways to save the deep-seated intuition that all consciousness is self-consciousness.[3] In other words I offer a way to overcome many of the problems in Sartre's defense of this fundamental thesis. But my aim in this book is not simply to examine Sartre's analysis of human consciousness in *Being and Nothingness* and to attempt to save his central thesis about consciousness. My primary concern is not with defending Sartre but with defending a position he has developed through phenomenology that helps to illuminate the nature of consciousness. I hope to show that science-based accounts of consciousness can strengthen and clarify Sartre's phenomenology-based account of consciousness. In appealing to the work of certain analytic philosophers as well as to that of scientists, I attempt to show, contra Sartre, how phenomenology and science can *both* be useful in our search for a fuller understanding of consciousness.

My approach to Sartre is not the traditional one. I do not examine his claim about the self-consciousness of consciousness in the context of his entire corpus, narrowing my focus to *Being and Nothingness* and to this one claim about consciousness as it is advanced in that work. Even more narrowly, I look at Sartre's belief in the reflexivity of consciousness primarily as he works it out at the level of pre-reflective and reflective consciousness. I ignore almost completely the self-consciousness involved in our existence for others, and hence I do not discuss the social dimension of consciousness. It is of course this latter dimension that unfolds in more and more detail in Sartre's later work; I ignore this aspect because I think it is grounded in a more primary (and in a sense a more primitive) form of self-consciousness that is rooted in the body. This book is directed toward an analysis of that form of self-consciousness. It is an examination of that form that I argue can save Sartre's analysis of consciousness in *Being and Nothingness*. I depart from a more traditional approach to Sartre in other ways as well. I examine his discussion and defense of the translucency of consciousness outside the context of the work of his immediate predecessors in both philosophy and psychology, many of whom exerted a direct influence on him.[4] Much work has already been done in that area. Nor do I discuss Sartre's work in light of those who are his more obvious descendants, for example, postmodern European philosophers.

My aim is to examine Sartre's defense of the self-consciousness of consciousness in light of recent work on consciousness rather than in light of recent scholarship on Sartre.[5] The accounts of consciousness that predominate at present, at least in the Anglo-American tradition, are purely objective ones, and phenomenology is thought to have little if anything to contribute to their development. The prevailing belief is that consciousness can be fully explained by an objective, scientific account.[6] This is, of course, at direct odds with Sartre's stance. A growing number of contemporary philosophers in Britain and the United States, however, are beginning to remember that it is the body which is the subject of consciousness, and it is this belief, I think, that renders them more sensitive to the contribution phenomenology can make to our understanding of consciousness. But there is little, if any, reference by these philosophers to the work of such phenomenologists as Sartre or Merleau-Ponty. What references exist are only very rare and brief. Although Sartre's analysis of consciousness in *Being and Nothingness* is one of the central ones in the phenomenological tradition, the details of it are unfamiliar to most philosophers outside that tradition. This book attempts to go some way toward rectifying this situation. I hope, therefore, that it will be of use not only to those interested in Sartre but to anyone interested in understanding the nature of consciousness.

I wish to provide the reader with a brief overview of the chapters that follow along with my rationale for proceeding in the way I do. Chapter 1 seeks to establish the importance in Western philosophy of the belief that all consciousness is self-consciousness and to place Sartre within the tradition of those who defend this belief. To that end I explore Descartes's, Locke's, and Kant's defenses of this claim. I focus on what Sartre's analysis of this claim shares in common with these predecessors and how it diverges from their analyses of this same claim. I choose just three of the numerous philosophers in the Western tradition who accept this claim about consciousness because I think it better to present in some detail the positions of three major philosophers rather than to run briefly over the views of many. And these three in particular set the stage for the discussion and defense of this claim in the nineteenth and twentieth centuries, and hence they influence philosophers who in turn influenced Sartre.[7]

Chapter 2 shows the foundational role the claim that all consciousness is self-consciousness plays in *Being and Nothingness*. Once the fundamental importance of this claim to Sartre's analysis of consciousness is established, it becomes clear how devastating to Sartre's entire analysis a failure to support his central claim would be. I examine in detail the role this central claim plays in each section of *Being and Nothingness*, not simply to establish its importance but also to acquaint those not familiar with Sartre's work with some of the basic points in his analysis of consciousness that must be understood to follow my critique of his view and my attempt to construct a way to save it.[8] In discussions with analytic philosophers, it became clear to me that even those who had some familiarity with *Being and Nothingness* did not understand central points in Sartre's analysis. This was true, for example, of Sartre's belief that the

Law of Identity fails to apply to the for-itself. This is the most important claim to follow from Sartre's belief in the reflexivity of consciousness, and yet it is an assertion that can baffle even those who are receptive to Sartre's analysis. I hope that Chapter 2 makes such points more intelligible to readers with little or no familiarity with Sartre's work.[9]

In Chapter 3 I engage in what I call an internal critique of Sartre's claim that all consciousness is self-consciousness. I do so by tracing Sartre's unraveling of this position about consciousness. In *Being and Nothingness* Sartre describes the various types of self-consciousness involved in our existence for ourselves as well as our existence for others. I examine these various modes of self-consciousness, focusing particularly on the self-consciousness of reflective and pre-reflective consciousness. Relying primarily on analysis and argument offered by Sartre on these topics throughout *Being and Nothingness*, I attempt to construct a coherent explanation of each type of self-consciousness. I conclude that Sartre has no unambiguous account of reflective and pre-reflective consciousness that allows him to maintain the distinction he wishes to make between various types of self-consciousness at the pre-reflective and reflective levels.

In Chapter 4 I examine evidence from contemporary research in neuroscience and psychology that appears to undermine the belief that all consciousness is self-consciousness. I utilize this evidence to develop an external critique of Sartre's thesis about the nature of consciousness. In examining three prima facie counterexamples to his claim that all consciousness is self-consciousness, I try to construct ways that Sartre might diffuse these counterexamples. My contention is that those ways fail.

I take a different tack in Chapter 5. Rather than turning to the actual text of *Being and Nothingness* for resources to defend Sartre's central claim about consciousness, I look beyond that work—to the work of philosophers as well as scientists who follow out the implications of the belief that it is the body which is the subject of consciousness. I argue that there are good reasons to think that at the level of bodily intentionality— at the level of perception and action as the most basic modes of the body's presence to the world—there is always a consciousness of self. That consciousness is a consciousness of one's body. And if one takes the most basic level of self-consciousness to be bodily self-awareness, one is in a much better position to defend the belief that self-consciousness is a part of the very nature of all consciousness. Sartre's denial that physiological processes contribute anything to consciousness, coupled

with his refusal to allow evidence from biology or neuroscience to contribute anything to our *understanding* of consciousness, bars him from
utilizing the kind of support for his thesis that I appeal to in this chapter.
But I contend that his refusal to accept such evidence shows he has
forgotten that it is the body which is the subject of consciousness. If he
had followed out the implications of that belief, he would have had much
stronger support for his belief in the reflexivity of consciousness. I argue
that it is because there is a form of self-consciousness present even in
our most primary contact with the world, our contact with it as sensorimotor organisms, that the intuition that all consciousness is self-
consciousness is so strong and deep rooted in Western philosophy.
Despite recent attacks on it, this intuition persists for many.[10]

By way of conclusion, in Chapter 6 I offer suggestions for ways of
using the notion of bodily self-consciousness developed in Chapter
5 to shore up some of Sartre's analysis of consciousness in *Being and
Nothingness* and to overcome some of the problems with that analysis
that I raised in Chapters 3 and 4. Although I argue that bodily self-
consciousness will not in the end serve to ground the kind of freedom
Sartre claims characterizes human consciousness, it does indirectly
ground a more limited notion of human freedom. And it certainly can
be used to ground the self-consciousness of consciousness. It is Sartre's
belief that self-consciousness is a defining feature of consciousness that
constitutes the scaffolding on which Sartre builds his analysis of consciousness in *Being and Nothingness*.

A last note on my methodology: I examine Sartre's work in light of
and in interaction with the work of many other thinkers because I believe
that philosophy is, as Socrates called it so long ago, a conversation. Thus
I approach Sartre as one figure in the midst of many others, all of whom
are engaged in a long and enduring conversation about the nature of
human consciousness. That is why this work is in some sense less a book
about Sartre and more a book about consciousness.

The Tradition

The view of consciousness which holds that consciousness cannot exist without being aware of its existence began with Descartes and finds its fullest development in Sartre. On this view consciousness is always self-consciousness. It is in Descartes that we find this thesis first articulated in modern form. It is an essential part of what Gilbert Ryle has called "the official doctrine" of the mind, a doctrine that springs, on Ryle's view, at least in part from Descartes's philosophy. There can be nothing presently in the stream of consciousness of which "the mind whose life is that stream might be unaware."[1] I wish to make it clear at the outset, however, that although I claim Sartre culminates a line of philosophers whose traditional view of consciousness goes back at least as far as Descartes, I am not contending that Sartre is in total agreement with the Cartesian analysis of consciousness. No, although a residue of Cartesianism remains in Sartre's analysis, he takes his analysis to differ in many important respects from the Cartesian one. In fact one of the targets of Sartre's account of consciousness in *Being and Nothingness* is Descartes. The exact nature of the differences between Sartre and Descartes will become clear in later chapters as I explore what Sartre means by the claim that all consciousness is self-consciousness. My purpose here is simply to place Sartre within a tradition, one now under careful scrutiny and indeed under attack on many fronts. It is Sartre's contention in *Being and Nothingness* that all consciousness is self-consciousness, which ties him to this tradition and leaves his analysis vulnerable to many of the attacks against the traditional view now being mounted by cognitive scientists.

DESCARTES

Descartes maintains in the First Replies to the objections raised against his *Meditations on First Philosophy* that "there can be nothing within me [as a thinking thing] of which I am not in some way aware."[2] He reiterates this view again in the Fourth Replies. "The fact that there can be nothing in the mind, in so far as it is a thinking thing, of which it is not aware . . . seems to me to be self-evident. . . . We cannot have any thought of which we are not aware at the very moment when it is in us."[3] In defining *thought* in the Second Replies, Descartes says: "I use this term to include everything that is within us in such a way that we are immediately aware of it. Thus all the operations of the will, the intellect, the imagination and the senses are thoughts."[4] It is because he defines thought in this way that Descartes claims in article 19 of part 1 of *The Passions of the Soul* "that we cannot will anything without thereby perceiving that we are willing it."[5] He makes this same claim in his letter to Mersenne, 28 January 1641: "For we cannot will anything without knowing that we will it."[6] He makes a similar claim in the Fifth Replies: "For does anyone who understands something not perceive that he does so?"[7] How are we to understand the quotes given above? What is it exactly that Descartes is claiming about the nature of thought?[8]

Robert McRae interprets statements like these as evidence that for Descartes all thought is self-conscious. That interpretation seems indisputable. What Descartes means by that claim still needs clarification, however. For McRae, Descartes's maintaining that thought is always conscious of itself makes explicit his adherence to the belief that "all consciousness of anything involves consciousness of the self as being conscious of that thing. . . . [For Descartes] all consciousness is self-consciousness."[9] But what does that claim come to for Descartes?

There are at least two different ways of interpreting Descartes's claim about consciousness. On one reading Descartes is interpreted as maintaining that every act of consciousness is accompanied by a second act of consciousness. The first act of consciousness has for its object a table, for example, and the second act has the first act of consciousness for its object. Bernard Williams in *Descartes: The Project of Pure Enquiry* is an example of a commentator who reads Descartes in this first way. He thinks the Cartesian claim about consciousness is a result of Descartes's confusing mere consciousness with reflexive consciousness.[10] Williams argues that for Descartes "all conscious processes . . . must themselves be the objects of a reflexive consciousness."[11] Seeing, which is the example of a conscious process that Williams uses to illustrate his point, involves, on the Cartesian analysis, not only seeing Lloyd George, for example, and seeing *that* Lloyd George is present but also judging reflexively that *one*(self) is seeing Lloyd George.[12] For Williams, Descartes's belief that all consciousness is self-consciousness is the belief that every act of consciousness involves the making of a reflexive judgment about oneself.

But there is another way to read Descartes's claim that links it directly to Sartre's claim in *Being and Nothingness* that all consciousness is self-consciousness. On this reading, Descartes is seen as holding that every act of consciousness is one with a consciousness of itself. Richard E. Aquila gives this reading of Descartes. Aquila contends that for Descartes perception and consciousness of perception are one and the same. For example, in the case where what one is conscious of is an external object, one's consciousness of oneself as conscious of a particular external object is not distinct from one's consciousness of that external object. According to Aquila, "Descartes proposes an *identification* of a certain kind of self-or inner-directed consciousness and a certain kind of cognition or perception of which it is a consciousness."[13] In other words, Descartes identifies consciousness with self-consciousness.[14] For Aquila this identification is at least implicit in Descartes, although he acknowledges that Descartes never developed the implications of it. Aquila thinks that "the most elaborate attempt at a formulation" of this identification of consciousness with self-consciousness may be Sartre's in *Being and Nothingness*.[15]

It is this second reading of Descartes's claim that all consciousness is self-consciousness which has the most textual support. Williams's reading of Descartes's position overlooks an important distinction that other commentators have argued is present, at least implicitly, in Descartes's work.[16]

The distinction between implicit knowledge and consciousness, on the one hand, and explicit knowledge and consciousness, on the other, is one that complicates and makes more subtle Descartes's claim that all consciousness is self-consciousness. It also ties the Sartrean analysis of consciousness more closely to the Cartesian tradition.[17] In an essay on innate ideas in Descartes, McRae details both the distinction Descartes draws between implicit and explicit knowledge and the use Descartes makes of it in answering his objectors. McRae points out that when accused in the Second and Fifth Objections of having deduced the *cogito ergo sum* from the general principle 'Everything that thinks exists', Descartes responds that we learn general principles from knowledge of particulars. Hence the *cogito ergo sum* is known by a primitive act of knowledge and is not deduced from the general principle. In section 10 of part I of *Principles*, however, Descartes maintains that when he asserted that the *cogito ergo sum* is the first and most certain belief that confronts one who philosophizes, he did not deny that one must first know, among other things, the general principle that everything which thinks exists. McRae refers to *Conversations with Burman*, in which Burman asks Descartes whether his assertion in the Second Replies that the *cogito ergo sum* rests on no syllogistic reasoning is consistent with his holding in the *Principles* that the general principle that everything which thinks exists is known before its application in the particular case. Descartes's response to Burman relies, as McRae makes clear, on the drawing of a distinction between implicit and explicit knowledge. My knowledge of the general principle is only implicit, so although it is presupposed and prior to my knowledge of the particular case, it is not made explicit prior to my explicit knowledge of the particular claim. According to Descartes, the reason for this is because I pay attention only to what is within me and hence direct attention to the *cogito ergo sum* but not to the general principle that everything which thinks exists.[18]

McRae also explains how Descartes utilizes the distinction between implicit and explicit knowledge in his discussion of certain ideas. McRae refers again to *Conversations with Burman*, in which Descartes claims that knowledge of the idea of God is implicitly present in one's explicit knowledge of one's imperfection. That is, one cannot have explicit knowledge of one's imperfection without having implicit knowledge of God (a perfect being), because all lack presupposes that of which it is a lack. On McRae's readings of these passages, Descartes is concerned with the transition from the implicit to the explicit within 'experience' or 'consciousness'. Descartes's entire activity in the first four *Meditations* of extracting the concepts of 'thing', 'thought', 'truth', 'substance', 'God', and 'freedom' is that of directing attention to or reflecting on what I am pre-reflectively conscious of in the cogito.

McRae supports this reading of Descartes by referring to the Sixth Replies, which begin with the assertion that the knowledge of what thought and existence are, a knowledge necessary for one's knowledge of one's own existence, is known not by reflective knowledge or by knowledge of reflective knowledge but "by means of that internal awareness which always precedes reflective knowledge." As McRae points out, for Descartes, each person has an implicit knowledge of the concepts necessary for knowledge of *cogito ergo sum* "from the mere fact that he thinks and is conscious of thinking." The self-consciousness of thought underlies implicit as well as explicit knowledge. According to McRae the distinction between implicit and explicit knowledge (and consciousness) of oneself is central to Descartes's notion of innate ideas. I am always implicitly conscious of myself for Descartes, but I can also become explicitly conscious of myself through reflection, and in that way I can come to explicit knowledge of innate ideas.[19]

Continuing his exposition of this reading of Descartes in his essay "Descartes' Definition of Thought," McRae claims that for Descartes "being conscious of what is occurring in the mind is not the same as thinking of what is occurring in the mind." To support his reading of Descartes, McRae points to an apparent inconsistency in Descartes's remarks, an inconsistency that can be resolved if one attributes to Descartes the drawing of a distinction between consciousness and reflection. McRae notes that in reply to an objection raised by Burnam, Descartes implies that "thought is not something of which we are *always* conscious." How are we to make that view consistent with Descartes's remark in the Fourth Replies that there can be no thought in us of which we are not conscious at the moment it is in us? McRae argues that the only way to reconcile these two apparently conflicting claims about thought is to see in Descartes a distinction between *consciousness and reflection*. Thought is always conscious of itself, but one does not always reflect on one's thought. I think the distinction is more clearly captured by referring to it as the distinction between *pre-reflective and reflective consciousness* rather than between consciousness and reflection, because Descartes clearly identifies reflection with consciousness in the passage McRae cites from *Conversations with Burnam*. This brings Sartre even closer to Descartes. On this reading Descartes would be seen as holding that although we are always pre-reflectively conscious of our thought, we are not always reflectively conscious of it. For Descartes that requires an act of attention, as McRae points out: "Explicit knowledge, that which we get from attending to what we are conscious of as being in ourselves is, then, the *clear and distinct perception* of what we are pre-reflectively conscious of."

McRae argues that attributing this distinction to Descartes allows one to reconcile Descartes's claim that many people are ignorant of their own beliefs with his claim that there is nothing in the mind of which it is not conscious. Ignorance, on this reading of Descartes, is associated with lack of explicit knowledge of one's beliefs. Descartes's explanation of why people can be ignorant of their beliefs even though consciousness is self-consciousness accords with McRae's reading of Descartes. As McRae notes, Descartes points out in *Discourse on Method* that believing and knowing one believes are two different mental acts, and so one can exist without the other. Hence one can be in ignorance of what one believes because one has failed to reflect on or attend to one's beliefs. Given the distinction between consciousness and reflection (or pre-reflective and reflective consciousness), Descartes can still maintain that belief as a kind of thinking is self-conscious and yet the person whose belief it is may lack reflective knowledge of his or her belief.[20]

In her book on Descartes, Margaret Wilson, in discussing Descartes's view of consciousness, grants that he distinguishes between implicit and explicit knowledge and between reflective and non-reflective cognition. But she disagrees with McRae in thinking that these distinctions allow Descartes to resolve all the inconsistencies which arise from his holding *both* that there is nothing in us as thinking things of which we are not conscious and that we can be ignorant of much that is in us as thinking things. In particular Wilson argues "that Descartes does not provide a coherent account of how we are both 'conscious of all that is in us' and possibly ignorant of mathematics and metaphysics." Nonetheless, she does grant the presence in Descartes of the distinctions on which McRae focuses. In her discussion of these distinctions, she attempts to make clear the connection between knowledge and consciousness in Descartes. In reviewing McRae's discussion of the distinctions Descartes uses to resolve inconsistency between certain claims he makes in his work, I left vague the relationship between the distinction he draws between implicit and explicit knowledge and between pre-reflective and reflective consciousness. Indeed, I occasionally used the two distinctions interchangeably. Wilson's discussion of the relationship between consciousness and knowledge in Descartes helps to clarify this relationship. She remarks that "it is hard to know what being conscious of x could be, if it did not in *some* way involve having knowledge of x—knowing that x exists or occurs. And it is clear that Descartes does regard the concepts of consciousness and knowledge as, at least, closely connected." In explicating what is involved in Descartes's claim that we are conscious of every thought in us, she quotes passages in which Descartes seems to treat as equivalent 'to be conscious of' and 'to know that'. This identification between consciousness and knowledge or at least the close connection between the two is reinforced by her argument that Descartes's distinction between implicit and explicit knowledge is *not* the distinction between actual and potential consciousness (a distinction he uses in the Third Meditation with regard to faculties of the mind). For Descartes, consciousness is involved with both explicit and implicit knowledge. Given this Cartesian view, the distinction between implicit and explicit knowledge is either equivalent to or closely connected with the distinction between pre-reflective and reflective consciousness.[21]

If we read Descartes as holding that knowledge and consciousness are closely connected, then, for Descartes, it is because we are pre-reflectively conscious of all our thoughts and ideas that we have implicit knowledge of them, and it is because we can be reflectively conscious of our thoughts and ideas that we can gain explicit knowledge of them. If, however, we read him as holding that knowledge and consciousness are identical, it would follow that pre-reflective consciousness of all our thoughts and ideas is just implicit knowledge of them and that reflective consciousness would be explicit knowledge. McRae reads Descartes as claiming identity between the two: "To be conscious is [for Descartes] . . . to know what we are doing or to know what is happening to us."[22] On either reading of the knowledge/consciousness relationship, it remains true that implicit knowledge of one's ideas and thoughts, on both Wilson's and McRae's interpretations of Descartes, can be made explicit—that is, we can become explicitly conscious of our ideas and thoughts by paying attention to that of which we are pre-reflectively conscious.

Wilson also discusses the distinction Descartes draws in the Sixth Replies between reflective knowledge and the internal cognition or awareness that always comes before reflection. She thinks "this distinction is very close to, if not identical with, that between explicit and implicit knowledge."[23] Her discussion makes it clear that for Descartes consciousness is self-conscious *before* reflection. That is, there is pre-reflective self-consciousness and hence implicit knowledge of what is in us as thinking things. She continues her discussion of Descartes's distinction between the internal cognition that precedes reflection and reflective (or attentive) consciousness in terms of a distinction between pre-reflective and reflective awareness.[24] This is close to the distinction Sartre makes in *Being and Nothingness* between pre-reflective and reflective consciousness. For both Descartes (at least implicitly) and Sartre (quite explicitly), there are two levels of consciousness, pre-reflective and reflective, and at both levels consciousness is self-consciousness.[25]

Although Sartre and Descartes share this important thesis about the self-consciousness of consciousness, I should point out at least a few of the important differences between their analyses of consciousness. One of the biggest differences is that for Descartes, at least on a traditional reading, what I am conscious of are ideas and thoughts *in my mind*. For Sartre what I am conscious of are not objects 'in the mind', because he denies there is a mind in the sense of an entity with contents. Rather, I am conscious of objects *in the world* or states of my own consciousness. Consciousness, for Descartes, is the mind's awareness of its activity. For Sartre it is the body's presence to the world. Perhaps the most important difference between the two philosophers is that the self for Descartes is an immaterial substance. Although critics argue over whether self-consciousness involves the direct intuition of the self for Descartes or whether the self is known through its attributes or by means of an inference to the fact of the thinker's existence from an experience of mental activity, none deny that Descartes believed that the subject of consciousness is an immaterial substance.[26] Sartre denies the existence of such a self.[27] Despite these differences and many others that exist between Sartre and Descartes, it remains true that Sartre is heir to one of the most basic claims of Descartes's philosophy: that all consciousness is self-consciousness.

LOCKE

Locke agrees with Descartes in maintaining that we cannot think without being conscious of it. "Our being sensible of it is not necessary to any thing, but to our thoughts; and to them it is; and to them it always will be necessary, till we can think without being conscious of it." The latter possibility cannot be realized since the soul "*must necessarily be conscious of its own Perceptions.*" It is logically impossible for the soul to think and for "the man" not to perceive it.

If they say, The Man thinks always, but is not always conscious of it; they may as well say, His Body is extended, without having parts. For 'tis altogether as intelligible to say, that a body is extended without parts, as that any thing *thinks without being conscious of it*, or perceiving, that it does so.

For Locke "thinking consists in being conscious that one thinks." Locke's attack on Descartes's belief that the soul is always thinking is grounded in his belief that all thought is self-conscious. What proof do those who maintain that the soul is always thinking have that a person is thinking even in sound sleep, Locke asks? If a person were thinking when sound asleep, then when he is awakened he should be conscious of such thinking. But Locke argues that when you wake someone from a sound sleep, the person is not conscious of any thoughts having occurred while he was sleeping. So how can one contend that the sleeping person was thinking? To maintain both (1) that all thought is self-conscious and (2) that the soul always thinks, one would have to claim that the person simply forgot thoughts he was conscious of at the time they occurred. Locke thinks it is more probable that the person was not thinking during dreamless sleep, for example, than that he was but forgot such thoughts before or upon awakening. The important point for our purposes is that to resolve the apparent inconsistency between the two claims, Locke jettisons the second claim and is adamant in maintaining that the first one is true. "Consciousness . . . is inseparable from thinking, and . . . essential to it: It being impossible for any one to perceive, without perceiving, that he does perceive. When we see, hear, smell, taste, feel, meditate, or will any thing, we know that we do so." Locke, like Descartes, uses thinking to cover the whole range of mental activities and believes all such activities must be accompanied by self-consciousness.[28]

What is this consciousness that must accompany all thinking? Locke defines it as "the perception of what passes in a Man's own mind."[29] Locke's use of the term *consciousness* is parallel to Sartre's use of the term *self-consciousness*. He does not use the word *consciousness*, as Sartre would, to refer to awareness of objects, for example. Being conscious of a particular object is, for Locke, equivalent to having an idea of that object. On Locke's analysis the having of such an idea or the thinking of the object must be accompanied by a consciousness of that idea or thought. So although Locke would not speak as Sartre does of the self-consciousness of consciousness, it is nevertheless true that Locke does maintain such a thesis.

But some important differences exist between the Lockean view and

Sartre's position—differences that make the link between Sartre and Locke weaker than that between Sartre and Descartes. None of these differences, however, defeat my claim that both Locke and Sartre, like Descartes, maintain that all consciousness is self-consciousness. To keep the exact nature of their agreement in focus, however, it is best to point out the most important of these differences. They are fourfold. First, although Locke certainly has a notion of reflection, there is no clear distinction present in Locke, either implicitly or explicitly, that corresponds in any exact way to the Sartrean distinction between pre-reflective and reflective consciousness. Locke argues instead for degrees of self-consciousness. Second, for Locke the self-consciousness of consciousness involves two mental acts: a thought, for example, and a perception of that thought. For Sartre (and possibly for Descartes, at least at the pre-reflective level), self-consciousness and the mental act of which it is aware are one. Perception and consciousness of perception are distinct for Locke, but not for Sartre. Third, for Locke but not for Sartre, self-consciousness involves not only consciousness of a mental act but consciousness of the *self* whose act it is. Finally, Locke separates the mental from the conscious. For Locke, one still has a mind even if one is unconscious. Descartes avoids this conclusion by arguing that the soul is always thinking and that the essence of the mind is thought. Sartre also refuses to separate the mental from the conscious, although his foundation for this refusal differs profoundly from Descartes's. For Sartre there is no mind or soul "underneath" conscious activity, as a substance or substratum within which acts of consciousness occur. Consciousness is simply the body's presence to the world.

I wish to examine these differences in more depth. Although Locke does not draw a clear-cut distinction between reflective and pre-reflective consciousness, he does hold that there are degrees of (self-)consciousness. Locke believes there are always ideas in the mind when a person is awake. But the mind pays different degrees of attention to these ideas. At times the mind studies an idea so intensely that it shuts out other thoughts and does not even notice impressions made on the senses that would ordinarily produce very vivid perceptions. At other times the mind "barely observes" the train of ideas in the understanding and does not direct or pursue any of them. And at still other times "it lets them pass almost quite unregarded, as faint shadows, that make no Impression." All thinking is accompanied by consciousness, and that consciousness is the perception of the ideas in one's own mind. To perceive the ideas in one's mind, one must pay attention to those ideas. One can, on Locke's view, pay close and careful attention or barely attend to the ideas in one's mind. So although for Locke it is logically impossible for one to have a thought without perceiving it—that is, without paying attention to it—the intensity or strength of one's attention may vary. There is, according to Locke, "a great variety of Degrees between earnest Study, and very near minding nothing at all."[30]

It is difficult to draw parallels between Locke's notion of degrees of consciousness and Sartre's distinction between reflective and pre-reflective consciousness. At first glance it might strike one that Sartre's notion of pre-reflective consciousness is akin to Locke's earnest study. In both cases one is absorbed in the object of consciousness. But the objects of consciousness in each case are radically different. For Sartre one is so intensely conscious of the world or so absorbed in one's own activity (of reading or counting, for example) that consciousness is not reflexively aware of its own activity or object. For Locke one is absorbed in paying attention to one's own ideas and hence one does not notice other impressions or events. Because consciousness for Locke is always of ideas and inner directed and because for Sartre consciousness is outwardly directed, it is difficult to draw comparisons between these two analysis of consciousness other than to point to the shared Cartesian belief that all consciousness is self-consciousness.[31]

Locke, of course, has a notion of reflection that plays an important role in his epistemology, but he is interested in reflection as an origin of ideas rather than as a type of consciousness.[32] But it is in his discussion of reflection that one finds the closest parallel with Sartre's distinction between reflective and pre-reflective consciousness, although once again Locke's emphasis is on consciousness of one's ideas and mental operations.[33] For Locke the operations of the mind are always conscious of themselves even prior to reflection, since all thinking is accompanied by consciousness of itself. However, reflection is necessary for us to form *ideas* of our mental operations. For Sartre, as well, all consciousness is aware of itself as such even pre-reflectively. Yet reflection introduces a new type or level of self-consciousness for Sartre as it does for Locke. At the level of reflection, consciousness, on Sartre's view, attempts to step back from itself and take itself as its own object. But as we shall see in Chapter 3, the nature and purpose of reflection in the Sartrean analysis of consciousness differ greatly from the purpose of Lockean reflection. So although there are superficial similarities between Sartre's and Locke's analyses of consciousness, any attempts to draw substantive parallels between Locke's notion of degrees of consciousness and his concept of reflection, on the one hand, and Sartre's distinction between reflective and pre-reflective consciousness, on the other, fail. They fail because they are undermined from the start by the important differences between the two philosophers, who vary not only in the analysis of consciousness and reflection they offer but also in the use to which they put these analyses. Although they share the belief in the self-consciousness of consciousness, profound differences exist between the two philosophers' ontologies and epistemologies. Consequently, their analyses of consciousness run in diverse directions. The very diversity of their analyses shows, however, that the traditional view of consciousness as luminous to itself runs deep enough below the surface in modern philosophy to bind together philosophies of mind that are, in all their surface detail, radically at odds with one another.

The second important difference between Locke and Sartre is that for Locke one's thinking and one's perception of one's thinking are distinct, which is not so for Sartre, as we will see in Chapter 3. Even at the level of reflection, Sartre believes self-consciousness involves only one act of consciousness. Self-consciousness for Locke, on the other hand, involves two mental acts: (1) the ideas in one's mind or one's mental activity, and (2) a perception of those ideas or that activity. Locke says that it is "impossible for any one to perceive, without perceiving, that he does perceive." For Locke all thinking is an action that cannot be done "without a reflex Act of Perception accompanying it." It becomes even clearer that two mental acts are involved in self-consciousness at the level of reflection. Locke calls reflection "internal Sense." Just as the operation of the senses produces ideas of whiteness and sweetness, for example, so too the operation of the internal sense produces ideas of mental operations such as understanding and remembering. Thinking of reflection on the model of sensation forces Locke into a conception of self-consciousness that involves two operations: the initial operations of the mind, and the reflexive mental act by which one "perceives" one's own mental activity. The kind of separation that Locke envisions between consciousness and its awareness of itself is present neither reflectively nor pre-reflectively for Sartre. There is no such separation for Descartes either, at least at the pre-reflective level.[34]

The third difference that divides Sartre from Locke is that for Locke the consciousness that must necessarily accompany all one's thinking is consciousness of oneself as well as consciousness of one's mental activity.

> For if I know *I feel Pain*, it is evident, I have as certain a Perception of my own Existence, as of the Existence of the Pain I feel: Or if I know *I doubt*, I have as certain a Perception of the Existence of the thing doubting, as of that Thought, which I call *doubt*. . . . In every Act of Sensation, Reasoning, or Thinking, we are conscious to our selves of our own Being.[35]

Sartre would reject the view that the self we are conscious of in prereflective consciousness is something over and above the activity of consciousness itself. Sartre denies the existence of an immaterial substance that is the owner of one's mental activities. For Sartre the self at the prereflective level is simply consciousness of the world. Hence, consciousness's awareness of itself is simply its awareness of itself as consciousness of the world. For Locke self-consciousness involves not only consciousness of one's conscious activities but consciousness of the self who is engaged in such activities.[36]

The final and in some ways most important difference between Locke, on the one hand, and Sartre and Descartes, on the other, is that although Locke agrees that all consciousness is self-consciousness, he does not identify, as do Sartre and Descartes, the mental with the conscious. First, unlike Descartes, who believes there can be nothing in the mind of which the mind is not conscious, Locke believes there can be mental contents of which the mind is not presently conscious. These would be ideas "lodg'd in the memory."[37] Such ideas were actual perceptions in the past and could be made actual perceptions again if the person draws them out of memory. At present, however, although they are in the mind, the person whose ideas they are is not conscious of them. Second, also unlike Descartes, who believes thinking is the soul's essence, Locke argues that thinking is probably the activity of the soul and not its essence.[38] Because thought is not the essence of the soul, Locke claims that the soul continues to exist even in dreamless sleep, when the soul is not thinking and hence the consciousness that must accompany all thinking is absent. Sartre returns to the Cartesian view and, unlike Locke, identifies the mental with the conscious; but he does so by rejecting the most basic of Descartes's ideas: the idea of the mind as a substance. Consciousness, for

Sartre, is presence to the world; *in itself* it is nothing. It is neither a substance nor the essence or activity of a mental substance. Hence there is nothing *mental* outside of consciousness. In later chapters I will examine Sartre's rejection of any notions of an unconscious or of nonconscious mental processes.

There are profound differences between Sartre and Locke. And although the link between Sartre and Descartes is stronger than the one between Sartre and Locke, profound differences exist between those two as well. Despite these differences, the three are bound together in a tradition in which consciousness is always self-consciousness. This shared belief is a strand that is woven in complex ways into the fabric of modern philosophy. The most compelling and influential development of this strand comes in the philosophy of Immanuel Kant.

KANT

Kant's analysis of self-consciousness is most fully developed in the Transcendental Deduction section of his *Critique of Pure Reason*.[39] Like Sartre, Kant distinguishes between types or modes of self-consciousness. For Kant there are two: empirical and transcendental.[40] He makes this distinction in both the first and second editions of the *Critique*. At A107 Kant distinguishes between transcendental apperception and "consciousness of self according to the determinations of our state in inner perception," which he says is merely empirical.[41] Such consciousness he names 'empirical apperception'. At B132, he again distinguishes between pure apperception and empirical apperception, both of which he regards as types or modes of self-consciousness. Empirical apperception occurs through self-affection. We are affected by ourselves because of our faculty of inner sense (B156). Outer sense is the means by which "we represent to ourselves objects as outside us" (A22/B37). Inner sense is the means by which the mind intuits its inner states.[42] This awareness of the states of one's own consciousness constitutes empirical self-consciousness for Kant.[43] Empirical consciousness of oneself through inner sense is not consciousness of a fixed and abiding self (A107). Inner sense, Kant says, "yields indeed no intuition of the soul itself as an object" (A22/B37). Empirical self-consciousness is consciousness of one's states of consciousness. It is in this way that one is *self*-conscious in an empirical sense. "We intuit ourselves only as we are inwardly *affected*," and because of this, inner sense "represents to consciousness even our own selves only as we appear to ourselves, not as we are in ourselves" (B152–53). The distinction that Kant so carefully draws between inner sense and pure or transcendental apperception (B153) provides the foundation for his distinguishing between empirical and transcendental self-consciousness.

This Kantian distinction between transcendental and empirical self-consciousness parallels in some ways the Sartrean distinction between pre-reflective and reflective self-consciousness. Although there are important differences between Kant's and Sartre's analyses of these modes of self-consciousness, as we shall see later in this section, they do agree in the relation they think holds between the two. For Kant the most fundamental mode of self-consciousness is transcendental apperception. For Sartre it is pre-reflective self-consciousness. For both philosophers the most fundamental mode of self-consciousness is a necessary condition for our ability to become aware of our states of consciousness.[44] Kant says at A116 that empirical consciousness is grounded in pure apperception. He repeats this claim in the second edition at B139–40. The clearest explanation of the relation between transcendental and empirical self-consciousness and hence of the relation between pure apperception and inner sense comes in section 24 at B150–57, where Kant states that it is through inner sense that self-affection occurs. Inner sense, which represents the self to itself in empirical self-consciousness, is determined, Kant says, by "the understanding and its original power of combining the manifold of intuition" (B153). "The understanding does not . . . find in inner sense such a combination of the manifold, but *produces* it, in that it *affects* that sense" (B155). The possibility of understanding itself rests in turn on transcendental apperception. Because self-affection cannot occur without the presence of self-activity (that is, the synthesis of the manifold of representations via the imagination and the understanding) and because such self-activity requires transcendental apperception, empirical self-consciousness requires and finds its foundation in transcendental self-consciousness.[45] As Norman Kemp Smith notes in his commentary on Kant's *Critique*, "The ultimate ground of the possibility of consciousness and therefore also of empiricial self-consciousness is [for Kant] the transcendental unity of apperception."[46]

In the most famous and often quoted discussion of transcendental self-consciousness in the *Critique*, Kant says, "It must be possible for the 'I think' to accompany all my representations" (B131). The transcendental unity of self-consciousness involves the ability to generate the representation 'I think' (B132). The ability that Kant claims characterizes transcendental self-consciousness is taken by most commentators to be the ability to generate ascriptions of experience to oneself. P. F. Strawson, for example, maintains that what Kant is after in B132 is not empirical but transcendental self-consciousness. Kant is interested, on Strawson's interpretation, in "the fundamental ground of the possibility of empirical self-ascription of diverse states of consciousness on the part of a consciousness capable of knowledge of its own identity throughout its changing (or its constant) determinations."[47] Actual ascriptions of experience to oneself constitute empirical self-consciousness. Hence, on this reading of transcendental apperception as the *ability* to ascribe experiences to oneself rather than the actual ascribing of experience, empirical self-consciousness is grounded in transcendental self-consciousness in the way the use of an ability is grounded in the presence of the ability itself.

We will see in later chapters that for Sartre the self-consciousness of pre-reflective consciousness makes possible self-consciousness at the level of reflection. He argues that the possibility of the self-ascription of experience (and its realization in specific instances) could exist only if consciousness were self-conscious from the beginning. Sartre and Kant agree in claiming that there is a mode of self-consciousness more fundamental than empirical or reflective self-consciousness. They agree as well in thinking that the more fundamental mode of self-consciousness grounds self-consciousness at another level and allows for its very possibility.[48]

The important question, however, is whether Kant subscribes, as Sartre does, to the view that all consciousness involves self-consciousness. The answer to this question is much more complicated than it is when the question is asked with regard to Descartes or Locke. What many consider the standard view of Kant does attribute this claim to him. In a commentary on Patricia Kitcher's essay "Kant's Real Self," Sydney Shoemaker says "it is customary to interpret Kant's principle of apperception as in some crucial way involving the idea that consciousness requires self-consciousness."[49] However, a close inspection of commentators on Kant's *Critique* reveals no general agreement over whether Kant held this thesis. Norman Kemp Smith, for example, argues that *both* empirical and transcendental self-consciousness are required for experience. According to Kemp Smith, Kant argues in the subjective deduction that self-consciousness is needed for experience because synthesis requires the recognition of reproduced images, and such recognition requires self-consciousness. Although he characterizes this self-consciousness in the way most commentators characterize Kant's notion of transcendental self-consciousness, Kemp Smith reads the self-consciousness required for recognition as empirical in nature. He thinks it is only in the objective deduction that Kant argues transcendental self-consciousness is required as a ground of empirical apperception.[50]

Strawson, on the other hand, contends that on Kant's view neither empirical nor transcendental self-consciousness is required for conscious experience. It is simply the *possibility* of both that is required. A necessary unity of consciousness is required for experience according to Kant. Strawson maintains that for Kant it is not necessary for a unity of consciousness, that is, "for different experiences to belong to a single consciousness, that the subject of those experiences should be constantly thinking of them as *his* experiences; but it is necessary that those experiences should be subject to whatever condition is required for it to be *possible* for him to ascribe them to himself as *his* experiences."[51] The condition that is necessary for the actual self-ascription of experience is transcendental self-consciousness. To see any particular representation *as mine* requires that I be conscious of the identity of myself through time, on Strawson's reading of Kant. Such consciousness of one's identity is transcendental self-consciousness, and it is that which grounds empirical self-consciousness, according to Strawson. But it is not *actual* transcendental self-consciousness that is needed for the mere *possibility* of empirical self-consciousness. It is the *possibility* of the latter type of self-consciousness that implies the *possibility* of the former. "Unity of the consciousness to which a series of experiences belong implies, then, the *possibility* of self-ascription of experiences . . . ; it implies the *possibility* of consciousness, on the part of the subject, of the numerical identity of that to which those different experiences are by him ascribed."[52]

Some commentators take a position that falls between Kemp Smith's and Strawson's, claiming Kant holds that experience requires, or at least involves in some way, the actual presence, not just the possibility of, *transcendental* apperception, although it does not require actual *empirical* self-consciousness. In *Kant's Theory of Self-Consciousness*, C. Thomas Powell maintains that Kant's position is that transcendental rather than empirical self-consciousness is necessary for experience.[53] Paul Guyer and Terence Wilkerson concur with this view, although both appear to have conflated Kant's notions of empirical and transcendental apperception.[54] Wilfred Sellars, in distinguishing the two types of self-awareness in Kant's

Critique, implies that it is only pure apperception which *always* accompanies consciousness, because such consciousness of ourselves as spontaneous—which is how Sellars characterizes Kant's notion of transcendental apperception—is given in the very act of synthesizing empirical objects. Because synthesis is necessary for experience, transcendental apperception, which accompanies all acts of synthesis, must always accompany experience.[55]

Other commentators read Kant's notion of self-consciousness solely in terms of *empirical* self-consciousness, the self-ascription of experience. These commentators, however, do not all take the same stand with regard to the question of whether, for Kant, consciousness requires (empirical) self-consciousness. Kitcher contends in *Kant's Transcendental Psychology* that for Kant consciousness can occur without (empirical) self-consciousness.[56] In *Kant's Analytic*, Jonathan Bennett implies that (empirical) self-consciousness is necessary for experience, on Kant's view.[57] As the discussion above shows, there is an amazing array of diverse views on the question of whether Kant believed that all consciousness involves self-consciousness.

One of the reasons for so many interpretations of Kant's doctrine of transcendental apperception and for the disagreement over whether the doctrine entails that all consciousness is self-conscious is that Kant has at least four ways of characterizing transcendental apperception. He refers to it as (1) the *identity* of the self through time (A116); (2) *consciousness* of such identity (A107, B135, B408–9); (3) "the *identity* of the *consciousness* of myself at different times" (A363, emphasis mine; see B133 as well); and (4) the representation 'I' that represents a transcendental subject of thought (A117 n, B135, A346/B404). Given the first characterization of apperception, Kant clearly thinks such identity is required for consciousness. He says at A116 that empirical consciousness is grounded in "pure apperception . . . the thoroughgoing identity of the self." He says later in the same passage that "the complete identity of the self . . . [is] a necessary condition of the possibility of all representations." Although it is not certain whether the identity of the self through time is, for Kant, equivalent to the unity of consciousness, it is at least the ground of such unity. And there is no debate among Kantian scholars that the unity of consciousness is necessary for experience. Hence the identity of the self through time must be necessary for experience. But does it make any sense to call this identity self-*consciousness*? I think not. It is only on the second characterization of transcendental apperception as consciousness of this identity that it makes sense to think of it as a consciousness of self. But why would consciousness of the identity of oneself through time be necessary for unity of consciousness and synthesis and hence experience? Why wouldn't the identity alone be all that is required? At times Kant seems to suggest that it is only the possibility of such self-consciousness that is required for experience, not its actual presence. He says at B133 that "it must be possible for the 'I think' to accompany all my representations." Yet in his discussion of transcendental apperception in a note to A117, Kant seems to be arguing that the *actual* thought of the logical identity of the subject through various representations is required for experience and hence that transcendental self-consciousness is required for experience. That is, experience requires not just the identity of the self through time but consciousness of that identity. But he adds at the end of the discussion that it does not matter "whether this representation . . . is clear or obscure, or even whether it ever actually occurs" (A117 n).

I think it is in the Paralogisms that we find a solution to the ambiguity in Kant's remarks about transcendental self-consciousness as well as a way to collapse into one all four characterizations of transcendental apperception given above. Kant argues that we cannot know the true nature of the thinking self, the subject of consciousness. We cannot know that it is numerically identical through time.[58] Consequently, it cannot be that the identity of the self through time is required for experience, on Kant's considered view. At A363 he even speculates that experience could occur even if the identity of the thinking subject were to change during the course of the experience. Given the arguments in the Paralogisms against rational psychology, it does not make sense to attribute to Kant the view that experience requires the actual identity of the self through time. We can never know whether there is such identity, and we can conceive of experience occurring without the identity of the subject of experience through time. What must be needed for experience to occur is not that the subject of experience is identical through time but only that the subject represents itself as such. It is the *representation* of the 'I' as the transcendental subject of thought that persists through time which must accompany all empirical consciousness. Kant says at A401 that transcendental "self-consciousness in general is . . . the representation of that which is the condition of all unity [in the synthesis of thoughts]"—that is, the representation of the self "as numerically identical at all times" (A402).[59] This representation of the self as identical through time is simply a consciousness of the self as such. Kant says at A346/B404 that the representation 'I' is "a bare *consciousness* which must accompany all concepts" (emphasis mine). The second and fourth characterizations of transcendental apperception are really one. Consciousness of the identity of the self just is the representation of the 'I' as the enduring subject of consciousness, a representation that must accompany all empirical consciousness. The third characterization is really no different from the first. "The identity of the consciousness of myself at different times" is equivalent to the identity of the self that Kant talks about in the Transcendental Deduction. That identity is the identity of a single self-consciousness through time as he refers to it in the note to A117: "All consciousness should belong to a single consciousness, that of myself." He makes this point again at B133: all representations must belong to one self-consciousness, and I must represent to myself the identity of this self-consciousness throughout all these representations. It is here Kant brings together the various characterizations of transcendental apperception. The self-consciousness that must accompany all empirical consciousness is not for Kant, in the final analysis, a consciousness of the self as identical through time. We cannot be conscious of that; such consciousness is beyond the capacity of human knowledge. The self-consciousness that accompanies all consciousness must be a *representation* of the thinking self as persisting through time. That representation must accompany all other representations not as a representation that distinguishes "a particular object, but [as] a form of representations in general" (A346/B404).[60]

Other reasons, in addition to the various and confusing ways that Kant characterizes transcendental apperception, lead commentators to deny that all consciousness involves self-consciousness for Kant. One of these additional reasons is that some commentators fail to take Kant's distinction between transcendental and empirical self-consciousness seriously, or they take transcendental self-consciousness to be nothing more than the possibility of empirical self-consciousness. For example, Kitcher, in *Kant's Transcendental Psychology*, denies that all consciousness requires self-consciousness for Kant because she reads his notion of self-consciousness either as empirical self-consciousness or as consciousness of a cogito or thinker. She thinks that for Kant, empirical self-consciousness—that is, consciousness of the states of oneself as one's own—is not required for experience and that in the Paralogisms Kant denies the possibility of consciousness of a cogito or thinker. It is because she separates the doctrine of apperception from any question of self-consciousness that she fails to see that there is, for Kant, a self-consciousness other than empirical and that there can be a consciousness of the thinker which is not consciousness of the self as an object. Kitcher ties the doctrine of apperception to the question of the unity of mind, but she separates that question from the question of self-consciousness. Because she ties synthesis to her interpretation of Kant's account of mental unity, she fails to see the relation between synthesis and transcendental self-consciousness. This failure leads her to deny that all consciousness involves self-consciousness for Kant. It blinds her to Kant's view that all consciousness involves *transcendental,* although not empirical, self-consciousness.

Some of those commentators who interpret transcendental apperception as simply the *possibility* of empirical self-consciousness, that is, the possibility of the self-ascription of experience, also deny that for Kant all consciousness involves self-consciousness. They do so because, on the one hand, they think that experience does not require the actual self-ascription of experience, while on the other hand, they think the possibility of the self-ascription of experience must actually be realized for self-consciousness to be present.[61] They are right, of course, that for Kant experience does not require empirical self-consciousness, the *actual* self-ascription of experience. It is true, in one sense, that given Kant's analysis of consciousness, all consciousness is consciousness of states of oneself. That is so because for Kant consciousness of the objective world just is consciousness of one's mental states that have been organized in a certain, rule-governed way.[62] Indeed, one of the central questions of the *Critique* is how representations of a *subject* can be representations of an *objective* world. But consciousness of the mental states of oneself does not by itself constitute empirical self-consciousness. Such self-consciousness requires consciousness of one's mental states *as one's own.* That is, empirical self-consciousness requires consciousness of representations *as mine.* Kant says that representations can exist that are mine without my being conscious of them as mine (B132). That is, I might not exercise my ability to ascribe my experiences to myself—I can have a conscious experience without making the judgment that *I* am having it. The commentators who claim that empirical self-consciousness is not required for experience, given Kant's account of experience, are correct. But they are incorrect when they go on to maintain that for Kant it is only when the possibility of the self-ascription of experience is actualized that self-consciousness occurs. Their mistake results from their failure to see that a characterization of Kant's notion of transcendental self-consciousness solely in terms of the possibility of the ascription of experiences to oneself is an incomplete characterization of Kant's crucial doctrine of transcendental apperception.[63] It is only in seeing the relation between transcendental apperception, synthesis, and consciousness of objects that Kant's notion of transcendental self-consciousness can be fully understood. For it is only in seeing the relation between these three that one can see that Kant has a notion of self-consciousness which goes beyond the idea of actual or possible *empirical* self-consciousness. It is only in light of the relation Kant draws between synthesis, transcendental self-consciousness, and consciousness of objects that it becomes clear that for Kant consciousness is always self-conscious. This relation also makes the connection between Sartre and Kant the most clear.

To understand the three-way relation among synthesis, transcendental apperception, and consciousness of objects, we must first clarify the often confusing discussions in the Transcendental Deduction of the relation between synthesis and transcendental apperception. The relation between these two cannot be understood without distinguishing at least two of the senses in which Kant uses *apperception*.[64] In some passages Kant uses *apperception* to refer to (1) the unity of consciousness, and in others he uses it to refer to (2) consciousness of that unity. On the one hand, when Kant says that apperception is necessary for synthesis, he is using the term in sense 1, an example of which comes at A113. There Kant says that for synthesis to yield empirical knowledge, the numerical identity that is inseparable from transcendental apperception "must necessarily enter into the synthesis of all the manifold of appearances." He makes a similar point at A116–17: "Pure apperception supplies a principle of the synthetic unity of the manifold in all possible intuition." Kant, on the other hand, uses *apperception* in sense 2 when he claims that only through synthesis is apperception possible. At A108 Kant notes the dependence of apperception on synthesis: "The mind could never think its identity in the manifoldness of its representations [transcendental apperception 2] . . . if it did not have before its eyes the identity of its act [of synthesis]." He remarks on this dependence relation again at A111–12: "In original apperception everything must necessarily conform to the conditions of the thoroughgoing unity of self-consciousness, that is, to the universal functions of synthesis, namely, of that synthesis according to concepts in which alone apperception can demonstrate *a priori* its complete and necessary identity." In the second edition of the *Critique* at B132–35, he once more emphasizes the need of synthesis for transcendental apperception: "The thoroughgoing identity of self-consciousness cannot be thought" without "a synthesis of the manifold given in intuition" (B135). The clearest statement of Kant's belief that the "synthetic unity of the manifold of intuitions . . . is thus the ground of the identity of apperception itself" (B134) comes at B133:

> Only in so far, therefore, as I can unite a manifold of given representations in *one consciousness*, is it possible for me to represent to myself the *identity of the consciousness in [i.e. throughout] these representations*. In other words, the *analytic* unity of apperception is possible only under the presupposition of a certain *synthetic* unity.

It is sense 2 of *apperception* that is equivalent to transcendental self-consciousness. Synthesis requires apperception in sense 1 and produces or is a means to apperception in sense 2. For synthesis to occur, the manifold that is to be synthesized must be united in a single self-consciousness. Synthesis unites the manifold of representations according to concepts, but to do so transcendental apperception 1 is required: "Apperception is itself the ground of the possibility of the categories, which on their part represent nothing but the synthesis of the manifold of intuition, in so far as the manifold has unity in apperception" (A401). One cannot, however, become conscious of the unity of apperception necessary for the synthetic unity imposed on the manifold of representations except through the activity of synthesis. It is only through this activity that the self becomes aware of its unity through time, which is why Kant claims at B133 that the analytic unity of apperception rests on and requires the synthetic unity of apperception. It is only through the self's activity that self-consciousness, "the *representation* of that which is the condition of all unity," arises (A401; emphasis mine).

There is a relation not only between synthesis and transcendental apperception but also between synthesis and consciousness of objects. As Kemp Smith notes, "Syntheses . . . presuppose a unity which finds twofold expression for itself, objectively through a concept and subjectively in self-consciousness." Synthesis of a manifold of intuitions requires in the first instance the use of the concept of an object in general. Because of this requirement, synthesis produces consciousness of an objective world. It is this linking of synthesis with consciousness of objects and an objective world that connects self-consciousness and consciousness of objects in Kant's analysis of experience. Kemp Smith does a good job of explaining Kant's belief in the mutual interdependence of self-consciousness and consciousness of an objective world. Kant claims, Kemp Smith says, "to have proved . . . the self can be thus conscious, even of itself, only in so far as it is conscious of objects." The reason this is so is because it is only through synthesis that consciousness of self is obtained. But synthesis also produces consciousness of objects at the same time. Hence, as Kemp Smith points out, it is through synthesis that both consciousness of self and consciousness of objects come to exist. Self-consciousness is possible only by means of the consciousness of objects that synthesis produces. There cannot be any such thing as pure self-consciousness for Kant. According to Kemp Smith, Kant believes self-consciousness is possible only through the consciousness of something that is not the self, for transcendental apperception has no contents of its own. The only way for it to be self-conscious is by means of a contrast between its pure identity and unchangeableness, on the one hand, and the constant variety and change in the contents of experience, on the other hand. However, "the variety can contribute to the conditioning of apperception only in so far as it is capable of being combined into a single consciousness. Through synthetic unifying of the manifold the self comes to consciousness both of itself and of the manifold." Thus it is that for Kant, "only through consciousness of both [self and object] simultaneously can consciousness of either be attained." Kemp Smith sees consciousness of self and consciousness of objects as connected because synthesis necessarily produces both. Consequently, consciousness of objects, one product of synthesis, will always be accompanied by consciousness of self, another product of synthesis.[65]

Jay F. Rosenberg, in *The Thinking Self,* sees the relation Kant draws between synthesis, transcendental self-consciousness, and consciousness of objects in a way similar to Kemp Smith's.[66] Rosenberg is interested in how Kant solves what Rosenberg calls "the problem of apperception." That problem is embodied, according to Rosenberg, in the question, How can there be self-consciousness if the self cannot be an object of consciousness? Rosenberg thinks that Kant attempts to solve this problem by distinguishing two forms of self-consciousness. The first, empirical self-consciousness, is the mind's awareness of its own states as its own when it is affected by them through inner sense. Not all consciousness, as we saw above, involves that kind of self-consciousness. Transcendental self-consciousness is the awareness of the identity of the self through time. It is an awareness, Rosenberg says, of the fact that the 'I' that thinks *x* is identical to the 'I' that thinks *y*. Synthesis is required for such awareness, on Rosenberg's reading of Kant. And all consciousness of an objective world involves this type of self-consciousness for Kant, according to Rosenberg. So, for Kant, all conceptual representation of an objective world is self-conscious. This self-consciousness is the awareness of neither the self as an object nor the mental states of one's self. It is the intellectual thought of the identity of the self through time. For Kant this awareness is part of the global structure, as Rosenberg calls it, of intentional consciousness. Hence all intentional consciousness is self-consciousness.[67] Representations must be constituted through synthesis as representations of both an objective world and a unitary self. This is the mutuality thesis that Rosenberg attributes to Kant.

> An objective "synthetic unity of experience" was . . . correlative to the (subjective) "transcendental unity of apperception." In other words, the conditions according to which an experienced world was constituted as an intelligible synthetic unity were *at the same time* the conditions by which an *experiencing consciousness* was itself constituted as a unitary self.[68]

On both Rosenberg's and Kemp Smith's readings of Kant, synthesis produces at the same time consciousness of objects and consciousness of self. Consciousness of self and consciousness of the world are born together in the activity of synthesis.

Aquila gives a much stronger reading to the connection between consciousness of self and consciousness of objects in Kant. He sees the two as identical and thus thinks consciousness just *is* self-consciousness rather than simply involving or requiring self-consciousness: "Any truly cognitive apprehension does not merely *entail*, nor is it merely entailed by, some mode of self-consciousness. Rather, it is originally *constituted* through the effecting of the latter." Consciousness, at least full-blown human consciousness, does not entail self-consciousness but is constituted by it. Indeed, Aquila argues that for Kant, transcendental self-consciousness, what Aquila calls "a pre-predicative mode of self-consciousness," is one with consciousness of objects. Consciousness of objects is not just a necessary condition for a determinate consciousness "of oneself as an individual distinguishable from others" but is also necessary for an indeterminate consciousness of self—that is, for transcendental self-consciousness. Indeed, the two turn out to be identical on Aquila's reading of Kant's *Critique*. In interpreting Kant, Aquila contends that to conceptualize appearances as appearances of objects, one needs to apprehend these appearances "through manifolds of one's own anticipations [of future experiences] and retentions [of past experiences]." This involves not only the combining of representations resulting from present sensory input with representations of my past experience and my (possible) future experiences but also the use of these imaginative anticipations and retentions to stretch present experience into the past and the future. Either because the *anticipations* and *retentions* are one's own or because the *experiences* anticipated or retained are one's own, Aquila seems to think that awareness of one's present experience (which includes awareness of one's past and future experiences) is simply self-awareness. This does not, however, involve awareness of oneself as an object, an empirically identifiable individual, although it is the ground of such empirical self-consciousness for Kant. Aquila argues that for Kant, apprehending appearances in a certain way constitutes both transcendental self-consciousness and consciousness of objects.[69]

On Aquila's reading of Kant, transcendental self-consciousness and consciousness of objects are identical to each other. Kemp Smith and Rosenberg attribute a weaker claim to Kant: the relation between transcendental self-consciousness and consciousness of objects is one of mutual entailment, not identity. The textual evidence is compatible with either reading. Indeed, these authors cite the same passages from the *Critique*—for example, A108 and B133–35—to support their conflicting interpretations of Kant. But the attribution of the stronger claim to Kant creates problems that can be avoided by attributing the weaker claim to him. Aquila's identification of transcendental self-consciousness with consciousness of objects leads him to conclude that transcendental self-consciousness is "the consciousness of oneself . . . as a kind of 'synthesis of representations.' "[70] Given this wording, it is unclear whether Aquila means to identify original self-consciousness with (1) consciousness of the activity of synthesis or (2) consciousness of the results of synthesis, that is, with a synthesized set of representations. Problems arise on either interpretation of Aquila's view of Kant. If Aquila means to identify Kant's notion of transcendental self-consciousness with consciousness of synthesis, then he will have difficulty reconciling this with his attribution to Kant of the claim that all consciousness is self-conscious. This is so because Kant is ambiguous about whether the activity of synthesis is itself conscious.[71] If synthesis itself is not always a conscious activity or does not have to be a conscious activity, then transcendental self-consciousness would not necessarily accompany all acts of consciousness. Aquila's attribution to Kant of the claim that all consciousness is self-conscious provides a good reason for thinking that Aquila means to be arguing that transcendental self-consciousness is consciousness of the results of synthesis. But that interpretation of Kant and the first interpretation both face a more difficult obstacle. Identifying transcendental self-consciousness with synthesis *or* its results ignores Kant's notion of a *subject* of consciousness, a problem that Aquila's interpretation shares with Strawson's and Kitcher's.[72] Strawson identifies transcendental self-consciousness with consciousness of synthesis or its exercise.[73] In *Kant's Transcendental Psychology*, Kitcher argues that the self for Kant is nothing other than mental states connected in certain ways. The only difference she sees between Hume's and Kant's notions of the self is that the connections between mental states are necessary for Kant, whereas they are not for Hume. Although Kitcher acknowledges that for Kant persons are not just heaps of perceptions as Hume thought, she maintains that for Kant they are "no more than contentually interconnected systems of cognitive states (at least as far as we can ever know)."[74] Kitcher does acknowledge that one can maintain that view of Kant's doctrine of apperception only by sacrificing other views he held about the self. She acknowledges as well that many passages in Kant fail to support a conception of the Kantian thinker as a contentually interconnected system of mental states. Indeed, many of those passages are precisely the ones that deal with Kant's notion of transcendental self-consciousness, a notion she all but ignores in her discussion of the Transcendental Deduction.[75]

The most important view sacrificed by Aquila's, Strawson's, and Kitcher's interpretations of Kant is his notion of a subject of consciousness. Powell makes this point clear in criticizing Kitcher's account.

> Kitcher does draw our attention to the kind of strategy Kant presses against Hume: that experience, if it is to *be* experience, must be systematic and orderly. Kitcher has forcefully argued—with Kant—for the necessity of a thoroughgoing interdependence of mental states. . . . What Kitcher misses—along with Hume—is that this order depends on, but *does not*

constitute, the existence of a logical *subject* of experiences. . . . Thus any equation of the transcendental unity of apperception with transcendental synthesis is too quick.[76]

Powell claims, and rightly so, that Kitcher's account obscures the role that Kant thinks the subject plays in experience. Aquila's account does the same. As Powell remarks in his introduction, "The possibility of the synthesis of a manifold (in experience) requires that the manifold be synthesized as thoughts of a unitary subject."[77]

To interpret Kant as identifying transcendental self-consciousness with consciousness of objects or the process that produces such consciousness (that is, synthesis), as Aquila does, creates this insurmountable difficulty for his interpretation.[78] It obliterates the tension Kant wishes to maintain between two claims: (1) transcendental self-consciousness is at the same time consciousness of objects, and (2) transcendental self-consciousness is not identical to (or reducible to) consciousness of objects. Transcendental self-consciousness is more than simply the apprehension of appearances in a certain way; it is the thought of a subject that persists through time. In the final analysis, however, the attribution to Kant of *either* the weak or the strong claim about the relation between transcendental self-consciousness and consciousness of objects commits Kant to two further claims: all consciousness is accompanied by transcendental self-consciousness, and consciousness is self-conscious in this most fundamental sense only by being consciousness of objects. On either reading, Kant falls within the tradition to which Sartre is heir.[79]

Sartre, like Kant, maintains both that all consciousness is self-conscious and that the relationship between consciousness of self and consciousness of objects is interdependent. Sartre, as we shall see in later chapters, argues that the self-consciousness of pre-reflective consciousness just is consciousness conscious of itself as consciousness of a particular object of consciousness. In pre-reflective consciousness, the self is simply consciousness of the world. Without an object of consciousness, no self-consciousness is possible. The reverse is also true. Consciousness of objects requires self-consciousness. To be conscious of a particular object, consciousness must be conscious that it is not that object, because to exist, consciousness requires distance and distinction from its objects. For consciousness to exist, Sartre argues, it must be aware not only of its object but also of itself as not being its object. Although there is a relation of dependence between consciousness of objects and self-consciousness, Sartre, like Kant, does not wish to collapse the two into one.[80]

No exact parallel exists between Kant's notion of transcendental self-consciousness and Sartre's notion of the self-consciousness of pre-reflective consciousness, yet there are striking similarities between the two philosophers' conceptions of this fundamental mode of self-consciousness. No reflection is involved in this mode of self-consciousness for either Sartre or Kant. For both it is a noncognitive mode of self-awareness.[81] The two philosophers maintain that this mode of self-consciousness as a necessary condition for consciousness serves a logical function. By separating apperception from inner sense, Kant makes it clear that transcendental self-consciousness is awareness of a self not as an object of consciousness but as a necessary condition of consciousness. Sartre contends, as I noted above, that for consciousness to be consciousness, it must be aware of itself as not being the object of which it is conscious. In the introduction to *Being and Nothingness*, Sartre argues that a consciousness not conscious of itself—that is, an unconscious—would be absurd.[82] The self is not an object of awareness at the level of pre-reflective consciousness.[83] For both philosophers this mode of self-consciousness involves the capacity to ascribe experiences to oneself. But, as I argued earlier in this chapter with regard to Kant, there is more to this fundamental mode of self-consciousness than simply a latent capacity. I will argue this point with regard to Sartre in Chapter 3. Both Kant and Sartre wish to distinguish a kind of self-consciousness that is different from the self-consciousness of reflective consciousness. In addition, both philosophers reject Descartes's notion of the cogito as substance. Kant argues in the First Paralogism that because we cannot know the true nature of the self, we cannot know whether it is a substance. Sartre's position is also anti-Cartesian, although he goes further than Kant does in rejecting Descartes's view. Sartre contends that consciousness is not and cannot be a substance. An additional point of comparison between the two philosophers is that a fundamental motivation behind their analyses of consciousness is that both want an interpretation of consciousness that allows for human freedom.

Several areas of agreement between Sartre and Kant are made clear in Sartre's discussion in *The Transcendence of the Ego* of Kant's notion of transcendental apperception. There Sartre aligns himself with Kant against Husserl. Sartre is right in thinking that Kant's analysis of consciousness, like his own, embodies no notion of a transcendental ego. As Sartre points out, Kant's notion of "transcendental consciousness is nothing but the set of conditions which are necessary for the existence of an empirical consciousness."[84] One of those Kantian conditions which Sartre discusses is that the 'I think' be able to accompany all consciousness. Sartre is correct in claiming that what this condition means for Kant is that the possibility of the self-ascription of experience must accompany all acts of consciousness. Kant does not think, however, as I argued earlier, that this possibility must be realized in every act of consciousness. Sartre is also correct in contending that for Kant the 'I' one meets in reflective consciousness is "made possible by the synthetic unity of our representations" (TE, p. 34). As I have pointed out, the analytic unity of apperception rests, for Kant, on the synthetic unity of apperception. There is no transcendental ego unifying one's representations. Sartre makes a similar point when he says, "The *I Think* can accompany our representations because it appears on a foundation of unity which it did not help to create; rather, this prior unity makes the *I Think* possible" (TE, p. 36). Sartre agrees with the Kantian points he discusses. There can be for both Sartre and Kant what Sartre calls a " 'pre-personal' " field of consciousness; one can conceive of "absolutely impersonal consciousnesses" (TE, pp. 36, 37). Likewise, the thought of the identity of the self through time that constitutes transcendental apperception for Kant is not the thought of one's *personal* identity.[85]

Sartre is correct, I think, in aligning himself with Kant, even though in a way there is an 'I' involved in Kant's characterization of transcendental apperception. In *The Transcendence of the Ego* Sartre clearly rejects the presence of an 'I' in consciousness. Sartre simply ignores this Kantian notion of an 'I', and hence he ignores Kant's notion of a subject of consciousness. I think this fact does not separate Sartre and Kant as much as it might at first appear to do. Earlier in this chapter I argued that transcendental apperception involves, for Kant, more than merely the possibility of the self-ascription of experience. Kant's claim that transcendental self-consciousness must accompany all acts of self-consciousness is a claim about the actual thought of a self enduring through time. But this characterization of transcendental apperception does not introduce a transcendental ego into Kant's analysis of consciousness. The 'I' that must accompany all empirical consciousness is a *representation* of an enduring self. This representation of the 'I' as the transcendental subject of thought is a bare and empty representation, the form of all representations. This characterization does not, as we have seen, commit Kant to a Cartesian ego. The Kantian claim that the thought of a subject of consciousness that is identical through time must accompany all consciousness does not entail for Kant that there be such a subject or that if there is it is anything more than the body. Kant makes this clear in the Paralogisms. Because Kant believes we cannot know the true nature of the subject of consciousness, such a subject may be the body, or it may be an immaterial substance (see, for example, A395). Sartre, of course, takes a more definitive stand on this question, maintaining that the subject of consciousness is the body.[86] Although there are points of disagreement between Sartre and Kant in their discussions of consciousness, points that Sartre conveniently overlooks, he is right in focusing on their points of agreement. These points do loom larger in the context of Sartre's discussion of the transcendental ego than the points of disagreement between the two philosophers.

The most important similarity between the two is their agreement that consciousness is self-conscious, even pre-reflectively. But significant differences exist in how Kant and Sartre conceive of the nature of this pre-reflective self-consciousness. All that Kant thinks transcendental self-consciousness amounts to is the thought of a thinking subject that persists through time. For Sartre, as we shall soon see, pre-reflective self-consciousness is consciousness aware of itself as a specific act or mode of consciousness. Sartre says in the introduction to *Being and Nothingness* that to say consciousness of a table, for example, is self-conscious is to say consciousness is *implicitly* (or non-positionally) aware of itself as consciousness of a table. Rosenberg makes this distinction between Kant and Sartre quite clear in *The Thinking Self.* For Kant, as Rosenberg points out, transcendental apperception does not involve awareness of either the self as object or states of one's self (or one's mind). As I mentioned earlier, Sartre too denies that self-consciousness at the pre-reflective level involves awareness of the self as an object. But he does think that such self-consciousness involves awareness of a particular consciousness (of X, for example). For both Kant and Sartre it is part of the structure of intentional consciousness that it be self-conscious. But they differ in what each thinks constitutes this self-consciousness. Although both contend that consciousness of objects involves consciousness of self and vice versa, the consciousness of self involved with consciousness of an objective world is not the same for the two philosophers. For Kant it is the thought of a self that is identical through time. For Sartre it is consciousness aware of itself as not being its object and as being consciousness of its object. It is the difference in the way they each unravel this 'mutuality thesis' and hence the difference in their analyses of pre-reflective self-consciousness that brings Sartre closer to Descartes than to Kant in the end. As Rosenberg notes, Sartre adheres to Descartes's transparency of mind thesis.[87] It is not that Sartre thinks one is always *explicitly* aware of one's state of consciousness, but he does contend that for one to be capable of ascribing experience to oneself, one must always be *implicitly* aware of one's state of consciousness. Although Kant says the 'I think' must be able to accompany all acts of consciousness and although transcendental apperception is the ground for this capability, transcendental apperception cannot be the implicit awareness of one's state of consciousness. It cannot be because inner sense is required for the apprehension of one's states of consciousness and because Kant distinguishes apperception from inner sense, as Rosenberg points out. Both Kant and Sartre agree in thinking that there could be acts or states of consciousness without reflective awareness of such acts or states. But for Sartre the absence of reflective self-consciousness does not entail that consciousness is not *in any sense* aware of itself. For Kant, although there cannot be consciousness unaccompanied by transcendental self-consciousness, there could be consciousness without empirical self-consciousness present even implicitly. For Kant there is a real qualitative distinction between transcendental and empirical apperception. Empirical apperception, as I noted early in this discussion of Kant, is consciousness of one's inner states of mind, whereas transcendental apperception is consciousness of the identity of the self through time. The former is intuitive; the latter, intellectual. One involves a quasi perception; the other, a thought. Sartre makes no such distinctions between reflective and pre-reflective self-consciousness. For Sartre, as we shall see in Chapter 3, there is only a quantitative difference between self-consciousness at these two levels. He says in *Being and Nothingness* that what distinguishes reflective from pre-reflective self-consciousness is a nothingness that separates consciousness from itself at the level of reflection which is deeper than at the level of pre-reflective consciousness. At both levels, consciousness is aware of itself as a specific consciousness (of a table, for example); but it pays attention to itself as such at the level of reflective self-consciousness. So although both Kant and Sartre believe that all consciousness is self-conscious, each envisions the nature of that self-consciousness in a different way.[88]

There is certainly a great deal more that could be said about the similarities and differences between Sartre and Kant. But let me once again make clear that my intention in this chapter is to set Sartre within a tradition, a tradition which is both broad and deep in Western philosophy and which maintains that all human consciousness is self-consciousness. I have no desire to deny the important differences between the philosophers who fall within this tradition. My task here is to paint a backdrop to the discussion of self-consciousness that follows. This backdrop should both enlarge the context of my discussion of Sartre's notion of self-consciousness and illuminate Sartre's analysis of consciousness in *Being and Nothingness*.

The Force of the Claim

To see the force of a critique of Sartre's claim that all consciousness is self-consciousness, even pre-reflectively, it is necessary to see the foundational role this claim plays in *Being and Nothingness*. It grounds every other major claim Sartre makes in this work. Before examining its foundational role, however, it is necessary to make clear the meaning of some of Sartre's basic terms, as well as the methodology he employs in his discussion of consciousness in *Being and Nothingness*.

Some of the terms that are most basic to Sartre's discussion of consciousness form pairs: (1) *being-in-itself* and *being-for-itself;* (2) *thetic* (or positional) *consciousness* and *non-thetic* (or non-positional) *consciousness;* and (3) *pre-reflective consciousness* and *reflective consciousness*. Sartre divides reality up into two categories: beings that have the capacity for consciousness and those that do not. When he refers to being-for-itself (or simply the for-itself), he is referring to humans as self-conscious beings.[1] Because his primary interest is consciousness, the terms *being-for-itself* and *consciousness* come to be used interchangeably by Sartre. But we must not forget that for Sartre it is the human body that is the subject of consciousness, even though his language sometimes makes it sound as though the for-itself as consciousness is free-floating and disembodied.[2] Sartre refers to nonconscious reality as being-in-itself.

Sartre also draws a distinction between what he calls thetic (or positional) consciousness and non-thetic (or non-positional) consciousness.

On the one hand, anything that falls within one's field of awareness and toward which one's attention is directed is an object that is posited by consciousness. Hence Sartre calls consciousness of this object thetic or positional consciousness. On the other hand, one has only a non-thetic or non-positional consciousness of anything that falls within one's field of awareness but to which one is not now paying attention. For Sartre every act of consciousness has both a positional and non-positional aspect because "every positional consciousness of an object is at the same time a non-positional consciousness of itself" (BN, p. liii). What he means by this becomes clearer when examined in light of the distinction Sartre draws between pre-reflective and reflective consciousness. Pre-reflective consciousness is a consciousness that is directed toward something other than itself (the glass on the table, for example) and so its awareness of itself is only non-positional. But in reflective consciousness, consciousness shifts its attention to itself and becomes a positional consciousness of an act of consciousness on which consciousness reflects. The consciousness that is doing the reflecting remains only non-positionally conscious of itself.[3]

The relationships between the members of these three pairs of terms are a great deal more complex than these brief explanations indicate. The nature of these relationships and their importance to Sartre's analysis of consciousness will be elucidated later in this chapter as well as in the chapters that follow.

To understand Sartre's methodology one must understand the influence that Husserl had on him and the ways in which Sartre agreed and disagreed with Husserl's phenomenology. Husserl developed the phenomenological method, a method he thought could be used to grasp the essence of objects. He believed that in reflecting on phenomena—that is, on being as it appears to consciousness—one could come to grasp the essence and the sense of the world. His focus was on being in the sense of essence rather than existence. In fact, for Husserl, the first step in using the phenomenological method was to engage in the phenomenological epoché or reduction that was a bracketing or suspending of one's belief in the existence of objects. What was left after such bracketing was, on Husserl's view, pure subjectivity (the transcendental ego) and its intentional objects. The task of the phenomenologist was to describe the phenomena without concern for whether objects as they appear to consciousness existed and without allowing any interpretive elements to enter one's description of intentional objects. The point was to describe the various ways in which a particular object could appear to consciousness until what was necessarily true of the object—its essence—revealed itself.[4]

Sartre uses the phenomenological method in *Being and Nothingness* to grasp the nature of being. Indeed, the subtitle of *Being and Nothingness* is *An Essay on Phenomenological Ontology.* When consciousness turns back and reflects on itself, it discovers, on Sartre's analysis, several things. Some of the most important are: First, consciousness is intentional. A phenomenological description reveals, for both Sartre and Husserl, that consciousness cannot exist without an object. Consciousness must always be of something. Second, consciousness must always be of that which is not itself, even when it takes itself as its own object. Hence consciousness must withdraw from and negate its objects to be conscious of them. Finally, consciousness must be self-conscious; how else could it become aware of itself through reflection? By reflecting on consciousness and its objects, we discover, according to Sartre, two distinct yet mutually dependent regions of being: being-for-itself and being-in-itself. *Being and Nothingness* is devoted to a detailed phenomenological description of these two types of being. As Sartre says in the introduction, "Ontology will be the description of the phenomenon of being as it manifests itself" to consciousness (BN, p. xlviii).

Although Sartre uses the phenomenological method in *Being and Nothingness*, important differences exist between his phenomenology and Husserl's. Two of the most important differences are Sartre's rejection of Husserl's bracketing of the belief in the existence of the phenomena and Sartre's rejection of Husserl's transcendental ego.[5] As an existentialist he is interested, of course, in existence, not just essence. As a phenomenologist he argues in *The Transcendence of the Ego* that a description of pre-reflective consciousness reveals no transcendental ego. As we saw in Chapter 1, at the pre-reflective level there is simply consciousness of this or that and a non-positional consciousness of consciousness, but there is no 'I' or ego in consciousness. For Sartre the ego is a construction that, although it exists *for* consciousness, is not part of the structure of consciousness.[6] So although Sartre was profoundly influenced by Husserl and his phenomenological method, his interpretation and use of this method differed from Husserl's in extremely important ways. However, to understand Sartre's task in *Being and Nothingness* and his method of defending many of his positions with regard to the nature of being in general and consciousness in particular, one must remember that Sartre's detailed descriptions are not a literary flourish imposed on a philosophical text but a philosophical method applied to questions of ontology.[7] Whether the method of phenomenology is adequate to the task of understanding the nature of consciousness is an issue that is still debated. But to approach the Sartrean text without any awareness of Sartre's methodology makes it impossible to assess his contribution to this task of understanding consciousness.

Armed with some acquaintance with Sartre's terminology and methodology, we can return to his claim that all consciousness is self-consciousness and to the role that thesis plays in *Being and Nothingness*. In one sense it is obvious that the self-consciousness of consciousness is central to Sartre's ontology and his phenomenological description of being. He refers, after all, to human reality as being-*for*-itself. But exactly what Sartre means by existence for oneself and how that truth about consciousness underlies all his other claims need to be spelled out much more carefully. Indeed, on a superficial reading of *Being and Nothingness*, the more obvious foundational claim about consciousness is one that appears quite strange when one first encounters it. This is Sartre's claim that the Law of Identity, which maintains that each thing is identical to itself, does not apply to consciousness. The fact that it does not, Sartre maintains, is the basis for distinguishing the for-itself from the in-itself. The Law of Identity applies to the latter but not the former. In addition, it is that same claim which grounds Sartre's analysis of consciousness as freedom, desire, lack, possibility, and the source of temporality, spatiality, and motion—indeed, the source of the world itself and its characteristics. But if one examines with care Sartre's grounding of that claim, one discovers that the Law of Identity fails to apply to the for-itself because consciousness is self-consciousness even pre-reflectively. Sartre argues that point in his discussion of the faith of bad faith in chapter 2 of part 1 of *Being and Nothingness*. Most of the commentaries on that chapter have focused on Sartre's characterization of bad faith and his repudiation of the Freudian unconscious. In the last section of that chapter as well as in the first section of the following chapter, however, Sartre offers a difficult and obscure discussion of the self-consciousness of belief. Within the context of that discussion, he puts forth the general claim that because consciousness is self-consciousness, even pre-reflectively, it is no longer identical to itself.

In this chapter I wish to examine in painstaking detail the use to which Sartre puts his assertion that all consciousness is self-consciousness.

I have no intention of elucidating all the intricacy and richness of Sartre's explication and defense of his belief in the reflexivity of consciousness. Nor do I wish to judge the adequacy of his defense of this belief. I leave those tasks for later chapters. My intent here is to establish that this thesis about consciousness is indeed *the* foundational one in *Being and Nothingness* and that it does ground every other major claim Sartre makes.[8]

There are dangers, however, in pursuing this task. In attempting to pull out the thesis that all consciousness is self-consciousness from the weave of the fabric of *Being and Nothingness*, I may perhaps do violence to the tightness and density of the work's design. Some threads may be broken or discounted. Yet this claim is central both to the analysis of consciousness in *Being and Nothingness* and to the history of modern philosophy (of mind). It is now receiving careful scrutiny in a wide variety of fields. For these reasons, taking the risk involved in the attempt to pull out one claim from the ground of the work and bring it to the foreground is, I think, amply justified.

THE PURSUIT OF BEING

It is in the introduction to *Being and Nothingness* that Sartre first asserts that consciousness is, in its very nature, self-consciousness. He begins *Being and Nothingness* by rejecting the dualism of being and appearance. The appearance for Sartre is not a film between subject and object. He rejects Descartes's indirect realism, which allows the subject direct access only to a representation of the object. He rejects as well Kant's distinction between the phenomenon and the noumenon. He supports instead a dualism of single appearance versus a series of possible appearances that constitute the object. What appears for Sartre is the object, not a representation of it. The essence of the object is not behind the appearance or hidden by the appearance but is the principle of the series of possible appearances. Because "the essence of the appearance is an 'appearing' which is no longer opposed to any *being*, there arises a legitimate problem concerning *the being of this appearing*" (BN, p. xlviii). This is the problem with which Sartre will begin. Is the being of the appearance to appear, he asks? Is Berkelian idealism, which holds that *esse est percipi*, correct? Sartre thinks not. There are two reasons why it cannot be correct. The first has to do with the nature of the perceiver, and the second, with the nature of the object perceived.

It is within his discussion of the first reason that Sartre first defends the claim that all consciousness is self-consciousness. According to Sartre, Berkelian idealism is intent on reducing being to the knowledge we have of it. Such an idealism first ought to give some kind of guarantee for the being of knowledge. But the being of knowledge cannot itself be measured by knowledge, Sartre argues. The foundation of being for the *percipere* and the *percipi* cannot itself be subject to the *percipi*. Sartre agrees with Berkeley, as well as with Descartes, Kant, and Husserl, that what underlies knowledge is consciousness. But Sartre rejects the position he attributes to the seventeenth-century rationalists, the position which argues that what grounds knowledge is self-knowledge, the reflective cogito. Sartre maintains that although it is true that consciousness can know itself, consciousness *in itself* is something other than a knowledge turned back on itself. If its *being* required being known, then we would have no foundation for knowledge, according to Sartre. The existence of consciousness would be dependent on being known if it were true both that self-consciousness is part of the very nature of consciousness and that such self-consciousness is in its original form self-knowledge. For Descartes the first thing I know with certainty in a logical reconstruction of knowledge is my own existence as consciousness, as knower or thinker. What self-consciousness comes to for Descartes, on the standard interpretation of his views, is self-knowledge, the reflective cogito.[9] Sartre denies this characterization of self-consciousness. What is known is the world. Consciousness is directed toward objects. Its *existence* is dependent on its positing of an object transcendent to consciousness and not on its being *known* by itself. He accepts Husserl's intentionality of consciousness thesis. However, Sartre still wishes to maintain the Cartesian thesis that all consciousness is self-consciousness. So he argues that consciousness of consciousness is initially pre-reflective, not reflective; that is, it is consciousness conscious of itself as consciousness of an object. Self-consciousness at the pre-reflective level is "an immediate, non-cognitive relation of the self to itself" (BN, p. liii). It is pre-reflective consciousness, not reflective consciousness, that is primary. In fact pre-reflective consciousness makes reflective consciousness possible. Self-consciousness at the pre-reflective level is one with the consciousness of which it is conscious. According to Sartre, it is part of the very nature of consciousness to be self-consciousness, in the same way that it is part of the nature of an extended object to be three-dimensional. For Sartre all consciousness, even at the pre-reflective level, is self-consciousness; but this primary level of self-consciousness does not constitute self-knowledge. Thus Sartre manages to maintain the thesis that all consciousness is self-consciousness while avoiding the positing of a foundation of knowledge that itself must be known in order to exist.

Sartre goes on in the introduction to contend that because of the nature of the objects of perception, idealism cannot be true. Just as the existence of consciousness is not dependent on its being known, so too the existence of the objects of perception is not dependent on their being known. The nature of the *percipi* is to exist in itself. Indeed, on Sartre's view, it is consciousness that is dependent on its objects for its existence rather than vice versa. Consciousness, for Sartre, is a relation to a transcendent being and as such requires a being independent of it for its existence. Consciousness must be a revealing intuition of something, or it is nothing. This something is being-in-itself. This repudiation of idealism reveals, Sartre claims, two regions of being: being-in-itself and being-for-itself, that is, consciousness.[10]

In the introduction, Sartre rejects traditional views about the relation between consciousness and its objects of knowledge. He rejects Cartesian dualism, Berkelian idealism, and Kantian transcendental idealism. He proposes to offer an alternative analysis of the nature of being and the relation between the two regions of being he has identified in the introduction. It will be the self-consciousness of consciousness that is the essential feature that distinguishes these two regions of being.

Sartre has already articulated the two essential features of the for-itself. As consciousness it must be self-consciousness, that is what it means to say it exists for itself, and it must have an object to exist.[11] In the last section of the introduction Sartre characterizes being-in-itself, and it is by means of contrast with the in-itself that he adds to his characterization of the for-itself. Being-in-itself, as its name implies, exists *in itself.* What this means, Sartre claims, is that "it does not refer to itself as self-consciousness does. . . . It is itself so completely that the perpetual reflection which constitutes the self is dissolved in an identity. . . . *Being is what it is.*" (BN, p. lxv). This self-identity does not apply to the for-itself. It is this distinction between the for-itself and the in-itself, the fact that the Law of Identity applies to the one and not the other, that is basic to Sartre's discussion of these two regions of being throughout *Being and*

Nothingness. And this distinction rests on the fact that being-for-itself is self-consciousness. It is the self-consciousness of consciousness that causes it to lack identity with itself. Why this is so becomes clear in the sections immediately following the introduction. The route to this conclusion, however, is circuitous, and to ease the passage I offer here an over-simplified reconstruction of the line of thought Sartre develops in the first three chapters of the book. Sartre maintains that nothingness originates with human reality. That is possible, he contends, only if human beings are free. He goes on to argue that the for-itself is free because the Law of Identity fails to apply to it and that is so, as I noted above, because consciousness is self-consciousness. This brief overview is meant to provide a road guide to the following three sections, which offer a detailed analysis of these chapters.

THE ORIGIN OF NEGATION

The entirety of *Being and Nothingness* is an attempt to discover the origin of nothingness and its relation to being. Sartre begins this task in the introduction by questioning Being, and this question reveals, as we have seen, two regions of being: the in-itself and the for-itself. He wonders about their relation, which in turn raises the question of what the meaning of the questioning attitude is. He sees that to be able to question is a human attitude, a way of facing being. But the fact that we can question being means that a negative reply is possible. Sartre contends that we could not question, especially with regard to being, if negation (non-being) did not exist. Negative judgments are possible, Sartre maintains, only because of non-being. Sartre rejects the view that negation is simply a quality of a judgment. For Sartre nothingness is a structure of the real and, as such, is the foundation for negation and negative judgments. A negative judgment does not cause non-being to appear; it simply reflects a prior revelation. "The necessary condition for our saying *not* is that non-being be a perpetual presence in us and outside us, that nothingness haunt being" (BN, p. 11). A triple non-being, Sartre claims, conditions every question: (1) "the non-being of knowing in man" (BN, p. 5)—one questions and does not know whether the reply will be affirmative or negative; (2) the possibility of the non-being of being—such a possibility will be realized if the reply to a question about the existence of some entity or state of affairs is negative; and (3) the non-being introduced by the fact that a question implies the existence of a truth. Truth involves the ruling out of certain possibilities. A particular possibility, *and not others*, is actually the case. But what is the nature of this non-being, this nothingness that the questioning attitude reveals? Sartre rejects both the Hegelian and Heideggerian positions with regard to the nature of nothingness. "Nothingness can be conceived neither *outside of* being, nor as a complementary, abstract notion, nor as an infinite milieu where being is suspended" (BN, p. 22). According to Sartre, the reason these conceptions of nothingness fail is because of the existence of certain types of realities that he calls *négatités*. These concepts involve non-being *and* being; negation is a necessary condition for their existence. Examples of such realities are absence, change, otherness, and distance. Pierre's *absence* from the café, for example, refers both to the *existent* Pierre and to a *nonexistent* state of affairs (Pierre's being in the café). Realities such as this one are supported by being, although they enclose non-being within themselves. That is why Sartre says "if nothingness can be given, it is neither before nor after being, nor . . . outside of being. Nothingness lies coiled in the heart of being—like a worm" (BN, p. 21). But from where does nothingness come? That is the next question Sartre addresses.

Nothingness cannot come from being-in-itself since being-in-itself is "full positivity" (BN, p. 22); it has no relation to non-being. It must come, therefore, from a being that does not exist within the region of being-in-itself. It must come from a being that is its own nothingness. A human being is such a being. In examining the human ability to question, that is, to engage in philosophic and scientific inquiry, Sartre claims we discover the existence of negation and non-being as an objective dimension of reality. Every question presupposes the possibility of a negative answer—in other words, it presupposes the possibility of nothingness. So every question involves "a nihilating withdrawal in relation to the given" (BN, p. 23) and hangs between being and nothingness. To question, the questioner must be able to detach herself from Being in order to allow for the possibility of non-being that a negative answer would realize. In doing so she detaches herself from the causal order of the world. What must a human being be for her to do that—that is, what must a human being be that nothingness may come to being through her?

Sartre's answer is that a human being must *be freedom* in order to question and hence to introduce nothingness into being.[12] Psychological determinism cannot be true because it returns consciousness to the causal order and to "a plentitude of being" (BN, p. 26). If one were part of the causal order, then on Sartre's view one would be full positivity and being, and the questioning attitude our freedom allows us to take toward reality would be impossible.[13] For human consciousness to introduce nothingness into being (as it does, for instance, when it sees a book as belonging to a person *who is absent*), there must, Sartre claims, be a break between one's past psychic state and one's present psychic state. If my present psychic state were causally determined by my past psychic state, then human freedom would be impossible. Anguish is the realization of one's freedom, and it is produced by the fact that consciousness experiences itself as cut off from its past and future being by nothingness. Although there is a relation between my present being and my past as well as my future being, that relationship involves a kind of nihilation. Sartre maintains that I am my past and future self in the mode of not being either of them. This is so because my past and the choices and actions that constitute it do not determine the choices I make in the present. Likewise, my present choices do not determine my future choices. Of course I am (now) the person who decided yesterday to climb Mont Blanc, but that choice does not determine whether I will actually climb the mountain today. If I decide today to postpone the climb until tomorrow, then I am related to a future self that my present choices create. But my change of mind today does not necessitate that I act in a certain way tomorrow. Tomorrow I might change my mind again. I am my past, for Sartre, in the sense that my present self has been created by my past choices; but because those past choices do not determine my present action, I am causally separated from that self, not by some other causal agent but by nothing. Likewise, my present choices are a projection of myself into the future and thus help create my future self. Yet just as my present self is not determined by the choices of a past self, so too my future self will not be determined by the choices I make in the present. This is why Sartre believes that the Law of Identity does not apply to the for-itself. Because it does not, human reality is freedom.

The examination of the human ability to question and of the negation that is introduced into being by such an ability has brought us, Sartre maintains, to human freedom. The foundation for such freedom is to be explicated, according to Sartre, in terms of two original nihilations: the nihilating structure of the pre-reflective cogito and the nihilating structure of temporality. The next three chapters of *Being and Nothing-*

ness concern these nihilating structures, both of which are structures of consciousness. To examine the first structure, Sartre will consider a particular human conduct that is open to us because of our freedom—that is, bad faith. "What . . . are we to say that consciousness must be in the instantaneity of the pre-reflective *cogito*—if the human being is to be capable of bad faith?" (BN, p. 45). Ultimately, the answer will be that human consciousness must be self-consciousness, even at the pre-reflective level, for bad faith to be possible. The route to this answer, however, is not direct. Sartre first argues in chapter 2 of part 1 of *Being and Nothingness* that it is because the Law of Identity fails to apply to the for-itself that human beings are capable of bad faith. But upon analysis it turns out that the reason the Law of Identity fails to apply to the for-itself is because of the self-consciousness of the pre-reflective cogito.

BAD FAITH

Sartre defines bad faith as a lie to oneself. In bad faith the liar and the one lied to are one and the same. If I engage in bad faith, I must hide the truth from myself. To do this, I must know the truth. So a paradoxical situation occurs when I engage in bad faith: I must know the truth to conceal it from myself. In addition, given the translucency of consciousness, Sartre claims that a person in bad faith must be pre-reflectively conscious of her bad faith. The question Sartre asks is how bad faith is possible given the translucency of consciousness and given that a person must at the same time know and conceal the truth *from herself.* How are we, he asks, to overcome or explain this paradox? Sartre argues that the paradox to which bad faith gives rise cannot be avoided by a retreat to the unconscious. Freudian psychoanalysis fails, on Sartre's view, to dissolve or explain the difficulties that the phenomenon of bad faith creates. For Sartre, bad faith is possible because the Law of Identity fails to apply to human beings. One is what one is not and one is not what one is. It is because this seemingly absurd conjunction is true that bad faith is possible. In bad faith a person refuses to accept one side or the other of this conjunction. A person either refuses to accept that she is not what she is, or she refuses to accept that she is what she is not. The examples Sartre gives to illustrate these two possibilities help to clarify his point here. Sartre describes the waiter who attempts to be a waiter in the way an inkwell is an inkwell as an example of a person who refuses to accept that he is not what he is. Although it is true that the waiter is a waiter (as opposed to being a diplomat or a soldier), he is not identical to what he is in the way an inkwell is. A person always transcends his role both because he is conscious of playing that role and because he freely chooses to play the role. Sartre's example of a person who refuses to accept that he is what he is not is the homosexual who refuses to accept that he is a homosexual and seeks to focus only on the fact that he transcends any such designation. For Sartre, facticity and transcendence are both properties of human beings. We must not attempt to suppress either property, or we will be guilty of bad faith.

Although the possibility of bad faith rests initially on the fact that the Law of Identity does not apply to the for-itself, it will become clear as Sartre begins to analyze the *faith* of bad faith that the reason human reality fails to coincide with itself is that consciousness is always, even pre-reflectively, self-consciousness. If we are to understand, in any complete sense, the possibility of bad faith, we must attempt to understand what it is in the nature of human consciousness that accounts for its capacity to deceive itself and, at the same time, to be conscious of such a deception.

Bad faith, Sartre claims, is nonetheless faith, and as such it involves belief. However, for it to be a lie to oneself but a lie one is conscious of engaging in, bad faith must involve a belief about oneself that one somehow believes and at the same time does not believe. That is, bad faith involves belief that is not quite belief. It is the self-consciousness of consciousness which is responsible for the fact that belief fails to be identical to itself. Sartre argues that because belief is conscious of itself at the pre-reflective level, it is not belief. "Thus the non-thetic consciousness (of) believing is destructive of belief. . . . One never wholly believes what one believes" (BN, p. 69).[14] The reason one does not is that consciousness of one's belief, even at the pre-reflective level, removes one just far enough from one's belief to turn one's belief into non-belief. What this transformation amounts to for Sartre becomes clearer in the next chapter of *Being and Nothingness*.

IMMEDIATE STRUCTURES OF THE FOR-ITSELF

In chapter 1 of part 2 of *Being and Nothingness*, Sartre examines what he calls the immediate structures of the for-itself. He claims first that the for-itself is, unlike the in-itself, presence to self. He examines such self-presence in terms of the pre-reflective cogito. It is in this section that Sartre makes most explicit his view that it is because consciousness exists as a witness to itself, even pre-reflectively, that the Law of Identity does not apply to it. Being-in-itself is what it is. This table, for example, is purely and simply this table, Sartre says. But this is not true of consciousness. For example, because it is a mode of consciousness for Sartre, belief is not identical to itself. The reason for this, Sartre claims, is because pre-reflective consciousness is self-consciousness. In other words, the for-itself exists as presence to itself. On his view, which Sartre develops in more detail in a later chapter on transcendence, to be present to something requires separation from that to which one is present. So there must be a separation of consciousness from itself. "If being is present to itself, it is because it is not wholly itself" (BN, p. 77). But what separates belief, for example, from consciousness (of) belief is nothing because "belief is *nothing other* than the consciousness (of) belief" (BN, p. 77). What usually separates, Sartre points out, is distance in space or time or psychological difference or the individuality of the two things present. But, he argues, if you introduced such things into consciousness to explain the distance between consciousness and itself, you would bring something into consciousness of which consciousness is unconscious. Sartre thinks a consciousness unconscious of itself is a contradiction in terms.[15] It is the being of consciousness, its being as self-consciousness, that introduces nothingness and negation into being. Sartre presents two major assertions in the beginning of his examination of the immediate structures of the for-itself. First, the Law of Identity fails to apply to the for-itself because consciousness is self-consciousness, that is, presence to self. Second, it is because pre-reflective consciousness is self-consciousness that human consciousness is the origin of negation and nothingness. Sartre thinks it is the self-consciousness of consciousness and the split between consciousness and itself that the reflexivity of consciousness requires which make a human being a being that is its own nothingness. In searching for the origin of nothingness and non-being and hence the foundation for negation and negative judgments, Sartre was looking for just such a being.

Sartre continues to examine the immediate structures of the for-itself and finds that the for-itself is lack, desire, value, and possibility. Lack, desire, value, and possibility exist in the world, and for such to be possible, Sartre argues, they must have their origin in a being that is itself lack, desire, value, and possibility. Because it is the for-itself that introduces these four into the world, then the for-itself must be lack, desire, value, and possibility. The reason that the for-itself is such, Sartre claims, is because the Law of Identity fails to apply to the for-itself. If the for-itself coincided with itself as being-in-itself does, it would be full being and hence could not be lack. Sartre contends that if the for-itself coincided with itself, it could not be desire, since desire is an appeal to the future, to what is not. Lack, desire, value, and possibility: all four surpass what is toward what is not. Only a being that does the same could be the source of these four. But if the for-itself coincided with itself it could not, Sartre claims, surpass what it is toward what it is not. As we saw above, the reason the for-itself does not coincide with itself is that as consciousness it is self-consciousness. Hence, nothingness is within the being of the for-itself, and thus the for-itself can introduce nothingness into the world in the form of lack, desire, value, and possibility.

The for-itself is a lack of being in that it nihilates both itself and the in-itself of which it is conscious. What underlies both these nihilations is the self-consciousness of consciousness. It is because consciousness is a witness to itself that there must be a separation of itself from itself and therefore a lack of coincidence with itself. This constitutes the first nihilation. In addition, it is a necessary condition, according to Sartre, for consciousness to be consciousness of something—for consciousness to be present to its object—that it be aware that it is *not the object of which it is conscious*. This constitutes the second nihilation. Given this double nihilation, what the for-itself lacks is "itself as in-itself" (BN, p. 89).

Sartre claims that "the existence of desire as a human fact is sufficient to prove that human reality is a lack" (BN, p. 87). Desire *is* only in relation to what it is not. Hunger, for example, in order to be hunger (that is, a desire for food), needs to transcend itself toward what Sartre calls "satisfied hunger." To constitute desire as desire, we must see *what is* versus *what is not*. Desire is a lack of being. It transcends itself toward what it is not. Human reality is desire. It is because human reality lacks a coincidence with itself that it lacks being-in-itself and desires such being. The for-itself desires to be a for-itself that is at the same time an in-itself, that is, it desires to coincide with itself without losing its nature as consciousness. Such a desire Sartre calls the desire to be God—in other words, the desire to be the foundation of one's own being and one's own freedom. Because the for-itself is a lack of being and the desire for what it lacks, it can introduce lack and desire into the world.

Sartre contends that the same sort of analysis applies to the for-itself as value and possibility. Because values and possibilities go beyond the facts, beyond what is, their origin must be in a being that also goes beyond what is. Such a being is the for-itself since it is not simply what it is. On Sartre's view the self-conscious nature of consciousness ensures that consciousness surpasses itself.

In examining the immediate structures of the for-itself, Sartre finds that we are taken beyond the instantaneity of the Cartesian cogito. The for-itself as lack, desire, value, and possibility surpasses being toward what is not. Such surpassing introduces considerations of temporality, which is the topic that Sartre examines next.

TEMPORALITY

Sartre contends that it is through the for-itself that the past, present, and future arrive in the world. Human consciousness, Sartre maintains, is the origin of time as both a totality and in terms of its three dimensions. The reason this is so is because human consciousness is self-consciousness and because, given the self-consciousness of consciousness, the Law of Identity fails to apply to the for-itself. In the final analysis, it is the self-consciousness of consciousness that allows it to escape from the instantaneity of the Cartesian cogito. It escapes, for Sartre, from instantaneity to temporality. Although, on Sartre's view, past, present, and future are the secondary structures of temporality as a totality, he begins this section with a phenomenological description of these three dimensions of time. He cautions, however, that they must "appear on *the foundation* of temporal totality" (BN, p. 107). This foundation, we will see, is human consciousness.

The Past

To connect the past and the present, Sartre maintains that we must see the past as a possession of a present. Paul's past, for example, is the past of the Paul of the present. It is the forty-year-old Paul, Sartre says, who *was* at the polytechnic when he was fifteen: "The past itself *is* in the sense that at present it *is* the past of Paul" (BN, pp. 111–12).[16] The past cannot *be* the present, however. Rather, it is the present that *is* its past, which is why Sartre rejects the view that explains memory by means of present states or modifications of the brain, the view that sees "the past as a present impression in the body" (BN, p. 108). If we construe the past in this fashion, we cannot get out of the present, Sartre claims. It is only through the for-itself, a being that transcends itself by failing to be identical to itself, that we can escape the present. Only a for-itself can 'have' a past. The for-itself, however, does not 'have' a past in the sense of having a possession. If that were the case, there would be only an external relation between the for-itself and its past. No, for Sartre the for-itself *is* its past. I *am* the person who went to Chicago last weekend. Because the in-itself is identical to itself, its present just is what it is. Its present is its present and nothing more. Its present cannot be its past. Consequently, the in-itself as such cannot 'have' a past on Sartre's view. It is the for-itself that confers a past on the in-itself.[17]

Because the Law of Identity fails to apply to the for-itself, it can transcend its present toward its past. Only a being that can transcend itself can introduce temporality into the world. It does so by transcending what it is toward what it was (and is no longer) and toward what it will be (and is not yet). Such a being is needed in order to see the in-itself in terms of a past or a future. The for-itself is responsible for the temporality of the world as well as of itself. Because the cogito is temporal in its very nature, it escapes the instantaneity of the Cartesian cogito. As Sartre noted in his discussion of its immediate structures, the origin of this self-transcendence of the for-itself lies in the self-consciousness of consciousness.

The Present

The meaning of the present, Sartre argues, is presence to the in-itself. Only the for-itself can be present to the in-itself. So, according to Sartre, the present enters into the world through the for-itself. The in-itselves are present only insofar as the for-itself is present to them. Presence to being means, for Sartre, that one is bound, by an internal negative bond, to the being to which one is present. To be present to a being, one must be *conscious of oneself* as not being the being to which one is present. So only a self-conscious being, only a for-itself, can be present to being. And since the meaning of the present is, for Sartre, presence to the in-itself and only the for-itself can be present to the in-itself, then the present comes into the world through the for-itself. The present is introduced into the world by a being that is self-conscious. It is because of the self-consciousness of consciousness that the for-itself can introduce the present into the world.

The Future

Just as with the past and the present, Sartre contends that the future arrives in the world only through human consciousness. In itself, something just is what it is. Without human consciousness there could be no notion that it will be something else. Sartre gives this example: the crescent moon just is what it is unless there is a self-conscious being to see that the crescent moon will become the full moon. "If the future is pre-outlined on the horizon of the world, this can be only by a being which *is* its own future" (BN, p. 124). This, of course, is the for-itself, the being that, for Sartre, comes to itself in terms of the future. In tennis, Sartre points out, the position I take on the court has meaning only through the future movement I make with my racket: serving the ball, for example. Sartre reiterates in this context a point he had previously made: I am a lack. I lack the future state that gives meaning to my present state. This is true for my conscious states as well as for my physical movements in tennis. "When I write, when I smoke, when I drink, when I rest, the meaning of my conscious states is always at a distance" (BN, p. 125). The for-itself as presence to being is a twofold flight: It is a flight from being in-itself to which it is present; it is *not* that being. And it is a flight from its past toward that which it is not yet, the future. The future that I am is the possibility of my being present to being in the future. But the future is also a lack because the future is not yet. But since the future, as future, never becomes present, I never merge with what I lack and hence I never become an in-itself. As we saw in the preceding section, the for-itself can be lack and possibility because it is not identical to itself, and this is so for Sartre because the for-itself is self-consciousness.[18]

The Ontology of Temporality

Sartre follows his discussion of past, present, and future with a section on what he calls "static temporality," in which he deals with the formal structure of temporality. Temporality, Sartre says, is a succession of befores and afters, that is, a succession of instants. In considering how unity is imposed on these instants, he examines the Humean answer and rejects it. Time, according to Sartre, separates and unites. To say that A is before B is to separate A from B; but it is also to unite the two as being related through a certain order. Hume and the Association school want to say that this unifying relation is external. What unites the mind's impressions are external bonds, of contiguity, for example. On this view, each impression is in itself what it is. Sartre points out that for Hume any impression one can find will never be anything in itself but itself. Sartre, however, denies Hume's claim that each moment of consciousness exists in itself. For Sartre, each moment of consciousness carries within it the past and the future. It is temporal in its internal structure. It flows out of the present toward both the past and the future. And it can do so because it is not what it is and is what it is not. If it *is* itself, as Hume believed, then it would be an in-itself and no unity between moments of consciousness would be possible. Sartre argues that the external relations that for Hume unify moments of consciousness are insufficient to establish such unity. Given a Humean analysis of instants of consciousness, consciousness remains nontemporal.

Sartre also rejects the position of several other thinkers with regard to temporality. In particular he rejects the Cartesian and Kantian positions, in which time is seen not in terms of an external relation but as a function of an *a*temporal witness. For Sartre, however, the unity of time still remains external to being on Descartes's and Kant's analyses. Sartre argues that the origin of temporality cannot be in an atemporal witness but must be in a witness that is itself temporal in its very structure. The for-itself is such a witness because its present carries with it its past and its future. That is so because, as we have seen, the Law of Identity fails to apply to the for-itself and most fundamentally because as consciousness the for-itself is self-consciousness.[19]

TRANSCENDENCE

In this section of *Being and Nothingness*, Sartre is concerned primarily with the question of the nature of knowledge, contending that self-consciousness is necessary for knowledge. It is necessary because, as Sartre noted in his previous chapter, self-consciousness is required for presence to being, and presence to being is what knowledge is for Sartre. Therefore, only a self-conscious being is capable of knowledge. Related to this point, Sartre argues that the for-itself as self-consciousness causes a *this* or *that* to appear—that is, the for-itself reveals the world and causes being-in-itself to *be there*. In this section I will try to delineate what Sartre means by these claims and how these points relate to his earlier discussion of the nature of the for-itself and temporality.

Knowledge, for Sartre, is a relation between the for-itself and the in-itself. It is "nothing other than the presence of being to the For-itself" (BN, p. 216). Thus for Sartre there is only intuitive knowledge, because intuition just is presence to ____.[20] Such presence to ____ requires, as Sartre remarked earlier, a consciousness that one is not the object to which one is present. For example, I cannot be aware of the table without being aware that I am distinct from the table. Only a being that is conscious of itself can have such awareness. The for-itself is such a being.[21]

The knower, Sartre says, "is nothing other than that which brings it about that there is a *being-there* on the part of the known, a presence—for by itself the known is neither present nor absent, it simply is" (BN, p. 177). Knowledge, Sartre claims, adds nothing to being; it only causes being 'to be there'. The for-itself, as presence to being, is not responsible for the existence of the in-itself, but it is responsible for the existence of a 'this' instead of a 'that'. It is also true for Sartre that totality comes to being only because of the for-itself. The for-itself reveals being as a totality and as a particular this rather than a particular that. The relationship between the totality and the particular 'thises', as Sartre calls them, is analogous to the relation between the figure and the ground in Gestalt psychology. The ground of the world is really the totality in Sartre's terminology. A particular 'this' appears on the ground of the totality (the all, the world), and the for-itself, as a negation of a particular 'this', appears on the ground of itself as radical negation. I make present the world and particular things in the world by *not being* this table or this glass, but I am a negation of those things on the ground of my being as a negation of being-in-itself. As nothingness, as a being that is not a substance, the for-itself is a radical negation of the totality of being. As presence to this object or that, it is the negation of the object to which it is now present. For a 'this' to appear as a figure on the ground of the world, all the other 'thises' must, Sartre says, withdraw into the background. Likewise, for the for-itself to be a negation of a particular this, the for-itself must, as a radical negation of the totality of being, withdraw into the background. "Negation can come to the *this* only through a being which has to be simultaneously presence to the whole of being and to the *this*" (BN, p. 183). To be presence, of course, the for-itself must be conscious of itself as not being that to which it is present. That is, it must be conscious of itself as not being the totality and not being the particular object to which it is now present. For being to rise up both as a totality and as a collection of individual entities distinguishable from one another on the ground of the world requires that being be present to consciousness. Such presence requires the self-consciousness of consciousness.

The for-itself as presence to being and hence self-presence reveals being as a thing, and in so doing, Sartre claims, it reveals the various structures of a thing: its thisness, its spatiality, its permanence, its essence, and its motion, among other characteristics. I wish to examine how it is that the for-itself is responsible for space and motion. It is within this discussion of transcendence that Sartre raises these issues.

Space, for Sartre, is the instability of the world inasmuch as it can always disintegrate into a multiplicity of individual entities. Space is neither the figure nor the ground. It is the exterior relation that holds between this particular entity and the ground on which it rests as figure. The relation is exterior because of the possibility of the ground disintegrating into multiple figures. It is the for-itself that introduces 'thises' and 'thats' and totality itself into existence. It is the for-itself as self-consciousness that introduces the figure and ground into the flat realm of being. Hence, it is the for-itself, on Sartre's view, that introduces space as the possibility of the ground collapsing into many figures.

Sartre's account of motion holds that when an object moves, it changes place without an alteration in its qualities. For Sartre, a for-itself is necessary for there to be motion, the reason for which becomes clear during Sartre's discussion of Zeno's paradoxes. According to Sartre the only way both to overcome the Eleatic paradox that an object in motion is also at rest and to maintain that the quality of a moving body remains unchanged is to see the body as exterior to itself. The Eleatics argued with regard to a moving arrow, for example, that when it passed a segment of space specified by a line AB, it was not only in motion but also at rest because in passing AB, it must *be* at AB and hence at rest. Sartre maintains that the moving object occupies a place "in so far as the 'this' is revealed as exterior to other 'thises' " (BN, p. 212). The arrow is other than the target. A for-itself is necessary for the 'this' to be so revealed. But there is also a passage at this place. Because motion involves the moving body being both in a place and passing that place, "motion is the being of a being which is exterior to itself" (BN, p. 212). But on Sartre's view it is impossible to define in terms of the in-itself alone a being that is exterior to itself, because being-in-itself by its very nature coincides with itself and does not go beyond itself. Such a paradoxical being can be revealed only by means of a being that is itself exterior to itself. Sartre contends that the for-itself which as self-consciousness transcends itself is for that reason exterior to itself and hence can reveal motion in the world.[22]

For Sartre, the for-itself is an affirmation of being-in-itself, and it can be such because it is a negation of itself. Such self-negation is self-consciousness on the pre-reflective level. The presence of being, its 'thereness', in Sartre's language, arises from the for-itself, which is a negation of being. The 'being there' of being as well as its worldliness, spatiality, motion, and temporality arise from a being that is consciousness of being. According to Sartre, "The world is human" (BN, p. 218).

Sartre ends his section on transcendence by explaining why he did not consider the body in his discussion of knowledge. The body, according to Sartre, appears first as known, and so we cannot refer knowledge back to it. Our body is essentially that which the other knows. I discover with my body another mode of being as fundamental as my being-for-myself. This is my being-for-others. Sartre's discussion of my being-for-others introduces a new dimension of self-consciousness.

THE EXISTENCE OF OTHERS

In his discussion of the existence of others, Sartre complicates and enriches his claim that all consciousness, even pre-reflectively, is self-consciousness. Sartre introduces his discussion of the other with a consideration of the experience of shame. Although the experience of shame is accessible to reflection, Sartre claims that it is not originally an experience of reflective consciousness. Shame is a pre-reflective consciousness, and as such it is a non-positional self-consciousness. That is, shame is consciousness (of) itself as shame. For Sartre, any consciousness exists *for itself* as non-thetic consciousness of itself. But with the experience of shame a new dimension of self-consciousness is introduced at the pre-reflective level. It is through shame that I am revealed to myself as existing for others.[23] In the experience of shame, there exists a non-thetic consciousness of self as existing for oneself *and* for others. My original apprehension of these two modes of my being occurs pre-reflectively. Sartre argues that it is this second dimension of self-consciousness at the pre-reflective level, the dimension made clear in the experience of shame, that reveals and makes certain the existence of the other.

Although Sartre acknowledges that the other is given to me as an object in perception, this objectness of the other is based on a primary relation between myself and the other. This is a relation in which the other is experienced as a subject. It is in my being as an object for the other that I am able to experience the other as subject. This aspect of my being is revealed to me through the look of the other. Sartre describes this new dimension of self-consciousness, which arrives with the other's look, in his long example of a person's being caught peeping through a keyhole. Before I sense someone looking at me, I am pre-reflectively self-conscious only in terms of the first dimension of self-consciousness. That is, consciousness is conscious of itself as consciousness of the keyhole, the furniture in the room being looked into, and so forth. No self, Sartre says, inhabits my consciousness. The world is presented as a set of instruments and obstacles. Things are what they are relative to my goals and purposes. There is no reflective consciousness of myself. Then I hear footsteps. Someone is looking at me. There is an essential modification in the very structure of my being. Considering the for-itself in isolation, Sartre claims that unreflective consciousness is not inhabited by a self. Considering the for-itself in isolation, it is the *reflective* consciousness that has the role of making the self present. But with the look of the other, the *unreflective* consciousness takes on this role. There is a difference, however, between these two types of self-consciousness. The reflective consciousness takes the self directly for an object. But "the unreflective consciousness does not apprehend the *person* directly or as *its* object; the person is presented to consciousness *in so far as the person is an object for the Other*" (BN, p. 260). Suddenly I experience myself escaping myself. I do so not because I am transcendence and my own nothingness but because I have a foundation outside of me, in the other. But neither myself nor the other is presented in this experience as an object. The other cannot be an object in this context. If she were she could not make me into an object. Only a subject can do that. My ego is also not present to my consciousness as an object, on Sartre's account. What is present to pre-reflective consciousness is the self *as an object for another.* I discover this self through the experience of shame. My relation to this self is one of being, not knowing. Neither dimension of self-consciousness at the pre-reflective level involves knowledge.

But what is my relation to the being that shame reveals to me if it is not a relation of knowledge? This is the question Sartre addresses next. Shame is my confession that I am this being thus revealed, but I am it in the mode of the in-itself rather than the for-itself. I am separated from this being, however, by a nothingness that is the other's consciousness, the other as freedom. Alone I cannot be what I am; I always escape myself. But the look of the other forces me to be what I am. However, I am what I am for the other and never for myself. Although the other's look fixes my transcendence and gives it a nature, an outside, "that very nature escapes me and is unknowable as such" (BN, p. 263). With the other's look, the one who is not identical with himself becomes, Sartre claims, a somebody in the midst of the world. The experience of shame throws me out onto the other and into the world, not as consciousness of the world but as an object in the world. The look of the other creates for me a consciousness of myself as an object in the world. It is this second dimension of self-consciousness that makes certain for me the existence of the other as another consciousness. "Just as my consciousness apprehended by the *cogito* bears indubitable witness of itself and of its own existence, so certain particular consciousnesses—for example, 'shame-consciousness'—bear indubitable witness to the *cogito* both of themselves and of the existence of the Other" (BN, p. 273). The self-consciousness of pre-reflective consciousness, in its two dimensions, makes certain the existence of my own consciousness as well as the existence of the other's.

It is the first dimension of the self-consciousness of pre-reflective consciousness that grounds the second dimension. Negation, Sartre says, is involved in my relation with the other as well as with the world. If there is an other, then "it is necessary . . . that I be the one who is not the Other" (BN, p. 283). By means of this negation, I make myself be, and I also make the other arise as other. This negation, like the negation of objects of which I am conscious, constitutes my being. I make myself be by negating that I am the world or the other. I do this, Sartre claims, on the grounds of my original self-consciousness as a consciousness that exists for itself. By refusing the other, by making itself not be the other, the for-itself does not, for Sartre, give being to the other but "gives to the Other its being-other" (BN, p. 283). Sartre draws a parallel between the fact that the for-itself's negation of the in-itself constitutes the world as an arrangement of instrumentalities and the fact that the for-itself's negation of the other constitutes the other as other. The for-itself has to be self-conscious at the pre-reflective level to negate the in-itself. That is, it has to be conscious of itself as *not being* the object of which it is conscious. So too, Sartre argues, the for-itself has to be pre-reflectively self-conscious to negate the other. Consciousness must be self-consciousness in its existence *for itself* for the other to arise as other. But the self-consciousness of consciousness in its existence *for others* also plays a role in the negation that allows the other to arise as other. Because there is nothing upon which to direct my fundamental negation of the other (given Sartre's position that consciousness is nothingness), this negation must be directed at my objectified self, which is created by the look of the other. I make there be an other, Sartre claims, by the paradoxical act of affirming a self that I refuse. In other words, I acknowledge that, in a sense, I am the self created by another's look, but I also affirm that I transcend that objectified self.

My response to the look of the other and to the shame it produces involves a second negation. I negate not only that I am the other but also the subjectivity of the other. I treat the other as an object. My ability to engage in this second negation is also rooted in the first dimension of the self-consciousness of pre-reflective consciousness. The non-thetic consciousness of myself as freedom allows me to transcend the other's transcendence and reassert, in pride, my existence as a subject, as a being that exists for itself.

The self-consciousness of pre-reflective consciousness is deeply woven into Sartre's discussion of the existence of others. His belief that all consciousness is characterized by reflexivity plays a foundational role here as elsewhere in *Being and Nothingness*.

BEING AND DOING: FREEDOM

Sartre returns to a discussion of freedom in this last section of *Being and Nothingness*. He argues that action must be intentional and thus freedom is the first condition of action. Given that every action must involve an intention, it follows that every action must also involve the recognition of an objective lack. How could Constantine, to use Sartre's example, form the intention of creating Constantinople as a rival to Rome unless he apprehended that a Christian city to balance pagan Rome was lacking? But if every action necessitates the apprehension of an objective lack on the part of the actor, then, Sartre claims, consciousness, from the moment it begins to conceive of an act, must withdraw from the world of which it is presently conscious. Consciousness must move to the level of non-being to perceive an objective lack at the level of being. This movement is necessary because a lack in the present state of things can be made manifest by consciousness only in the light of some ideal state of affairs that does not now exist. Sartre gives an example: For a worker to revolt against his situation, he must first withdraw from his present situation and posit an ideal state of affairs in which his socioeconomic class is happy. That ideal state of affairs illuminates the present state, and the worker perceives, against the backdrop of what is not but could be, the fact that he is not now happy. He perceives this lack only in light of what is not. It is, of course, because consciousness is self-consciousness that it is capable of withdrawing from being and introducing non-being and hence lack into the world.[24]

Sartre claims that it follows from the fact that all action is intentional and hence requires the apprehension of an objective lack that no factual state can motivate, by itself, any act. On Sartre's analysis of action, to act is to project oneself toward an ideal state of affairs to overcome a lack in the present state of affairs. In acting, the for-itself projects itself toward what is not. But what is, Sartre claims, cannot determine by itself what is not. The factual state alone cannot reveal an objective lack that might spur action. Only the for-itself, which can apprehend what is in light of what is not, can constitute the present situation as one that is lacking. Action involves both a recognition of a lack and a projection toward what is not. But the for-itself can project itself toward what is not because it does not coincide with itself. That is so because consciousness is self-consciousness, and hence the self-consciousness of consciousness allows the for-itself to act.

In addition to arguing that no factual state, by itself, can motivate action, Sartre also argues that no factual state can determine consciousness to apprehend it as a lack. To apprehend a present state as lacking, consciousness must first constitute the present state of affairs as an isolated system. It does so by means of the nihilating power of the for-itself. Sartre contends that to act, consciousness must withdraw not only from the world in general but from a specific state of affairs as well. The worker, for example, to revolt, must withdraw from the state of affairs that Sartre describes as "worker-finding-his-suffering-natural" (BN, p. 436). He must transcend this state of affairs by denying it. "It is by a pure wrenching away from himself and the world that the worker can posit his suffering as unbearable suffering and consequently can *make of it the motive* for his revolutionary action" (BN, p. 436). Consciousness must tear itself away from its past, and in projecting itself toward the future, toward an ideal state of affairs, it must constitute the very meaning of the past. The worker, in seeing his past in light of a projection of himself toward the future, constitutes his past and makes of it a motive for his action. Given Sartre's analysis of action, it follows that the past by itself cannot motivate action.

The perception of a lack in the present situation and the positing of an end toward which the for-itself projects itself are necessary conditions for action, on Sartre's analysis. Nihilation is required to satisfy both those conditions. The past and present states of affairs are nihilated with regard to the end posited. If the end is the happiness of the working class, then the past and present states of affairs are seen as situations in which the working class *is not* happy. The end posited is nihilated with regard to the past and present because it *is not* yet existent. The actor must be free, however, to nihilate the past and present in relation to an end toward which she projects herself. If the actor were bound to being or immersed in being-in-itself, she could not withdraw from being to negate the past and present states of affairs.

In claiming that a person must be free so as to act, Sartre does not deny that an act must have a motive. Indeed, he says that without a motive a person's behavior would not be intentional and thus would not be an action. But it is the for-itself that constitutes the past and present states of affairs as a motive for action. And it does so not in terms of another existent but in terms of non-being. That is, "the motive is understood only by the end" (BN, p. 437), which does not yet exist. By way of illustrating this point, Sartre gives the example of the person who accepts a low salary because of fear. Fear of dying of starvation is the motive of the action. For this fear to have meaning, however, the person must posit the ideal end of preserving one's life by avoiding starvation. This fear is understood, Sartre argues, in relation to the value that the actor gives to her or his life and its preservation. The motive is understood and indeed constituted by means of the future, which is ideal and nonexistent. Only a being which is its own future and which transcends being can introduce non-being into the world. Without such non-being, action is impossible. For a being to be able to introduce non-being into the world, it must itself be non-being. Action requires a being that transcends the world and itself, a being that can withdraw from and nihilate being-in-itself. But because it transcends the causal order of the world, such a being is free. Hence freedom, on Sartre's analysis of action, is the fundamental condition of the act. But as Sartre's earlier discussion of freedom indicates, the for-itself is free because it fails to coincide with itself. It lacks coincidence with itself because consciousness, even pre-reflectively, is self-consciousness. From its very upsurge into the world of being, consciousness, as a presence to the world, is a presence to itself. Thus underlying Sartre's entire discussion of action and the conditions necessary for action is the fact that the for-itself is self-consciousness. Only such a being can be free and thus act. "Man is free because he is not himself but presence to himself" (BN, p. 440). Such presence to oneself is the ultimate and most fundamental of the conditions for action.

Central to his discussion of action is what Sartre calls a person's fundamental project or choice. This is the foundational project or end toward which a person strives and which structures all her other choices and actions. It is only in light of a person's fundamental project that any particular action can be fully understood. Sartre contends that the French writer Jean Genet's fundamental project was to be a thief. One can understand all his actions and secondary goals only in light of this most fundamental choice of a way of being. The causes and motives that guide our actions are created, on Sartre's view, by our fundamental choice. We may not be reflectively conscious of this choice, but we are always pre-reflectively conscious of it, Sartre believes. This choice of a goal or end or way of existing is indeed what the self is on the pre-reflective level. Hence pre-reflective self-consciousness is the non-positional awareness of one's fundamental project. Because I create the world through my choice and through the ends toward which I project myself, the world and indeed my own body are a reflection of my fundamental choice. They are a transcendent image of me. The clothes I wear, the furniture I buy, the street and the city in which I live—all these can give me a positional consciousness of my fundamental choice. But this positional consciousness is possible because on the pre-reflective level I have a non-positional consciousness of myself as a fundamental choice.[25]

Underlying Sartre's discussion of freedom, both in the first part and again in this last section of *Being and Nothingness*, is his contention that all consciousness is self-consciousness. This remains true in Sartre's analysis of the relationship between freedom and facticity. "Freedom [which is another way Sartre refers to the for-itself] is originally *a relation to the given*" (BN, p. 486). It is a lack of being, a nihilation of being-in-itself. The paradox of freedom, Sartre says, is that there can be freedom only in a situation, and there can be a situation only through freedom. Sartre is reiterating his earlier point that consciousness needs being-in-itself to exist and that being-in-itself needs consciousness to exist *as a world*. Hence facticity is required for the existence of consciousness as freedom, and freedom is required in order that the given be illuminated and made meaningful in light of the ends and projects of the for-itself. Sartre discusses the elements of facticity out of which I constitute my situation: my place, my past, my environment, and my existence for others. Each of these is constituted by the for-itself. The for-itself is free because it can transcend the given from which it arises and create the meaning of the world by negating and transcending the world. It can do so because it is self-consciousness from the start and hence nothingness.

My place, Sartre says, can be determined only in relation to an end. It is only through my free choice of an end that my place takes on meaning as an obstacle or a refuge, for example. That the place I occupy is near to or far from another place is relative to my end. Moscow may seem very far away from New York if I long to visit Moscow but lack the financial means. But if I long to escape the old places and memories associated with Moscow and yet news and relatives keep arriving from there, Moscow may seem much too close. The same is true for my past. Sartre contends that I constitute my past by my choice of ends. It is my fundamental project, ultimately, that decides what the past means. Sartre holds that whether the mystic crisis a person experienced at fifteen was an accident of puberty or a first sign of conversion will depend on choices and ends he chooses at a later date. If, for example, the person converts at twenty or thirty, the crisis becomes the first sign of conversion. The future decides the meaning of the past. My environment, like the other elements in my situation, is also constituted by my projection of myself into the future. Imagine, Sartre says, that I wish to get to the next town on my bicycle as quickly as possible. But I find my tire is flat, the sun is too hot, and the wind is blowing against me. All these elements are part of my environment. But it is only relative to my ends that the wind is a head wind, that the sun is too hot, and so on. The presence of the given is not an obstacle to freedom, Sartre argues. Rather it is in negating the given that consciousness arises in the midst of being and makes of being a world. That is why, for Sartre, "I am absolutely free and absolutely responsible for my situation" (BN, p. 509).

Sartre discusses the fact that someone might object to his analysis of freedom and argue that it is not the individual who creates the meaning of things through her choice of ends but that the individual finds herself in a world already full of meanings. Sartre acknowledges that each person finds herself in a world of meanings that she did not create. It is in such a world that the for-itself must be free. I exist for others as well as for myself. And to exist in a world with others is to exist in a world full of meanings which I did not create but which I must still make sense of in light of my ends.

I am able to create my place, my past, my environment, and indeed the world as a whole because I can transcend being and project myself toward what is not. As the review of earlier sections of *Being and Nothingness* has made clear, this is so because I lack identity with myself, and that lack of identity arises from the fact that consciousness is self-consciousness. In the background of this discussion of the elements that for Sartre create one's situation is this fundamental claim.

DOING AND HAVING

Sartre begins this section with a discussion of existential psychoanalysis. Because on Sartre's account of human reality a person defines herself by the ends she pursues, the proper task of the psychoanalyst is to study these ends and reach the irreducible end that will explain all the others. Sartre rejects, for example, an attempt to offer an exhaustive explanation of Flaubert's life as a writer by an appeal to his ambition alone. He argues that one cannot provide a complete explanation of a person's history by appeal solely to such factors as heredity, environment, or education. He rejects these explanations as insufficient because they utilize factors that are not irreducible; these factors need explanation themselves. Sartre contends that the irreducible end, in terms of which all other ends must be understood, is the desire of being. The for-itself lacks being-in-itself and hence, as we saw earlier, desires to be a being-in-itself that is its own foundation. The task of the psychoanalyst is to uncover the fundamental choice that is the manifestation, on the part of a particular subject, of the for-itself's desire for being.

Sartre's claims that the irreducible desire of the for-itself is the desire for being and that the ultimate task of psychoanalysis should be to uncover the fundamental choice that is an expression of this desire rest on his analysis of the for-itself as a lack of being. As a lack of being the for-itself is a projection into the future; it is freedom, nothingness. The for-itself lacks being because as consciousness it is self-consciousness and thus cannot achieve the identity with self that characterizes being-in-itself. Once again it is the claim that consciousness is self-consciousness that grounds Sartre's discussion, this time of existential psychoanalysis.

As we shall see in more detail in Chapter 4, the self-consciousness of consciousness is also the reason that the subject of psychoanalysis can recognize the image of herself presented to her by the analyst. For Sartre, the fundamental choice is consciousness itself as a projection toward ends. Therefore because all consciousness is non-thetically self-aware, consciousness as choice must be conscious of itself as such. The enlightenment of the subject, Sartre remarks, is "understandable only if the subject has never ceased being conscious of his deep tendencies; better yet, only if these drives are not distinguished from his conscious self" (BN, p. 574).

In this section on doing and having, Sartre discusses both existential psychoanalysis and possession.[26] His fundamental claim about consciousness underlies both these discussions. Possession, including appropriation and the desire to have, is a type of relation between the for-itself and the in-itself. It is a relation between the possessed and the possessor, and that relation, on Sartre's view, is an *internal* bond. The possessed in-itself, Sartre argues, is defined by a sufficiency of being unlike the possessor who lacks being. I create the objects I possess in the sense that "I am responsible for the existence of my possessions in the human order. Through ownership I raise them up to a certain type of functional being" (BN, p. 590). *My* lamp is not just the bulb, the shade, and the base. It is a power of lighting *this* desk and *these* books and papers, according to Sartre. "It is animated, colored, defined by the use which I make of it; it *is* that use and exists only through it" (BN, p. 590). On Sartre's view, possession requires a being that lacks being and hence can pursue ends and project itself into the future. The for-itself, as I have mentioned repeatedly, can do so because as consciousness it is self-presence.

Not only does my use of objects define them as possessions of mine, but my possession of objects defines me. I am the objects I possess. Because I am my thrust toward the future and because that is how these objects are created as *my* objects, then I am my possessions. Again, it is because I lack being that these objects are my being. The things in my environment become mine by the use I make of them. Even natural objects, the mountain outside my window, for example, become mine when, in the case of the mountain, I scale it or use it for contemplation or solace. Insofar as I use the object for my purposes and in relation to my ends, I create it as mine and in doing so create myself. But as the object appears in my world, it is both wholly me and independent of me, Sartre claims. This is another expression of his claim that the for-itself is what it is not and is not what it is. I am my possessions, and yet I am not. They are me, and they are not me. The possessed object, as possessed, as mine, is created by me, yet it exists in itself and is independent of me. It exists without me and when I go away. Possession, Sartre says, is a magical relation: "I *am* these objects which I possess, but outside, so to speak, facing myself" (BN, p. 591). This is so because I am always outside myself, an incompleteness, Sartre says, which makes itself known to itself by what it is not. That is, one way the for-itself makes itself known to itself is by means of its possessions.

The for-itself is an insufficiency of being that finds its completion, on Sartre's view, in the objects it possesses. I found my being as being-in-itself by creating, as a for-itself, the objects I possess. Because I am the objects I possess and create the objects I possess *as mine*, I create myself. Consequently, I am my own foundation as a being-in-itself. This is precisely the ideal being I desire to be. The in-itself-for-itself. In possession, I realize my ideal of being a for-itself that in itself is its own foundation, but Sartre claims I realize such only in a *symbolic and ideal* way because I can never fully realize my appropriation of an object. It would take a lifetime and beyond to utilize the object and hence possess it. In addition the in-itself, even when used by the for-itself to fulfill its purposes, still has a life of its own. It still has existence independent of human reality. Thus possession is never complete. I attempt in the possession of a particular object to possess the world. So the for-itself is a desire to be the world. Possession realizes this desire ideally. The desire to have, for Sartre, is really the desire to be. In possessing, the for-itself attempts to be a conscious being which exists for itself but which is its own foundation. Its attempt to possess the world, to create itself in creating the world, is the attempt to be God. This attempt, of course, meets failure. Consciousness, since it is self-consciousness, remains a lack of being.

We have seen how Sartre's claim that all consciousness is self-consciousness undergirds all his other major claims. As the foundation for his belief that the Law of Identity fails to apply to the for-itself, it indirectly supports all the claims that rest on this latter belief. Therefore, it indirectly grounds Sartre's analysis of human consciousness as freedom and hence his assertion that human consciousness is the origin of nothingness within the realm of being. It also indirectly supports his claim that human consciousness, because it lacks coincidence with itself, is desire, lack, value, and possibility as well as the origin of these four in the world. In addition, it underlies his analysis of bad faith, which is made possible for human beings because the Law of Identity fails to apply to the for-itself. Finally, the thesis that consciousness is self-consciousness is the ultimate, if indirect, foundation of Sartre's contention that temporality is introduced into the world through the for-itself because the for-itself can transcend and thus constitute its past and its future.

This central thesis about consciousness also directly supports Sartre's analysis of knowledge and his claim that the for-itself is responsible for the existence of the world and its features. It functions as well as the foundation of his discussion of our existence for others and of his analysis of human action and the freedom and fundamental choice such action requires. Finally, it underlies his exposition of existential psychoanalysis.

In the conclusion to *Being and Nothingness*, Sartre reiterates once more that consciousness as presence to the world is presence to self. To be present to being, as we have seen above, requires, for Sartre, that one be other than being, and "to be other than being is to be self-consciousness" (BN, p. 618). It is the claim that consciousness is self-consciousness that grounds the ontology Sartre defends in *Being and Nothingness*.

An Internal Critique

The central tenet in the ontology Sartre describes and seeks to defend in *Being and Nothingness* is that being divides into the for-itself and the in-itself. As I made clear in Chapter 2, what characterizes being-for-itself and distinguishes it from being-in-itself is its self-consciousness. What it means for a being to exist *for* itself is that it is self-conscious. But what does self-consciousness come to for Sartre in *Being and Nothingness*? There is no simple answer to this question. For Sartre there are really several levels of self-consciousness: the self-consciousness of consciousness at the pre-reflective level, at the level of reflection both pure and impure, and at the level of being-for-others. A profound difference exists between the self-consciousness of being-for-others and impure reflection, on the one hand, and the self-consciousness of pure reflection and pre-reflective consciousness, on the other. With being-for-others and impure reflection, self-consciousness involves the attempt to grasp the self as an object for consciousness. Although the nature of this attempt and the reasons for its ultimate failure differ at each level, these levels are bound together by a common sense of self-consciousness as a consciousness of the self as an object. At the level of pure reflection and pre-reflective consciousness, self-consciousness no longer involves the attempt to grasp the self as an object. On these two levels the for-itself attempts to grasp itself as consciousness, and because consciousness just is, on Sartre's view, presence to the world, it is consciousness's attempt to be conscious of itself as consciousness of the world. I will argue that on the level of being-for-others and impure reflection, self-consciousness, given Sartre's account of it on these levels, cannot be achieved. Sartre acknowledges these failures of self-consciousness and explains why such failures must be the case, given the nature of consciousness. It is on the level of pure reflection and pre-reflective consciousness that problems arise. Here Sartre contends that self-consciousness is possible. But I will argue that Sartre's account of self-consciousness at the level both of pre-reflective consciousness and of pure reflection fails. I will maintain that the account of self-consciousness at the level of pure reflection fails because Sartre does not offer a characterization of reflective self-consciousness that keeps it distinct from the self-consciousness of pre-reflective consciousness, on the one hand, and from the attempt at self-consciousness on the level of impure reflection, on the other. The account of self-consciousness at the level of pre-reflective consciousness fails as well because Sartre is unsuccessful in maintaining, without inconsistency, his claim that pre-reflective consciousness as self-consciousness must be dual yet one.

Because I wish to examine first the failures of self-consciousness that Sartre acknowledges before examining the unrecognized failure of his account of reflective and pre-reflective self-consciousness, I deal with the levels of self-consciousness distinguished in *Being and Nothingness* in an order the reverse of Sartre's. I begin by examining Sartre's account of self-consciousness in terms of our being-for-others and why for Sartre such self-consciousness is not attainable. Next I do the same with self-consciousness at the level of impure reflection. Following this, I argue that Sartre's account of self-consciousness on the level of pure reflection fails and, finally, that his account of self-consciousness at the pre-reflective level fails as well.

BEING-FOR-OTHERS

Self-consciousness on the level of our being-for-others involves for Sartre consciousness of the self as an object. It is a consciousness that ultimately eludes the self that has been objectified.[1] Although I can experience, through the look of the other, my revelation as an object in another's world, I cannot apprehend the object I am for the other. The self that is made present to me through my experience of the other's gaze is a self that escapes me and exists for the other. This self is the objectified self, the ego. I can recognize and acknowledge this self as myself. Indeed, Sartre claims the shame I experience when captured by the regard of the other is a confession that I am this self. But although I can acknowledge this me that comes to be in the look of the other, I can never apprehend that self as *myself*. It is an aspect of my existence that escapes me. So the *self* of self-consciousness at this level escapes into the world of the other. I am conscious that there is a dimension of my being that belongs to the other, but I cannot be conscious of the self which inhabits that dimension. The very being of self-consciousness, Sartre claims, is "the radical exclusion of all objectivity. I am the one who can not be an object for myself" (BN, p. 241).

What the other confers on me by her look is an outside, a nature. But because I am, as a for-itself, "pure interiority" (BN, p. 241), I cannot grasp my outside. That is why I experience the existence of the other as an alienation from myself. The other's look transforms me into an in-itself. I am somebody, but a somebody "who on principle escapes me" (BN, p. 263). I am transformed into a me, but a me that is "outside my reach, outside my action, outside my knowledge" (BN, p. 268). I am consciousness, a being that exists for itself, and as such I cannot apprehend *myself* as an object. So although I can accept that that object is me and can even conceive of myself as a being with objective properties once I have been seen by the other, I cannot grasp that object *as myself*. "Thus the Me-as-object-for-myself is a Me which *is not* Me. . . . Even if I could see myself clearly and distinctly as an object, what I should see would not be the adequate representation of what I am in myself and for myself" (BN, p. 273).[2] It is precisely because the other is other that she can confer an outside on me. She can take a point of view on me that I cannot. I am consciousness and interiority and as such cannot distance myself sufficiently from myself to make myself an object for my own consciousness. This becomes clear in Sartre's discussion of self-consciousness at the level of reflection.[3]

REFLECTION

For Sartre, reflection is a consciousness positing a consciousness (TE, p. 62). Thus, Sartre says, reflective consciousness is a positional consciousness of the consciousness reflected on. It is an attempt on the part of consciousness to recover itself by wrenching itself away from itself.

In reflection the for-itself attempts to regain itself by putting "itself inside its own being" (BN, p. 153). On the pre-reflective level, consciousness "has lost itself outside itself" (BN, p. 153) in its past, in the object to which it is present, and in its future. In reflection it attempts to find itself again. There are two important points to remember about Sartre's description of reflection: first, reflective consciousness involves a unity and a duality, and second, self-consciousness is involved in several ways at the level of reflection. In the end these two points come together in Sartre's account of reflection in a rather convoluted fashion. Although reflection involves a reflective consciousness and a consciousness reflected on, these two must remain one. On Sartre's view there must be an "absolute unity" (BN, p. 150) of reflective consciousness with the consciousness on which it reflects; they must be one in being with each other. Otherwise, the certainty of reflective consciousness would be lost, and Sartre wishes to maintain a version of the Cartesian thesis that reflection yields certainty. Sartre maintains that if we think of reflective consciousness as separate from the consciousness on which it reflects, the bond between them will be external only. Reflective consciousness will possess at most an image or representation of the act of consciousness on which it reflects. This conception of reflection would push us toward accepting a perceptual model of introspection. Just as in perception (construed on a Cartesian model) one is related to a representation of the object perceived, so in introspection, conceived of on a perceptual model, reflective consciousness would possess only a representation of the consciousness reflected on—a sensation of a sensation, so to speak. But then the kind of skepticism and lack of certainty that haunt the Cartesian view of perception would also haunt this view of introspection as a kind of quasi perceiving. "Reflective knowledge, and in particular the *cogito* would lose their certainty and would obtain in exchange only a certain probability, scarcely definable" (BN, p. 151). To maintain that reflection is infallible, Sartre claims that "reflection—if it is to be apodictic evidence—demands that the reflective *be* that which is reflected-on" (BN, p. 151).[4] Unfortunately, in this description of reflection in general, Sartre often ascribes to reflection as a whole characteristics that he later claims apply only to one of the two forms of reflection he distinguishes: pure and impure. In this case, the infallibility and certainty that Sartre attributes to reflection in general apply, as Sartre later points out, only to pure reflection. He does, however, continue to maintain that the unity that exists between reflective consciousness and the consciousness on which it reflects cannot be broken even at the level of impure reflection. For consciousness to remain consciousness, it must be one with itself; otherwise, Sartre fears, something will be introduced into consciousness of which consciousness is unconscious. That would destroy the translucency of consciousness and by introducing an unconscious something into consciousness involve one, Sartre thinks, in a contradiction. So the consciousness that reflects and the consciousness reflected on must be one and the same.

However, there must be a duality within this unity. "To the extent that reflection is *knowledge*, the reflected-on must necessarily be the *object* for the reflective; and this implies a separation of being" (BN, p. 151). Reflection, as the self conscious of itself, must involve, as all consciousness does on Sartre's view, a separation between consciousness and that of which it is conscious. This is true at every level of consciousness, given Sartre's analysis of consciousness as a presence to being that necessitates a withdrawal from being. Every consciousness is a nihilation. Reflection for Sartre is a stage of nihilation in between the pre-reflective existence of the for-itself and its being for others. In my existence for others, the nihilation necessary for consciousness to be a witness to the self as object is a nihilation performed, at least in the first stages of my existence for others, by a consciousness other than my own—by the consciousness of the other that like my own is, as a presence to being, non-being, a nothingness. What separates me from myself as an object at the level of existence for others is a nothingness that I am not, a nothingness that is other than myself. At the level of reflection, reflective consciousness is separated from the consciousness reflected on by a nothing that is itself: hence, duality within unity.

The second point to remember about Sartre's description of reflection is that reflection involves self-consciousness in several ways: (1) *the consciousness reflected on* is pre-reflectively self-conscious—that is, from the start it is both a thetic consciousness of an object and a non-thetic consciousness of itself as consciousness of an object; (2) *reflective consciousness* is itself pre-reflectively self-conscious—that is, as consciousness it is thetically aware of the consciousness on which it reflects and non-thetically aware of itself as that consciousness; and (3) *the very act of reflection* causes the non-thetic self-awareness of pre-reflective consciousness to become thetic consciousness of self. It is this third sense of self-consciousness to which I will be referring throughout my discussion of pure and impure reflection.

For Sartre, all self-consciousness involves duality within unity. Even at the level of pre-reflective consciousness there must be a duality within the unity of consciousness. For consciousness to be present to itself, even non-thetically, as it is at the pre-reflective level, it must withdraw from itself, and yet for consciousness to maintain its translucency, a trait that Sartre argues is essential to consciousness as consciousness, it must be one with itself. To accommodate these conflicting demands, Sartre contends that what divides consciousness from itself at the pre-reflective level is nothing. Hence, in reflection there is a nothingness that divides reflective consciousness from itself (since it is non-thetically self-conscious); there is a nothingness that divides the consciousness reflected on from itself (because it is also non-thetically self-conscious); and there is a nothingness that divides the reflective consciousness from the consciousness on which it reflects.[5]

Beyond giving this description of reflection in general and the self-consciousness involved at the reflective level, Sartre distinguishes pure from impure reflection. These two levels of reflection aspire to self-consciousness in different ways. I wish to examine the distinction Sartre draws between the self-consciousness of pure and impure reflection, arguing that both types of reflective self-consciousness fail. I begin with impure reflection because it is a type of reflective self-consciousness that Sartre agrees must fail.

Impure Reflection

Although pure reflection is the original structure of impure reflection, it is the latter, Sartre claims, that is given first in daily life (BN, p. 159). Impure reflection is the attempt "to apprehend the reflected-on as in-itself in order to make itself be that in-itself which is apprehended" (BN, p. 160). In impure reflection the reflective consciousness tries to take a point of view on the consciousness reflected on and thus attempts to view the reflected consciousness as an object. That is why Sartre holds that impure reflection is in bad faith. It is "an abortive effort on the part of the for-itself *to be another* while *remaining itself*" (BN, p. 161).[6] Reflective consciousness tries to separate the consciousness reflected on from itself and make it an object, an in-itself, while also claiming that it *is* that very same consciousness. The object with which consciousness at the level of impure reflection tries to claim identity is what Sartre calls the ego, the psyche, the psychic object. The nature of this object, the ego, is spelled out in both *Being and Nothingness* and in *The Transcendence of the Ego*. It is an object apprehended but also constituted by reflective consciousness. The ego is the totality of the states and qualities and actions of the person. Sartre gives hatred as an example of a state of a person. Although hatred is given through moments of consciousness, it transcends any one moment and has a permanence they lack. It is given as continuing even when the person who hates is absorbed in other things and has no consciousness that reveals the hatred. "Hatred . . . is a transcendent object" (TE, p. 63) that is constituted by impure reflection. Although qualities such as "ambitious" or "hard working" are latent dispositions, unlike states that actually exist, they too, along with actions, are transcendent. The same applies to the ego, which is the transcendent unity of states, qualities, and actions (TE, p. 70). Because impure reflection goes beyond consciousness to a transcendent object, it is fallible. It can be mistaken, for example, in the states or qualities it attributes to itself. But the more important problem is that this ego which consciousness attempts to claim as itself is the for-itself reduced to a thing. The ego is a shadow, Sartre says, cast by the for-itself. It is created by consciousness's attempt at the level of impure reflection to give to itself an outside and claim that outside is strictly identical to itself. It is what is revealed to me, on Sartre's view, when I wish to see myself, but because it is only a faint image of myself, only a shadow, my apprehension of myself as a psychic object does not amount to substantive self-consciousness. It is not consciousness conscious of itself as a for-itself but rather as something outside consciousness, a transcendent object, an object fit for the study of psychologists but not for the creation of self-consciousness. Such an object eludes the consciousness that constitutes it, for consciousness cannot grasp itself from the outside. As we have seen, only a consciousness other than oneself can grasp one's ego, and then what the other grasps is dust: oneself reduced and degraded, a mere shadow.

Pure Reflection

Sartre acknowledges the failure of self-consciousness at the level of both being-for-others and impure reflection. Is self-consciousness possible at the level of pure reflection? Before we can answer that question, we must clarify what the self-consciousness of pure reflection amounts to for Sartre. Sartre describes pure reflection as "the simple presence of the reflective for-itself to the for-itself reflected-on" (BN, p. 155). Although Sartre says in the section on reflection in general that the goal of reflection is for consciousness to recover itself and establish itself as a given (BN, p. 153), he modifies this claim in the section on pure reflection. There he says pure reflection does not deliver the reflected-on as a given (BN, pp. 155, 156). What pure reflection does is to make a being that is already "a revelation" (that is, non-thetically self-conscious) exist for itself (BN, p. 156). In pure reflection consciousness does not attempt to be present to itself as an ego, a transcendent object, that partakes of psychic temporality and has a past, present, and future congealed into states, qualities, and actions. No, in pure reflection consciousness attempts to be present to itself as a present moment of consciousness, a moment that partakes of the original temporality of the for-itself. Pure reflection grasps the historicized, unreflective for-itself dragging its past with it, pointed toward its future, and directed outward toward the world. Pure reflection is, Sartre says, "the pure and simple discovery [on the part of the for-itself] of the historicity which it is" (BN, p. 159). Pure reflection is an attempt on the part of consciousness to be present to itself without attempting to take a point of view on itself as it does in impure reflection. In pure reflection the consciousness reflected on is not presented as something outside reflection, nor is it presented as a being "in relation to which one can realize a withdrawal" (BN, p. 155). And yet because pure reflection is consciousness conscious of itself, because it is, for Sartre, the wrenching away and turning back of the self on itself, there must be a withdrawal of consciousness from itself. But for Sartre to maintain his claim that consciousness at the level of pure reflection is translucent and infallible about itself, he argues that reflective consciousness and the consciousness reflected on are one—that is, what separates consciousness from itself at the level of pure reflection is nothing (BN, pp. 150–51). Thus Sartre characterizes the self-consciousness of consciousness at the level of pure reflection as a consciousness conscious of itself and yet separated from itself by nothing. But because pre-reflective self-consciousness, on Sartre's account, is also a consciousness conscious of itself and separated from itself by nothing, Sartre needs to distinguish pure reflection from pre-reflective self-consciousness. He also claims that consciousness is separated from itself by nothing at the level of impure reflection. What distinguishes pure from impure reflection is the attitude each type of reflection takes toward this nothingness. Impure reflection attempts to grasp, in bad faith, this nothing as something, as an in-itself, whereas pure reflection attempts to grasp the nothing as a for-itself. Sartre must distinguish pure reflection from pre-reflective consciousness in an unambiguous way that manages at the same time to avoid destroying the distinction he draws between pure and impure reflection. How is he to do so? The answer is crucial to deciding whether Sartre's account of self-consciousness on the level of pure reflection is successful.

Perhaps one could characterize the difference between pre-reflective self-consciousness and the self-consciousness of pure reflection in terms of latency. Sartre suggests this interpretation in both *The Transcendence of the Ego* and *Being and Nothingness*. As I noted in Chapter 1, Sartre argues in *The Transcendence of the Ego* that Kant's claim that the 'I think' must accompany all our representations means that "I can always regard my perception or thought as *mine*" (TE, p. 32). It does not, however, mean that I do always do so. It doesn't mean that an 'I' must accompany every act of consciousness. Kant's dictum refers, on Sartre's view, to a *possibility* of reflective consciousness. It refers to a capacity, an ability not always realized. It is this notion of a capacity that remains latent at the pre-reflective level that comes into play in the cigarette-counting example Sartre utilizes in *Being and Nothingness* in discussing the self-consciousness of pre-reflective consciousness. The fact that consciousness is self-conscious even at the pre-reflective level means, at least if the cigarette-counting case is to be taken as paradigmatic, that if asked what I am doing, I can reply. In the example of counting cigarettes, it is not that I am explicitly, thetically conscious that I am counting. No, I am only explicitly aware of the cigarettes and their number. But I have the ability or the capacity to become reflectively aware that I am counting cigarettes. This capacity may remain latent, or it may become activated if, for example, someone asks me what I am doing. We must keep in mind, however, that in answering such a question, a person has abandoned the level of pre-reflective consciousness and has moved to the level of reflection. Will a characterization of the difference between the self-consciousness of pre-reflective consciousness and that of pure reflection in terms of latency provide us with an account of the self-consciousness of pure reflection that distinguishes it from pre-reflective consciousness and keeps it from collapsing into impure reflection?

The problem is that this account appears to be inconsistent with Sartre's characterization of the self-consciousness of pre-reflective consciousness as a realization and not simply a capacity. For Sartre, "to be and to be aware of itself are one and the same thing for consciousness" (TE,

p. 83). He repeats this view in his discussion of pre-reflective consciousness in *Being and Nothingness*. Pre-reflective consciousness *actually* is consciousness of itself as consciousness of an object. One way to resolve this
seeming inconsistency is to argue that for Sartre the self-consciousness
of pre-reflective consciousness is both a realized self-consciousness and a
capacity for another level of self-consciousness. The self-consciousness
that is actual at the pre-reflective level is a consciousness conscious of
itself as consciousness of an object. Here consciousness is not conscious
of itself as an 'I' or an ego but rather simply as consciousness. The
capacity for another level of self-consciousness is a capacity for attribution
of ownership. It is the capacity to be conscious that *I* am conscious of
an object. So because the realization refers to one level of consciousness
and the capacity to another, there is no inconsistency in claiming that
the self-consciousness of pre-reflective consciousness is a realized self-
consciousness and a capacity for self-consciousness. Yet this solution fails
to draw the distinction between pure reflection and the self-consciousness
of pre-reflective consciousness without at the same time collapsing the
distinction between pure and impure reflection. Because impure reflection involves the introduction of the ego into our thought about ourselves, if pure reflection is identified with the realization of the capacity
to attribute conscious activity to an 'I' or ego—to an owner—pure reflection reduces to impure. But if pure reflection is thought of as consciousness conscious of itself not as an ego but simply as consciousness
conscious of an object, then it becomes indistinguishable from the actual
self-consciousness of pre-reflective consciousness. Unless we can find another reading of this latency account, Sartre will need a different characterization of the distinction between the self-consciousness of
pre-reflective consciousness and pure reflection.

Because Sartre argues in the introduction to *Being and Nothingness*
that the self-consciousness of pre-reflective consciousness is not a knowledge, he could distinguish pure reflection from the self-consciousness of
pre-reflective consciousness by maintaining that pure reflection is a
knowledge. He begins his discussion of pure reflection by making just
such a claim. Pure reflection "is a knowledge; of that there is no doubt"
(BN, p. 155). Sartre, however, immediately begins to reconsider his attribution of knowledge to pure reflection. He realizes that on his analysis
of knowledge, "to know is to *make oneself other*" (BN, p. 155) and that
if pure reflection is a knowledge, then the possibility of self-consciousness
at this level will be destroyed. The subject/object dyad associated with

knowledge in the introduction to *Being and Nothingness* will reduce pure reflection to an attempt on the part of consciousness to grasp itself as an object. This is precisely what consciousness tried and failed to do at the level of impure reflection. Knowledge objectifies, and a for-itself objectified is, for Sartre, no longer a for-itself. So if pure reflection involves knowledge, it will fail as surely as consciousness's attempt to know itself as consciousness failed at the level of impure reflection and being-for-others. Describing pure reflection as knowledge will also destroy the distinction Sartre wishes to draw between pure and impure reflection. Both would become the for-itself's attempt in bad faith to make itself an object and claim that object as itself. In addition, if pure reflection is knowledge, because knowledge involves a duality between knower and known for Sartre, the unity he thinks necessary for the infallibility of pure reflection will be lost. Because of these manifold consequences of maintaining that pure reflection is knowledge, Sartre begins to weaken his original claim. Now he says pure reflection is a recognition, not a knowledge (BN, p. 156). It is "never anything but a quasi-knowledge" (BN, p. 162). It involves not an object as knowledge usually does but only a quasi object (BN, p. 155). It is a "lightning intuition" of oneself but does not involve the taking of a point of view as knowledge typically does (BN, p. 155). But what is this "lightning intuition" that reveals us to ourselves not as something other and not as an object but merely as a quasi object? What is this intuition of the self that can come to us without our having to withdraw far enough away from ourself to call our position a point of view? Sartre doesn't give many hints. He does say that this intuition "must be won by a sort of katharsis" (BN, p. 155), but later in this section on reflection, when he repeats this claim, he says it is not the place to discuss this catharsis, and he never returns to this question again.[7] What Sartre needs here is an explication of this quasi knowledge, of this "lightning intuition," in terms which are both clear and unambiguous and which distinguish pure reflection from the self-consciousness of pre-reflective consciousness without causing it to collapse into impure reflection.

He attempts to do so by arguing that the nothingness that separates consciousness from itself on the level of pure reflection is a deeper and more profound nothingness than that which separates consciousness from itself at the pre-reflective level. Reflection is a dissociation on Sartre's account, and it "is made by the deepening of the nothingness which separates the reflection (reflet) from the reflecting (reflétant)" (BN,

p. 161). What are we to make of this enigmatic claim? Is there a way to clarify this claim that maintains and illuminates both his characterization of pure reflection as a quasi knowledge and the distinction he draws between pre-reflective consciousness, pure reflection, and impure reflection?

A distinction to which Sartre refers, albeit rather obliquely, in various places in *Being and Nothingness* and one which may be of some use to him here is the distinction between a consciousness of oneself that involves no conceptualization and one that does involve the use of concepts. The presence or absence of concepts may be what distinguishes the self-consciousness of pre-reflective consciousness from self-consciousness at the level of pure reflection. It is not until late in *Being and Nothingness*, in the section dealing with existential psychoanalysis, that Sartre does much with this distinction. He utilizes it in the context of his discussion of the difference between consciousness and knowledge. He distinguishes between consciousness and knowledge to explain how existential psychoanalysis works and how it differs from traditional psychoanalysis. For Sartre the task of existential psychoanalysis is to bring to light the fundamental project of the person under analysis. This does not mean bringing it forth from the unconscious. For Sartre, the person is always *conscious* of the fundamental project that she is. What is lacking is *knowledge* of this project. "If the fundamental project is fully experienced by the subject and hence wholly conscious, that certainly does not mean that it must by the same token be *known* by him" (BN, p. 570). But what is this knowledge that existential psychoanalysis provides, and how does it differ from the consciousness each person has of her fundamental project? An essential difference for Sartre between consciousness and knowledge is that consciousness lacks conceptualization, whereas knowledge does not.[8] When he explains why reflection cannot serve as the basis for existential psychoanalysis, although it provides the brute materials on which such analysis works, he claims that what reflection lacks are "the means which would ordinarily permit *analysis* and *conceptualization*" (BN, p. 571) of the fundamental project. Reflection lacks the "techniques necessary to isolate the choice symbolized, [and] *to fix it by concepts*" (BN, p. 570; emphasis mine). The task of existential psychoanalysis, which involves the gaining of knowledge of the subject's fundamental project, is "a deciphering, a determination, and a conceptualization" (BN, p. 569). Now how will this distinction between consciousness without conceptualization and consciousness with conceptualization help Sartre to distinguish pure reflection from pre-reflective self-consciousness? There is no simple way to apply this distinction and keep pure reflection distinct from both pre-reflective self-consciousness and impure reflection. If we distinguish pre-reflective self-consciousness from pure reflection by claiming the former is consciousness without conceptualization and the latter is consciousness with conceptualization, then pure reflection becomes knowledge, given Sartre's identification of consciousness that involves conceptualization with knowledge. If pure reflection becomes knowledge and involves the attempt at the self-objectification that characterizes impure reflection, then the distinction between the two collapses. If instead we characterize pure reflection as consciousness without conceptualization to keep it distinct from impure reflection's attempt to know itself, then nothing remains to distinguish pure reflection from pre-reflective self-consciousness. Sartre's solution is to reassert his earlier claim that reflection is only a quasi knowledge. What sense can we make of this claim in light of the distinction between knowledge and consciousness drawn above? Reflection, Sartre argues, differs from the knowledge gained in existential psychoanalysis because it fails to grasp the fundamental project as it is symbolically expressed by concrete behavior. It grasps only the behavior itself (BN, p. 570). Given the fact that knowledge involves conceptualization, perhaps Sartre claims reflection is a quasi knowledge because although it applies concepts, it applies them only to the behavior and not to the fundamental project the behavior reveals. If we think of reflection for Sartre as a conceptualization that goes just halfway, we can understand why he placed it between the self-consciousness of pre-reflective consciousness and the self-knowledge attainable through existential psychoanalysis.[9] On this interpretation of Sartre, the distinction between the self-consciousness of pre-reflective consciousness and the self-consciousness of reflection would become the distinction between a consciousness that is a nonconceptualized consciousness of itself and a consciousness whose consciousness of itself involves conceptualization but not knowledge. Does this way of drawing the distinction clarify the difference between these two levels of self-consciousness in a way that is unambiguous and useful?

At least prima facie it is easier to comprehend the difference between a self-consciousness that utilizes concepts from one that does not than it is to comprehend the difference between a self-consciousness that involves a nothingness and one that involves a deeper nothingness. But problems remain. On the one hand, is consciousness without conceptualization possible? If Sartre wishes to hold that it is, he needs to offer an argument to support that claim; but he offers no such argument. On the other hand, can pure reflection involve a self-consciousness that utilizes conceptualization and yet does not objectify the self in a way that splits consciousness from itself and destroys the unity and hence the translucency and infallibility Sartre maintains are characteristics of pure reflection?[10] Existential psychoanalysis, whether it is performed by the subject herself or another, takes, Sartre says, the point of view of the other toward the self and brings to light *as an object* the fundamental project that one is (BN, p. 571). Now, if the reason for this is because existential psychoanalysis is a knowledge, then reflection, which is not a real knowledge on Sartre's view, can escape this description. However, if for Sartre this description applies to existential psychoanalysis because it involves conceptualization, then reflection, which also involves conceptualization, would likewise be the viewing of oneself from the point of view of the other. That is what impure reflection tries and fails to accomplish. If reflection reduces to that attempt, Sartre's account has once again lost the ability to distinguish pure from impure reflection. The attempt to utilize the distinction between a self-consciousness that utilizes concepts from one that does not in order to characterize reflection in such a way that it remains distinct from the self-consciousness of pre-reflective consciousness, on the one hand, and impure reflection, on the other, is not without its own problems. Without a reading of *Being and Nothingness* that allows us to overcome these problems, this solution fails. We are left either with an account of self-consciousness at the level of pure reflection that is ambiguous because it fails to distinguish pure reflection from the self-consciousness of pre-reflective consciousness or with an account of a self-consciousness that is unattainable because the self-consciousness of pure reflection would simply collapse into the failed attempt at self-consciousness on the level of impure reflection.[11] Sartre's problem is that at the level of pure reflection he does not have a clear enough notion of a knowledge that isn't a subject/object relation or of a self-consciousness that isn't just pre-reflective to provide a clear account of the self-consciousness of pure reflection that distinguishes it from both pre-reflective consciousness and impure reflection. Similar problems haunt his account of the self-consciousness of pre-reflective consciousness.

PRE-REFLECTIVE CONSCIOUSNESS

Sartre first discusses the nature of pre-reflective self-consciousness in *The Transcendence of the Ego*.[12] He does the negative labor of clearing away false notions of self-consciousness before articulating his own view. As we saw in Chapter 1, self-consciousness at the pre-reflective level is not consciousness of an 'I' or an ego that stands behind or is a substratum for the activity of consciousness. There is no 'I' that inhabits pre-reflective consciousness.[13] Indeed, there is nothing in consciousness; it has no content. So the self-consciousness of pre-reflective consciousness cannot be consciousness conscious of its content. Consciousness is defined, Sartre says, by intentionality (TE, p. 38); it always has an object. But the objects of consciousness transcend consciousness, and therefore, self-consciousness at the pre-reflective level is consciousness "aware of itself *in so far as it is consciousness of a transcendent object*" (TE, p. 40).

In *Being and Nothingness* Sartre expands but does not alter his conception of the nature of self-consciousness at the pre-reflective level. Self-consciousness at this level is still characterized as consciousness conscious of itself as consciousness of an object. Sartre asks in the introduction to *Being and Nothingness* what this consciousness of consciousness is, answering first in the negative. As we saw in Chapter 2, it is not a knowledge. If self-consciousness at the pre-reflective level were self-knowledge, that would involve consciousness taking itself as an object, resulting in either an infinite regress or a regress stopped only by accepting a non-selfconscious consciousness.[14] Neither alternative is acceptable. Consequently, Sartre rejects in his analysis of self-consciousness at the pre-reflective level the subject/object duality that characterizes knowledge. As he pointed out in *The Transcendence of the Ego*, "To be and to be aware of itself are one and the same thing for consciousness" (TE, p. 83). The self-consciousness of the pre-reflective cogito does not break its unity. Every positional consciousness of an object just is a non-positional consciousness of itself. Sartre emphasizes the unity of pre-reflective consciousness over and over again in the introduction to *Being and Nothingness*. "Consciousness of consciousness . . . is one with the consciousness of which it is consciousness" (BN, p. liv). If an intention, a pleasure, and a grief, for example, are not things in consciousness, then Sartre must ensure the self-conscious nature of these modes of consciousness by uniting pleasure, for instance, with consciousness of pleasure. "Pleasure can not be distinguished—even logically—from consciousness of pleasure" (BN, p. liv). It cannot be that pleasure exists first and then becomes conscious of itself, for that would make the psychic event into a thing, something unconscious, which is then made conscious. On the other hand, Sartre rejects the possibility of consciousness existing and then receiving the quality of pleasure. Consciousness is in itself nothing; for Sartre it is not a substratum or substance that can take on the quality of being pleasurable or grief-stricken. No, for Sartre, the self-consciousness of pre-reflective consciousness is not something added to consciousness; it is part of its very nature. "An intention, a pleasure, a grief can exist only as immediate self-consciousness" (BN, p. liv).

Although in the introduction to *Being and Nothingness* Sartre rejects in his analysis of pre-reflective consciousness the duality that knowledge introduces, he does argue that a certain duality is necessary in pre-reflective consciousness if it is to be self-conscious. Just as consciousness of the world is, on Sartre's view, a nihilating withdrawal of consciousness from the world of the in-itself, so too self-consciousness is a nihilating withdrawal of consciousness from all that it is: a withdrawal from its present object, from its past, and from its future. For Sartre, as the discussion in Chapter 2 made clear, it is because consciousness is self-consciousness, even at the pre-reflective level, that the Law of Identity does not apply to it. That is why bad faith is possible for humans. Because faith or belief as a mode of consciousness must be self-conscious, belief fails to be identical to itself. Even pre-reflectively, belief must be consciousness (of) belief.[15] But the non-thetic self-consciousness of belief is destructive of belief. "Belief is a being . . . which can manifest itself to itself only by denying itself. . . . To believe is not-to-believe" (BN, p. 69). As I indicated in Chapter 2, these remarks are clarified somewhat by his discussion of presence to self in the chapter immediately following the one on bad faith.

In discussing the immediate structures of the for-itself, Sartre contrasts the unity and self-identity of the in-itself with the duality at the heart of the for-itself. As we saw in Chapter 2, for a being to exist for itself— that is, for a being to be self-conscious—it must not be itself. Presence to self requires a withdrawal from self. Because the self at the pre-reflective level is simply consciousness of objects or modes of consciousness, then belief (as the example Sartre continues to use) is present to belief. Belief is pre-reflective consciousness of belief. Consciousness is always a witness to itself even from the start. And just as reflection alters the object of reflection, so too, Sartre argues, pre-reflective self-consciousness alters the consciousness of which it is a witness, even though it is this same consciousness. Sartre desires here to maintain the view he espoused in *The Transcendence of the Ego* and in the introduction to *Being and Nothingness* that self-consciousness does not destroy the unity of the pre-reflective cogito at the same time as he defends the claim that the Law of Identity does not apply to consciousness. To reconcile two seemingly conflicting claims—that consciousness is unified yet dual—he contends (as he does on the level of reflective consciousness) that what separates consciousness from itself is nothing.

Elsewhere I have argued that Sartre's account of self-consciousness at the pre-reflective level as a duality within a unity fails.[16] It fails because to maintain the duality, he introduces cognitive elements into pre-reflective consciousness. But he has rejected those elements in his analysis of pre-reflective consciousness in the introduction to *Being and Nothingness* to save the unity and thus the translucency of pre-reflective consciousness. As I explained in Chapter 2, Sartre contends that because belief is self-conscious even pre-reflectively, it is somehow no longer belief. In explicating what this duality amounts to, Sartre introduces epistemological considerations. "To believe is to *know* that one believes, and to *know* that one believes is no longer to believe" (BN, p. 69; emphasis mine). He wants to claim that belief *is and is not* what it is. Belief is belief, but because it is self-conscious, it is not belief. Sartre argues that once I know I believe, I see my belief as purely subjective and thus my belief is undermined; it is no longer directed outward toward its object. Although Sartre has here introduced elements of knowledge, in the introduction we have seen that he clearly rejects an analysis of the self-consciousness of pre-reflective consciousness in terms of knowledge. He acknowledges that he has "forced the description of the phenomenon [of belief] by designating it with the word *to know*; non-thetic consciousness is not to *know*" (BN, p. 69). Yet he dismisses this inconsistency on his part by simply repeating his claim that pre-reflective consciousness, in its translucency, is at the origin of all knowledge. From that fact alone he concludes that "the non-thetic consciousness (of) believing is destructive of belief" (BN, p. 69). Sartre's contention that pre-reflective consciousness is at the origin of knowledge appears to motivate his introduction of epistemological elements into his analysis of the self-consciousness of belief on the pre-reflective level. But his argument that because belief knows itself it is fractured within itself is undermined by his discussion of pre-reflective consciousness in the introduction to *Being and Nothingness.* There he contends that it does not follow from the primacy of the pre-reflective cogito and the fact that it underlies knowledge that it is a *knowing* consciousness in terms of itself. Sartre maintains in the introduction that pre-reflective consciousness does not *know* itself, although it is self-conscious. Prior to reflection, considerations of knowledge do not arise. For the Sartre of the introduction, pre-reflective consciousness is noncognitive. And yet it is the introduction of knowledge into the translucency of the pre-reflective cogito that underlies his argument, in the chapters on bad faith and the immediate structures of the for-itself, that "to believe is not to believe" (BN, p. 69).[17]

In his discussion of the self-consciousness of pre-reflective consciousness as well as in his discussion of pure reflection, Sartre introduces epistemological elements that on second thought he wishes to reject. He never resolves this problem. The reason it arises, I think, is because Sartre wants to distinguish self-consciousness from self-knowledge, but to do so he must first distinguish consciousness from knowledge. However, he fails to offer a coherent account that makes these two distinct. In fact, he characterizes both as presence to _____, and although in the introduction and in the section on existential psychoanalysis he claims they are distinct, the distinction begins to collapse in his discussion of the self-consciousness of pre-reflective consciousness in the section on bad faith and the one on the immediate structures of the for-itself as well as in his discussion of pure reflection. He ends up, in these latter sections, characterizing self-*consciousness* as a knowledge or a quasi knowledge, although he rejects that characterization elsewhere.

In the early sections of *Being and Nothingness*, Sartre characterizes consciousness as a presence to being, a revelation of the in-itself. As such it must withdraw from being. To be present to being, a witness to being, consciousness must be non-being. Likewise, self-*consciousness*—that is, consciousness conscious of itself—is characterized as a presence of the self to itself and hence a withdrawal of the self from itself.[18] "Presence to self . . . supposes that an impalpable fissure has slipped into being. If being is present to itself, it is because it is not wholly itself. Presence is an immediate deterioration of coincidence, for it supposes separation" (BN, p. 77).

In the chapter on transcendence in *Being and Nothingness*, Sartre applies this same analysis to knowledge. At the beginning of that chapter, he claims that there is only intuitive knowledge and that "intuition is the presence of consciousness to the thing" (BN, p. 172). "Knowledge therefore is of the type of being which we described in the preceding chapter under the title 'presence to _____' " (BN, p. 172). This type of being is the for-itself, so knowledge "is the very being of the for-itself in so far as this is presence to _____" (BN, p. 174). Knowledge as presence, as the presence of the for-itself to a certain being, involves negation. "Presence incloses a radical negation as presence to that which one is not. What is present to me is what is not me" (BN, p. 173).

Sartre fails in this section to distinguish consciousness of an object from knowledge of an object. Consequently, in his analysis of the self's consciousness of itself, he introduces epistemological elements before he even realizes it. He has trouble articulating a view of the duality he thinks necessary to presence to _____ without introducing cognitive elements and hence the subject/object duality of knowledge, a duality he wants to avoid at the level of pre-reflective consciousness and pure reflection. Unless he can make a clear distinction between consciousness of _____ and knowledge of _____, he will not be able to give a coherent account of self-consciousness at the pre-reflective level or even, as we saw above, at the level of pure reflection. His attempt, in the section on existential psychoanalysis, to distinguish them by associating conceptualization with one and not the other runs into the problems discussed earlier in this chapter. Even if he could distinguish consciousness from knowledge, he would still be left with the problem of distinguishing the noncognitive presence of consciousness to itself at the level of pure reflection from consciousness's self-presence at the level of pre-reflective consciousness.[19]

Self-consciousness as an attempt to grasp oneself as an in-itself, as ego, as an object, fails both at the level of being-for-others and at the level of impure reflection. Sartre, of course, acknowledges that there are objective dimensions to one's being. Persons can be objectified and thought of in objective terms. I can learn to think about myself in those ways, but then the dimension of myself I am thinking about is a dimension that essentially, on Sartre's account, escapes me (my being-for-others) or is one that is simply a shadow I cast (in impure reflection). In thinking about myself objectively, I fail to grasp the for-itself as such, the self as consciousness of the world, as a presence to being. It makes sense, given Sartre's distinction between the for-itself as consciousness and the in-itself as object, that an attempt to grasp oneself as object would fail, because the for-itself as consciousness is what is not the in-itself; it is a nihilation of the in-itself. But the problem for the Sartrean account of the self-consciousness of consciousness is that his account of self-consciousness as an attempt to grasp oneself as a for-itself—as consciousness or presence to the world—fails as well, both on the level of pure reflection (thetic self-consciousness) and on the level of pre-reflective consciousness (non-thetic self-consciousness). It fails on the level of pure reflection because Sartre offers no account of self-consciousness on this level that succeeds in distinguishing pure reflection from the self-consciousness of pre-reflective consciousness without at the same time causing the collapse of his distinction between pure and impure reflection. We have seen above that if we accept a latency account of the self-consciousness of pre-reflective consciousness to distinguish it from pure reflection, we must either accept an interpretation of this latency that is inconsistent with Sartre's overall characterization of self-consciousness at the pre-reflective level or we must interpret the latency in a way that destroys our ability to distinguish pure reflection from both pre-reflective self-consciousness and impure reflection. If we seek instead to distinguish pre-reflective self-consciousness from pure reflection by the presence or absence of epistemological elements, we face similar problems. If we attempt to read Sartre's distinction between the two in terms of a difference in the depth of the nothingness that divides consciousness from itself at each level, we are left with a claim so enigmatic as to be useless. If we attempt to dispel the mysteriousness of this claim by unraveling it in terms of a self-consciousness that utilizes concepts from one that does not, we find we've simply replaced one problematic claim with another. The account of self-consciousness at the pre-reflective level is also unsuccessful because Sartre maintains that for consciousness to be conscious of itself, it must be one with itself and yet separate from itself. To defend his claim about the unity of consciousness, he rejects the notion that pre-reflective consciousness is a knowledge, and yet in describing the duality at this level of consciousness, he introduces epistemological elements.

Although one of Sartre's most basic theses in *Being and Nothingness* is that all consciousness must be self-consciousness, he gives no unambiguous account of a self-consciousness that is attainable by the for-itself. On the one hand, his account of self-consciousness on the level of being-for-others and impure reflection is unambiguous, but the self-consciousness of which it is an account is unattainable by the for-itself. On the other hand, his account of a level of self-consciousness that is attainable by the for-itself is ambiguous and fails to maintain the tripartite distinction he wishes to draw between pre-reflective self-consciousness and the self-consciousness of pure and impure reflection. The underlying problem is twofold: First, Sartre fails to develop a theory of consciousness in *Being and Nothingness* which allows him to draw a distinction between knowledge and consciousness that is clear enough to sustain the tripartite distinction mentioned above. Second, he fails to develop a theory of consciousness's noncognitive presence to itself that allows him to distinguish when this self-presence is reflective from when it is not. If my criticisms of Sartre's analysis of self-consciousness are correct and if we can find no alternate reading of the text which presents us with a clear and consistent account of self-consciousness that can be achieved by the for-itself, then the ontology developed in *Being and Nothingness* has been seriously undermined.

In Chapter 6 I return to these problems that undermine Sartre's discussion of self-consciousness in *Being and Nothingness*. Utilizing a notion of bodily self-consciousness that I develop in Chapter 5, I explore ways in which appeal to bodily self-consciousness can offer possible avenues for overcoming many of the deficiencies in Sartre's account of self-consciousness that I have examined in this chapter.

An External Critique

S artre's acceptance of the claim that consciousness is self-consciousness, even pre-reflectively, motivates his belief in the total translucency of consciousness. "The being of consciousness is consciousness of being" (BN, p. 49). Sartre repeats this claim throughout *Being and Nothingness*: knowing is consciousness of knowing (BN, p. 53); belief is consciousness of belief (BN, p. 74); seeing is consciousness of seeing (BN, p. 316). Pleasure, Sartre argues, is logically indistinguishable from consciousness of pleasure (BN, p. liv). As explained in Chapter 2, it is Sartre's belief in the translucency of consciousness that grounds his rejection of the Freudian unconscious as a way of explaining self-deception. For Sartre, a lying consciousness must be consciousness of itself as lying. This does not mean, however, that consciousness must always be conscious of itself reflectively, that it always has knowledge of itself. As we saw in Chapter 3, in the introduction to *Being and Nothingness* Sartre distinguishes knowledge and consciousness. Self-consciousness on the pre-reflective level is consciousness conscious of itself, but noncognitively.

But are all cases of consciousness cases of (at least) pre-reflective self-consciousness? In this chapter I wish to examine possible counterexamples to Sartre's thesis that all consciousness, including pre-reflective consciousness, is self-consciousness. I will, however, bypass the central counterexample Sartre focuses on in *Being and Nothingness*—the Freudian unconscious. Much has been written on Sartre's critique of the

Freudian unconscious. I do not wish to add to that literature. I will focus instead on three other prima facie counterexamples to Sartre's thesis, also considering possible replies to these counterexamples that are open to Sartre. First I examine dreaming consciousness. The advantage of treating this counterexample first is that Sartre has a long discussion of such consciousness in *The Psychology of Imagination*, in which he offers a defense of his view that as consciousness, dreaming consciousness must be self-consciousness. I lay out his argument for this claim and raise objections to that argument. Next I examine two possible counterexamples to Sartre's thesis that can be found in more recent literature on the nature of consciousness. The first is D. M. Armstrong's example of a long-distance truck driver who suddenly 'comes to' after a long period in which he has apparently been unaware of what he has been doing. The second involves people with blindsight, a phenomenon first reported in the 1970s by experimental psychologists.[1] I examine two arguments Sartre might use against describing such cases as ones of consciousness that lacks self-consciousness, contending that his arguments are unconvincing if left unbuttressed by further support. Finally, I consider whether Sartre could simply avoid such cases as counterexamples by claiming that these are not cases of consciousness at all, an alternative I believe to be unavailable to Sartre because it conflicts with his rejection of psychological determinism.

DREAMING

Given Sartre's thesis that all consciousness is self-consciousness, dreaming consciousness ought to be consciousness of dreaming. But this seems counterintuitive. Yet Sartre claims in *The Psychology of Imagination* that dreaming consciousness is consciousness of itself as dreaming. Sartre argues that my reflective certitude of dreaming is proof that dreaming consciousness is consciousness of dreaming. I can have such reflective certitude, Sartre contends, only if "my primitive and non-reflective consciousness [of dreaming] . . . [contained] in itself a sort of latent and non-positional knowledge which reflection then made explicit."[2] I can therefore infer from my reflective certitude of dreaming that dreaming consciousness must have been consciousness of itself as dreaming. Sartre's reason for believing that my reflective certitude of dreaming must derive from the existence of a latent knowledge of dreaming on the pre-reflective level is that if such knowledge did not exist pre-reflectively, the dreamer would have to derive his reflective certitude "from reasonings and comparisons which would show him the incoherence or the absurdity of his images" (PI, p. 234).[3] But to engage in such reasonings, he would have to be awake. So, Sartre says, such reasonings can support only the past-tense judgment that I *was* dreaming and not the present-tense judgment that I am dreaming. At this point in the discussion Sartre equates my reflective certitude of dreaming with the making of the *present*-tense judgment that I am dreaming. But Sartre repeatedly claims that reflection destroys the dream: "So long as the dream lasts consciousness is unable to engage in reflection" (PI, p. 244). For Sartre there is no possibility of reflective consciousness within the dream because reflective consciousness always destroys the dream, if only momentarily (PI, p. 233). Sartre associates reflection with waking up (PI, p. 254). Indeed, what distinguishes dreaming consciousness from perceiving consciousness, for Sartre, is that perception, unlike the dream, is not destroyed by reflection. Given Sartre's position that reflective consciousness cannot occur within the dream and given his claim that the present-tense judgment "I am dreaming" cannot occur pre-reflectively, only reflectively (PI, p. 234), it follows that such a judgment must be made when awake. So why couldn't it rest on reasonings and comparisons just as well as on latent pre-reflective knowledge? How is it that I can even make, on the level of reflection, the present-tense judgment that I am dreaming? Given Sartre's view that reflection destroys dreaming, all such reflective judgments would have to be made in the past tense and presumably then while awake. If that is so, isn't it just as possible for such judgments to rest on reasonings as on a latent knowledge of dreaming that is present pre-reflectively? Isn't Sartre's argument in defense of the self-consciousness of dreaming consciousness weakened considerably by his conflicting claims? Sartre, I think, might reply that although the making of the reflective judgment that I am dreaming destroys the dream and wakes the dreamer up, the dreamer is insufficiently awake at that moment to be in the "full possession of his discursive faculties" (PI, p. 234). He might continue to argue that such full possession is needed to make the reflective judgment based on the reasonings and comparisons mentioned above. Consequently, such a judgment, although made while awake, must still rest on a latent knowledge of dreaming present within pre-reflective dreaming consciousness. Even if we accept this reply, there are other objections to Sartre's position.

Sartre's argument for his claim that I can come to believe that I have been dreaming only if dreaming consciousness contains within itself the non-positional knowledge of itself as dreaming implies that there are only two possible sources for such a belief: reasoning or latent knowledge on the pre-reflective level. He rules out the first, so the second must be the case. For Sartre, the judgment that I have been dreaming simply makes explicit an implicit knowledge of dreaming present within the dream. But is that the only way to make sense of my ability to judge reflectively that I have dreamed? Certainly Norman Malcolm in *Dreaming* thinks not. For Malcolm, the explanation of the judgment 'I was dreaming' *cannot* be as Sartre envisions it. Dreams, Malcolm contends, are not conscious experiences, and so my judgment upon awakening that I was dreaming cannot be derived from a latent knowledge present within dreaming consciousness, as Sartre claims it is. Malcolm rejects what he calls the "received view" that dreams are conscious experiences we sometimes recall upon awakening. He argues such a view involves conceptual confusion.

> When someone says he dreamt so and so, he does not imply that while he was sleeping he was aware of being asleep or was aware of dreaming. When he says 'I dreamt so and so' he implies, first, that it seemed to him on waking up as if so and so had occurred and, second, that the so and so did not occur. There is simply no place here for an implication or assumption that he was aware of anything at all while asleep. His testimony that he had a dream does not involve that nonsensical conclusion.[4]

Without going into the details of Malcolm's argument, let it suffice to say that he uses Wittgensteinian-style language analysis to defend his view that dreams are not conscious experiences and that one's reports of one's dreams cannot then be based, as Sartre claims, on a pre-reflective awareness of dreaming.

It is certainly true that much can be said against Malcolm's arguments. Indeed, Hilary Putnam thinks Malcolm's attack on the received view of dreaming is unsuccessful because the linguistic doctrines that are *used* but not *stated* by Malcolm are oversimplified or false.[5] In his 1976 article "Are Dreams Experiences?" Daniel Dennett noted that the arguments set forth by Malcolm in 1959 against the received view hadn't done much to dislodge it.[6] But despite Malcolm's lack of followers, his position still needs a solid refutation to clear the way for Sartre's conclusion. Even the existence of such a refutation wouldn't do the trick. If there is any other possible explanation for my ability to make the reflective judgment that I was dreaming besides the one Sartre proposes, then it doesn't follow without additional support that Sartre's analysis of the grounds for that ability is correct. In the article mentioned above, Dennett develops a position with regard to the received view that, although indebted to Malcolm's work, differs from it considerably. Malcolm's rejection of the received view of dreams would rule out as unintelligible Sartre's explanation of our ability to report reflectively that we had been dreaming. This is because Sartre's explanation utilizes the notion of dreams as conscious experiences. Dennett, however, argues that although the received view may be true, it may not be true, for there are other possible scenarios. Our dream reports may be based on memories of conscious experiences, or they may be based, for example, on the unconscious composition and recording of dreams that would require no conscious presentation of dream events. On Dennett's view, armchair philosophizing will prove nothing. The received view is just one of several possible theories, and only empirical investigation and evidence could prove which one is correct, if any, and which are false.

It is conceivable, to some philosophers at least, that my belief that I have been dreaming could be based on something besides the self-consciousness of dreaming consciousness. In fact, it is conceivable to both Malcolm and Dennett that such a belief be present without there having been dreaming *consciousness* at all. If that is so, then Sartre's argument fails. Sartre has not established, by the argument he presents in *The Psychology of Imagination*, at any rate, that dreaming consciousness, if it is consciousness at all, is self-consciousness. Of course, if dreams are not conscious experiences, then they can hardly stand as either an example or a counterexample to the thesis that all consciousness is self-consciousness. Let us look elsewhere for further possible counterexamples to Sartre's central claim.

THE LONG-DISTANCE TRUCK DRIVER AND
PEOPLE WITH BLINDSIGHT

In *The Nature of Mind*, D. M. Armstrong describes the case of a long-distance truck driver who, after driving for a long period of time, suddenly 'comes to' and realizes that he has been driving for some time apparently without being aware of what he's been doing. This case has been widely discussed in more recent literature about consciousness. Armstrong uses it as a way of making clear the distinction he draws between what he calls *perceptual* consciousness and *introspective* consciousness. The truck driver before he 'comes to', Armstrong argues, is perceptually conscious but lacks introspective consciousness. Although Armstrong admits it may be natural to say that in one sense of the term *consciousness* (the sense he calls introspective consciousness) the truck driver was unconscious before he 'came to', it is hard to deny that in some sense he was conscious. Armstrong asks us to consider the sophistication of the activities performed by the truck driver before 'coming to'. The truck driver drove the car along a road during that time, presumably using the clutch and brake at the appropriate times, maneuvering past other vehicles, and staying on the road.

> Above all, how is it possible to drive a car for kilometres along a road if one cannot perceive that road? One must be able to see where one is going, in order to adjust appropriately. It would have to be admitted, at the very least, that in such a case, eyes and brain have to be stimulated in just the same way as they are in ordinary cases of perception. Why then deny that perception takes place?[7]

For Armstrong, the truck driver does not lack consciousness altogether. What he lacks is introspective consciousness. He lacks awareness of his own activities—in particular, awareness of perceiving.[8]

The phenomenon called *blindsight* was discovered in patients who had suffered lesions to the striate cortex, the part of the cerebral cortex that usually receives visual inputs first. "Lesions in any particular region of the striate cortex cause restricted regions of 'blindness' in the visual field. . . . It was thought for a long time that those regions were absolutely blind. Patients typically say they do not see lights or patterns projected into such a 'blind' region of their fields." However, Lawrence Weiskrantz, who, along with colleagues, was among the first to study this condition in humans, found on testing such individuals that "if required to respond by forced-choice to visual stimuli projected into their 'blind' fields, [they] can discriminate those stimuli, even though they may fervently deny that they 'see' them." When told of the high degree of accuracy of their answers, these people express surprise and many claim to have thought they were simply guessing. How are we to describe such cases?[9]

The three most obvious choices for describing such cases as Armstrong's long-distance truck driver or those with blindsight are to describe each of them as (1) a case of perceptual consciousness that is pre-reflectively self-consciousness, (2) a case of perceptual consciousness that is unconscious of itself, or (3) a case of nonconscious perceptual activity or processing. Given these three possibilities, there are two alternatives open to Sartre if he wishes to diffuse these possible counterexamples to his thesis that all consciousness is self-consciousness. He must show of each case that (1) it is a case of perceptual consciousness that is pre-reflectively self-consciousness or (2) it is not a case of perceptual *con-sciousness* at all. Sartre makes it clear in the introduction to *Being and Nothingness* that he holds that perceptual consciousness must be consciousness of perceiving. "This spontaneous [pre-reflective] consciousness of my perception is *constitutive* of my perceptive consciousness" (BN, p. liii). If he chooses to treat these cases as cases of consciousness, then to defend his claim about the nature of perceptual consciousness, he must argue that these cases cannot be described as cases of perceptual consciousness that lack consciousness of perceiving. I will examine this line of defense first. Later in this chapter, I will discuss whether, given Sartre's characterization of consciousness in *Being and Nothingness*, it is open to him to redescribe these cases as cases of nonconscious perceptual processing as some have done. If these are not cases of consciousness, then of course they would fail as counterexamples to Sartre's thesis.

The Argument from Reportability

Can Sartre defend his thesis that all consciousness is self-consciousness while treating these cases as cases of consciousness? Does he have an argument that would support a characterization of each of these examples as a case of perceptual consciousness that is pre-reflectively self-consciousness? Could he apply to these cases the kind of argument he used to prove dreaming consciousness is consciousness of dreaming? Recall that in discussing dreaming consciousness, Sartre argued that my ability to judge reflectively that I was dreaming and to make that judgment with certitude is possible only if my pre-reflective consciousness had a latent knowledge of itself as dreaming consciousness (PI, p. 234).

In the introduction to *Being and Nothingness*, Sartre uses a similar sort of argument to establish the self-consciousness of pre-reflective consciousness. If I am engaged in the activity of counting, then although I don't *know* myself as counting, I do have a pre-reflective *consciousness* of counting. Sartre offers as proof that I am pre-reflectively conscious of counting the fact that if asked, " 'What are you doing there?' I should reply at once, 'I am counting' " (BN, p. liii). Sartre's position is not that such reflection is necessary for the existence of self-consciousness. Rather, the capacity to report on my conscious activity, even if unused, is proof that consciousness is, even at the pre-reflective level, conscious of itself. He uses an analogous argument, again in *Being and Nothingness*, to show that the subject in psychoanalysis has always been *conscious* of his drives and of his fundamental choice. Psychoanalysis, Sartre contends, does not bring to light what has been buried in the unconscious. No, the fact that the subject "*recognizes* the image of himself which is presented to him" (BN, p. 573) indicates that he must always have been conscious, albeit pre-reflectively, of the choice that underlies this image. How else, Sartre asks, could he recognize it when it is presented to him in the course of analysis?[10] In these cases of dreaming, counting, and psychoanalysis, the ability to report on one's conscious activity or the ability to recognize another's 'report' of one's choices or drives is taken by Sartre as proof of the presence of pre-reflective self-consciousness.

Could Sartre use a similar argument to establish that the perceptual consciousness of the long-distance truck driver and the individuals with blindsight is consciousness of perceiving? Let's look at the truck driver first. When he 'comes to', the truck driver is unable to report *spontaneously*—that is, without having to use inference—that he had been driving and hence presumably perceiving. He would have to *infer* from the fact that he is in the truck, behind the wheel, and moving along the road that he must have been driving the truck in the time preceding his 'coming to'. Because the present evidence suggests that he was driving without running off the road or without accident, he could infer that he must have been perceiving. But such an inference (or series of them) wouldn't prove he was pre-reflectively conscious of perceiving. Although Sartre acknowledges that it is possible at times to infer one was dreaming, such an inference is not what supports his contention that dreaming consciousness is consciousness of dreaming. Sartre uses instead the fact that I am sometimes able to make the judgment that I am dreaming without any inferential process (spontaneously, so to speak) to support his claim that I am pre-reflectively conscious of dreaming. Upon what else, Sartre asks, could such a spontaneous report be based? A similar move seems to be at work in his discussion in the introduction to *Being and Nothingness* of counting consciousness, and the same holds true for the subject of psychoanalysis. It is the subject's spontaneous recognition of the image of himself presented by the analyst that supports Sartre's claim that the subject was always conscious of his drives and fundamental choice. If the subject were incapable of such recognition and instead had to *infer* from the evidence presented by the analyst that the analyst's judgment of the subject's drives and complexes was correct, the subject's agreement with the analyst's judgment would no longer support Sartre's claim that pre-reflective consciousness is conscious of itself.

One might protest that the long-distance truck driver was aware of what he was doing and perceiving during the time preceding his 'coming to' but that he subsequently forgot. Could the truck driver simply have *forgotten* both what he perceived and indeed that he did perceive during a certain period of time? That is, does the fact that after he 'comes to' he is unable to report spontaneously his conscious activity in the period before he 'came to' prove that he was not pre-reflectively self-conscious during that period? No, of course it doesn't. As Alan Allport in "What Concept of Consciousness?" points out, one's ability to remember or report from memory actions and events is "reliable only as a *positive* indicator" of phenomenal awareness.[11] It does not follow that if a person is unable to recall or report past actions or events that we would say they were not aware of them. Such absence of recall, he thinks, leaves us uncertain about what to say.[12]

Dennett, however, thinks the long-distance truck driver is "a case of rolling consciousness with swift memory loss."[13] He describes the case this way because he believes that if, during the time preceding his 'coming to', the truck driver had been asked about his current experience, he could have reported at least some of the details of his perceptions. Max Velmans, in arguing for the existence of nonconscious cognitive activity, presents a case, similar in some ways to that of the long-distance truck driver, in which a driver engages in very fast and sophisticated actions to avoid an auto accident. He thinks the actions happened too fast for the driver to be conscious of them, and after the event, the driver may be unable to report what he actually did.[14] Ned Block, in commenting on Velmans's article, argues that this case could be one of phenomenal consciousness-plus-quick-forgetting.[15] That would explain the driver's inability to report after the event what he actually did to avoid the accident. Block would no doubt characterize the long-distance truck driver in a similar way. The problem is that no way exists to prove the long-distance truck driver, during the time preceding his 'coming to', was actually conscious and able to report on his actions and perceptions. Block argues against Dennett, who says that in many cases phenomenal consciousness-plus-quick-forgetting cannot in principle be experimentally distinguished from nonphenomenal consciousness. Block refers to work by experimental psychologist Mary C. Potter and her colleagues that offers experimental evidence of cases in which there is conscious understanding and quick forgetting.[16] To determine whether a picture in a sequence was momentarily understood and then forgotten, the experimenters contrasted the usual delayed test of recognition memory with a procedure in which the subject responded at the time of viewing. They found that subjects were able to understand and identify a picture, although interference from subsequent pictures blocked storage in long-term memory. But even if such cases could be established as cases of *conscious* understanding, a problem remains. Such studies may prove the *possibility* of consciousness-plus-quick-forgetting, but they do not offer any evidence toward establishing that the case of the long-distance truck driver was actually a case of consciousness-plus-quick-forgetting. That is, there is no way to be certain that if asked the truck driver would have been able to report on his immediate perceptions and actions. There is no way to be certain that he could even have reported on whether he were perceiving or not. In the absence of his ability to report after he 'came to', we have no way to establish that he was pre-reflectively self-conscious during the time preceding his 'coming to'. As a consequence Sartre cannot use the kind of arguments he used to establish the self-consciousness of pre-reflective consciousness in the cases of dreaming, counting, and psychoanalysis to establish that the truck driver was self-conscious during the period before he 'came to'. The reason he cannot is that in the cases Sartre examines there is the ability to report spontaneously or to recognize a report of one's conscious activity or drives, but there is no proof that such ability exists in the case of the long-distance truck driver.

The question of whether the individuals with blindsight can spontaneously report what they are perceiving is more complex and puzzling than such a question raised with regard to the truck driver. It is true that such individuals appear to be able to report with a high degree of accuracy the occurrence and location of visual events in their 'blind' field of vision. But they do so only when prompted. They do not spontaneously report such events and are unaware when making these "reports" that they are doing anything but guessing. There is not, as there is in the case of psychoanalysis, any recognition on the part of the subjects in the blindsight experiment when they are later told the high degree of accuracy of their answers to questions about visual events occurring in their 'blind' field of vision. The subjects claim to have no awareness of visual perception in their blind field. If we take their word as truth, then it is hard to use their ability to report these occurrences as proof that they are pre-reflectively conscious of perceiving. For Sartre it is the ability to report that one was dreaming or is counting or perceiving that establishes that pre-reflective consciousness is self-consciousness. But in the case of blindsight, individuals are not able to report that they are perceiving. It is not clear, however, that such inability establishes that self-consciousness on the pre-reflective level is absent. There is much controversy over the relation between reportability and consciousness. Velmans and Dennett both think that reportability is a criterion of consciousness. They both argue that if an experience is conscious, then it must be reportable. Dennett says that "a hallmark of states of human consciousness is that they can be reported (barring aphasia, paralysis, or being bound and gagged, for instance)."[17] Given this view, the inability of those with blindsight to report that they are perceiving would be proof that they lack consciousness of their perceiving.

But others claim that nonreportable consciousness may well be possible. Jeffrey A. Gray argues that if we deny such a possibility, we appear "to rule out a priori the presence of consciousness in species lacking language."[18] Dan Lloyd also questions Dennett's "assumption that consciousness is best operationalized as accurate memory reporting."[19] Graham F. Wagstaff speculates that our repertoire of verbal and nonverbal responses may be inadequate for describing the contents of consciousness.[20] Perhaps we have experiences of which we are aware but which we cannot report. Unless we could rule out the possibility of nonreportable consciousness, the fact that people with blindsight are unable to report that they are perceiving would not constitute proof that they are not conscious of perceiving.

Sartre's position in his discussion of dreaming consciousness and consciousness of the activity of counting falls between these two positions. His argument does not rest on the claim that if an experience is conscious, it must be reportable. He appeals to a weaker claim: if an experience is reportable, then it must have been conscious. Given this weaker claim, the lack of the ability to report on one's perceptual activity would not constitute proof that one was unconscious of such activity. But in the absence of such ability, Sartre does need a stronger argument than that from reportability to establish that if these cases are cases of conscious perceptual activity, then as such they must be cases of self-consciousness. Does he have such an argument, and can it counter the suggestion that these cases are simply cases of unconscious acts of consciousness—that is, perceptual consciousness that is unconscious of itself as perceiving consciousness?

The Argument from Logic

Yes, Sartre offers such an argument in the introduction to *Being and Nothingness*. It is an argument rooted in logic rather than in the empirical data of a subject's ability to report on the occurrence of present or past perceptual or dreaming consciousness. He contends in the introduction, as noted in earlier chapters, that a consciousness unconscious of itself is absurd, a contradiction. He claims that it is a necessary condition for consciousness to be consciousness of the table, for example, that it be conscious of itself as consciousness of the table. If that were not so, "it would be a consciousness ignorant of itself, an unconscious—which is absurd" (BN, p. lii). But is a consciousness that is not self-consciousness absurd, a contradiction? If it is so, it is certainly not self-evident to at least some contemporary philosophers, psychologists, and natural scientists who write about consciousness. Much controversy exists in the current literature on consciousness over whether it is of the nature of consciousness to be self-consciousness.

There are certainly people who would agree with Sartre. David Rosenthal in "Two Concepts of Consciousness" argues for what he calls a higher-order thought theory of consciousness.[21] Rosenthal contends that what makes an experience conscious is that it is the object of a higher-order thought that may itself be unconscious (that is, unaccompanied by any third-order thought that takes it as its object). The difference between a conscious and an unconscious state is simply the difference between a state that is accompanied by a thought about itself (that is, a state which is conscious of itself) and one that is not. Keith Oatley claims that because all consciousness involves a model of the self, all consciousness is, explicitly or implicitly, self-consciousness.[22] Robert Van Gulick develops a functionalist account of self-consciousness such that it again becomes the centerpiece of mentality.[23] For Roderick Chisholm all consciousness is self-consciousness, at least in the first of the two senses of self-consciousness that he distinguishes.[24] Don Locke argues that it is analytically true that we cannot think or perceive without knowing (or being in a position to know) that we do.[25]

There are, however, many who would disagree with the claim that it is the nature of consciousness to be self-consciousness. Armstrong certainly distinguishes consciousness from self-consciousness in drawing his distinctions between *minimal, perceptual,* and *introspective* consciousness in *The Nature of Mind.* Fred Dretske argues that an experience of an object, for example, is conscious not because the perceiver is aware of that experience but because that experience makes the perceiver aware of the object and its properties. It may be that a person is conscious of her experience of the object, but that is not necessary for her experience of the object to be itself a conscious experience. There can be, he argues, awareness without awareness of awareness.[26] In "What Is It Like to Be an Homunculus?" Stephen L. White argues as well that a distinction can be drawn between consciousness and self-consciousness.[27] He uses a long and extended example which he calls "the group fusion example" to support the logic of this distinction.[28] Kathleen V. Wilkes, in discussing "the four disparate bunches of phenomena" that she thinks the term 'conscious(ness)' includes, implies that with at least certain uses of the term, we distinguish consciousness from self-consciousness.[29] In his consideration of blindsight Thomas Natsoulas utilizes such a distinction.[30] Marcel Kinsbourne distinguishes experience from awareness of experience and sees self-consciousness as the most elaborate level of consciousness.[31] Along with Kinsbourne, Carlo Umilità also distinguishes between consciousness and self-awareness.[32] Karl H. Pribram in "Mind, Brain, and Consciousness: The Organization of Competence and Conduct" argues that although "self-consciousness is what we ordinarily refer to as 'consciousness,'" on the basis of clinical neurological observations, self-consciousness can be "dissociated from other forms of consciousness."[33]

This disagreement among the current writers on consciousness about whether it is logically possible to distinguish consciousness from self-consciousness does not disprove Sartre's claim that a consciousness unconscious of itself is absurd and a contradiction, but it does require that Sartre and others who hold such a view offer a defense of this position. It is not obvious to all that the notion of a consciousness unconscious of itself is contradictory. What support does Sartre offer for the position he articulates in the introduction to *Being and Nothingness*?

Presence to Being

It is Sartre's characterization of consciousness as a presence to being that provides, I think, the major support for his claim that a consciousness unconscious of itself is absurd, although Sartre himself never directly connects the two. He claims that the for-itself arises from the in-itself by constituting itself as a witness to being (BN, pp. 172–73). As we saw in Chapter 2, for Sartre such presence involves negation. For consciousness to arise as presence to being, it must "constitute itself as *not being* the thing" (BN, p. 174) of which it is conscious. That is why Sartre claims that "the For-itself's Presence to being implies that the For-itself is *a witness of itself* in the presence of being as not being that being" (BN, p. 122; emphasis mine). It is because Sartre characterizes consciousness in this way that it follows that a consciousness which is not self-consciousness is absurd. For Sartre it is a necessary condition, part of the definition of consciousness, that it be self-consciousness—that is, conscious of itself as not being that to which as consciousness it is present. Consciousness is not a substance for Sartre. It exists only as a presence to being. Sartre argues that because such presence is possible only if the for-itself posits itself as other than the object to which it is present, consciousness must be self-consciousness. If his characterization of consciousness as presence to being is correct and if his claim that presence requires that consciousness posit itself as *not being* its object is also correct, then his claim that a consciousness unconscious of itself is a logical absurdity would be grounded. But the question remains whether his characterization of consciousness is correct. Can his characterization cover such cases as the long-distance truck driver and the people with blindsight? Do cases such as these stand as counterexamples to his characterization? If they do, could Sartre save his characterization of consciousness from these possible counterexamples by simply claiming that these cases are not cases of consciousness at all? Let us first examine whether his characterization of consciousness can cover these cases.

If consciousness, for Sartre, requires presence to the world and hence to the self (as *not being* the world), it is difficult to characterize the truck driver during the time prior to his 'coming to' and the individuals with blindsight with respect to their 'blind' field of vision as conscious. It may seem reasonable to claim the truck driver was present to the world of traffic, road patterns, signs, and so forth. Indeed, one might argue, as Armstrong does, that it is necessary to attribute such presence to the world to the truck driver in order to account for his behavior in the period preceding his 'coming to'. But it seems far less plausible to claim he was pre-reflectively present to himself during that period. The main criterion Sartre uses for attributing such self-consciousness is absent, as we noted above, in the truck driver case. That is, he cannot report from memory what he was perceiving during the period before he 'came to'. Although that doesn't prove he was not self-conscious during that period (he may have forgotten), I think it does render the attribution of self-consciousness less convincing. It seems implausible to describe the individuals with blindsight as present in any sense to the visual events occurring in their 'blind' field of vision. Given that they adamantly deny seeing anything in this field, it is hard to claim they are present to that part of the world contained within their 'blind' field of vision. One may, however, want to offer an argument akin to the one offered in the case of the truck driver, one that points to the truck driver's behavior as evidence of his being conscious of the world. One may wish to argue that the behavior of the people with blindsight—that is, their ability to answer accurately, when forced to answer, most questions about events occurring in their 'blind' field—necessitates attributing presence to those events to these people as well. However, the fact that they are unable to report experiencing or perceiving these events *even while the events are occurring* makes it less plausible than in the truck driver case to claim there is conscious perception. It is more difficult to maintain that the individuals with blindsight simply forget from moment to moment what they are perceiving. In addition, if conscious perception requires consciousness of perceiving, as Sartre argues, then to claim that blindsighted people are present to certain visual events would also be to claim they are pre-reflectively aware of such presence. But again their denial that they are perceiving these events undermines the desire to attribute conscious perception to them.

It does not appear plausible, at least initially, to claim that the truck driver and the people with blindsight are present both to the world and to themselves. Given that initial implausibility, Sartre would have to offer some argument other than the one that relies on a person's ability to report his or her conscious activity to establish that these cases can be assimilated to his characterization of consciousness. I leave undecided for now the question of whether he could do so, returning to it in Chapter 6. Instead I wish to address the question of whether there is a more direct way open to Sartre for defusing these possible counterexamples. Can Sartre simply deny that the truck driver in the period before he 'came to' and the person with blindsight with regard to events in his or her 'blind' field are conscious?

NONCONSCIOUS PERCEPTUAL PROCESSING

There is controversy among more recent commentators over whether to characterize these cases as cases of consciousness at all. Although Armstrong clearly thinks the long-distance truck driver is conscious, at least perceptually, Wilkes reports that when psychologists at a conference in Bielefeld were questioned about a case similar to Armstrong's truck driver, they split about equally over whether the driver was conscious.[34] In their article "Attention to Action," Donald A. Norman and Tim Shallice draw a distinction between the performance of an action when it is automatic and when it is under deliberate conscious control.[35] They might well classify Armstrong's truck driver as a person performing a series of actions automatically, that is, in the absence of deliberate conscious control. Peter Carruthers, in his article on experience, treats this kind of case as one of nonconscious experience.[36] There is even more controversy over the individuals with blindsight. Colin McGinn thinks blindsight is an example of a conscious experience with the phenomenal surface of the experience absent. The person is still having a conscious visual experience of the events in his or her 'blind' field of vision, but what is lacking is the seeming-to-the-subject that he or she is having a visual experience. Because of this the subject has no self-conscious access to these experiences.[37] Natsoulas argues that awareness can occur unaccompanied by self-awareness, positing that there can be acts of consciousness (perception, for example) which "are not *conscious* acts of consciousness."[38] He characterizes the perceptions of people with blindsight as nonconscious visual perceptions. Because he holds that "perceptions are uniformly acts of consciousness" of a certain type, it follows for Natsoulas that those with blindsight experience nonconscious acts of consciousness.[39] His characterization of blindsight is, however, uncommon. Weiskrantz treats at least the classical cases of blindsight as cases of a capacity disconnected from the awareness or experience on which it normally rests.[40] In these cases subjects are capable of reporting on visual events without experiencing or being aware of—that is, conscious of—such events. Velmans interprets blindsight as analysis of visual stimuli without visual awareness.[41] Christof Koch and Francis Crick argue that given their neuronal theory of consciousness, they can in principle explain the nonconscious nature of blindsight.[42] Patricia Smith Churchland, in "Consciousness: The Transmutation of a Concept," treats people with blindsight as capable of making perceptual judgments without consciously available perceptions. The accuracy of the subjects' responses to questions about visual events occurring in the 'blind' portion of their visual field indicates, for Churchland, that nonconscious rather than conscious visual data are figuring in those responses.[43] Carruthers and Wilkes in their articles mentioned above as well as Anthony J. Marcel in his studies of conscious and unconscious perception all appear to agree that blindsight does not involve the use of conscious perceptions that are unconscious of themselves.[44] Rather, it involves nonconscious perception or perceptual activity.[45]

Could Sartre then take a different tack in the face of these two cases? Rather than argue that as cases of consciousness they are cases of self-consciousness, could he contend instead that they are not cases of consciousness at all? Could Sartre in this way avoid the problem of these cases standing as possible counterexamples to his thesis that all consciousness is self-consciousness? Perhaps he could argue along the following lines: The truck driver in the period before he 'comes to' and the person with blindsight with regard to the visual events in his or her 'blind' field of vision lack self-consciousness. But self-consciousness is constitutive of consciousness (BN, p. liv). Hence these cases are not cases of consciousness. I have already mentioned how debatable the second premise of this argument is. That problem aside, however, there is another, more pressing problem that would arise first for Sartre if he considered taking such a tack. Wouldn't this tack leave Sartre committed to nonconscious perceptual processing or activity? Without such a commitment, how is one to account for the truck driver's ability to drive successfully while lacking perceptual consciousness? And how is one to account for the blindsighted person's ability to report accurately visual events occurring in his or her 'blind' visual field? Sartre is adamant in *Being and Nothingness* in his rejection of the unconscious, but what about the nonconscious? He rejects the notion of psychic events that *become* conscious (BN, p. liv). But what about nonconscious events or entities which themselves never become conscious but which may underlie consciousness? Would the philosophical positions Sartre develops in *Being and Nothingness* allow him to countenance the existence of nonconscious entities or activities that underlie behavior and at times consciousness? I think not. A commitment to the existence of such entities or activities would fly in the face of his arguments against psychological determinism.

The tack I have been proposing that Sartre might use against these two cases as counterexamples to his central thesis does not, of course, treat them as cases of perceptual consciousness. In the case of the long-distance truck driver, the nonconscious perceptual processing would not be affecting conscious behavior. But if we allow for nonconscious processes underlying behavior unaccompanied by consciousness in the truck driver case, it is difficult to see how to bar the view held by many at present that these nonconscious processes underlie conscious behavior as well.[46] And in the case of the person with blindsight, the nonconscious perceptual processing would be affecting the individual's conscious behavior, that is, the answers given to questions asked about events in the 'blind' field of vision. But if we accept a model of consciousness that sees it as dependent on nonconscious processing and causally connected to such processing, then Sartre's characterization of consciousness and its connection to freedom is undermined. For Sartre, freedom is an all-or-nothing affair. Human beings are either wholly determined or wholly free (BN, p. 442). The only bond consciousness could maintain with mechanical processes would be one in which consciousness "*produces itself by an internal negation directed towards these existents*" (BN, p. 442). It must deny identification with these processes. Otherwise consciousness becomes an in-itself and "a determined consciousness—i.e., a consciousness externally motivated—becomes itself pure exteriority and ceases to be consciousness" (BN, p. 442). Sartre argues that if we identify consciousness with a causal sequence, we transmute it "into a plentitude of being" (BN, p. 26), into an object, a thing. For Sartre, consciousness "can be limited only by itself" (BN, p. lv). This determination of consciousness by itself is an essential characteristic of consciousness (BN, p. lv). It is impossible, Sartre argues, "to assign to a consciousness a motivation other than itself. Otherwise it would be necessary to conceive that consciousness to the degree to which it is an effect, is not conscious (of) itself. It would be necessary in some manner that it should be without being conscious (of) being" (BN, p. lv). In attempting to defend his central thesis that all consciousness is self-consciousness by denying that the truck driver and blindsight cases are cases of consciousness, Sartre would end up destroying his central thesis. Such a defense would allow for the existence of nonconscious processes that one might argue underlie consciousness as well as unconscious behavior. If consciousness is motivated by nonconscious processes, then, on Sartre's view, as the quotation above indicates, it is no longer pre-reflectively self-conscious. But it is precisely the claim that consciousness is always self-consciousness even pre-reflectively that Sartre is trying to save from these proposed counterexamples. Therefore, an appeal to nonconscious processes underlying behavior as a way to dispel the proposed counterexamples to Sartre's thesis would create more problems for him than it would solve.

The two alternatives open to Sartre for diffusing the long-distance truck driver and people with blindsight as counterexamples to his belief in the self-conscious nature of consciousness both present him with problems. The latter alternative—treating them as cases of nonconscious perceptual processing—undermines the very thesis he wishes to defend. The former alternative—claiming they are cases of self-conscious consciousness—lacks sufficient support in the face of arguments against such an interpretation. To meet these counterexamples, Sartre needs a notion of self-consciousness that is more primary than the self-consciousness that exists at the level of the pre-reflective cogito. I attempt to provide him with such a notion in Chapter 5.

Remembering the Body

Sartre believes—and I think by now most Western philosophers would agree—that it is the body that is the subject of human consciousness. Sartre, however, fails to take seriously enough his belief that intentionality and consciousness are embodied. He fails to follow, with sufficient detail, the implications of this belief, and many of the problems I raised in Chapters 3 and 4 are a result of this failure. If we take seriously, more seriously I think than Sartre himself does, the belief that it is the body which is the subject of consciousness, we can, at the very least, explain the pervasiveness and persistence of the belief that all consciousness is self-consciousness. I think we can also offer a firmer grounding for this belief than Sartre provides.[1]

Given that it is the body that is the subject of consciousness, we need a theory of consciousness rooted in the body. The predominant model of mind in Anglo-American philosophy in recent years has been and continues to be an information-processing model, a model based on a computational theory of the mind. Functionalism is probably the best-known example of a theory based on this model of the mind. There is, however, a kind of residual idealism and Cartesianism in functionalism, because it purposefully separates the mind from its material basis. The functionalists see the material basis of the mind as simply the hardware on which the software of the mind runs. Such hardware might be a live human brain or it might be an electronic computer. It makes no difference. The focus is on the software, the program, whether it runs on neuronal circuits or on electronic, silicon-based ones. In their attempt to avoid a species-specific theory of mind—in their attempt, that is, to achieve some kind of ultimate objectivity—functionalists forget the body. There have been, however, continual criticisms raised against functionalism. One of the most well known and persistent of the critics of functionalism and computer models of the mind is John Searle. In his frequently anthologized article "Minds, Brains, and Programs," Searle argues that functionalist accounts tell us little about mental activities because they tell us about programs and not about the machine on which the programs run. Intentionality, Searle reminds us, is a *biological* phenomenon.[2] For Searle, intentionality must be tied to the human body, the brain in particular. A similar criticism comes from a different quarter, from neurobiologist Gerald Edelman. In *Neural Darwinism*, Edelman develops a theory of brain function by means of which he attempts to provide an understanding of the biological basis of perception. He argues against information-processing and computational models, in particular when such models are used to explain perceptual categorization. He wants a biologically based theory of perception that will explain how an individual animal with rich brain structure can engage in perceptual categorization in a complex world with no instruction and how it can use this categorization to govern its responses to the world.[3] He wants a theory that can account for perceptual categorization without using homunculi or programs and without assuming an already labeled world. In the more recent *The Remembered Present: A Biological Theory of Consciousness*, Edelman once again attacks functionalist theories of mind. He argues for a "brain-based theory of consciousness."[4] He wants to offer, albeit as informed speculation rather than as established scientific theory, a theory of consciousness based on biological grounds. On Edelman's view, functionalism fails as an account of the mind because "there is no effective procedure by which *all* possible events and relations in a world consisting of the interacting conscious animal and econiche can be represented in a computer or a Turing machine."[5]

These arguments in favor of a biologically based theory of consciousness go some way toward correcting the prevailing computational theories that disregard the body altogether. But they are too limited themselves because they focus on the brain and forget the rest of the body. Of the two writers just discussed, Searle is particularly guilty of this.[6] One of the values of Sartre's analysis of consciousness, as well as that of other phenomenologists, is its emphasis on the body. There are too many philosophers who talk as though the brain or the neurons were conscious.[7] But it is the body, the organism as a whole, that is conscious. Just as a jet engine needs wings and tail and other parts to generate flight in the aircraft, so too the brain needs kidneys and lungs and blood and air to generate consciousness. Sartre is right that it is the body (not the brain) that is the subject of consciousness.

There are other, current criticisms of functionalist accounts of the mind that make this same point. Of course, prior to these current criticisms, one finds in both the phenomenological and the analytic traditions philosophers besides Sartre who stress the role of the body in consciousness. Wittgenstein, for example, in the *Philosophical Investigations*, particularly in his argument against the possibility of a private language for sensations, emphasizes the role of the body in our ascriptions of states of consciousness to ourselves and others.[8] It is clear from the later Wittgenstein's account of the language of mental states that it is a live human body to which we ascribe states of consciousness. Merleau-Ponty is famous for pushing Sartre's point that the body is the subject of consciousness much further than Sartre himself does. One finds references to Merleau-Ponty's work among more recent critiques of functionalist and brain-based theories of consciousness. Such references are found in the work not only of Continental philosophers but of Anglo-American analytic philosophers as well. Later in this chapter I will return to the work of Merleau-Ponty.[9]

More recently there are philosophers, again in both the analytic and phenomenological traditions, who in criticizing computational theories of mind emphasize the role of the entire body in cognition and in consciousness in general. Mark Johnson, acknowledging his debt to the European phenomenologists of the nineteenth and twentieth centuries, is one such philosopher.[10] He argues in *The Body in the Mind* that understanding, for example, "is very much a matter of one's embodiment, that is, of perceptual mechanisms, patterns of discrimination, motor programs, and various bodily skills."[11] Johnson believes that understanding, rationality, and indeed consciousness in general are rooted in our bodily existence, which he argues any theory of mind must acknowledge. Natika Newton, in her article "The Sensorimotor Theory of Cognition," claims that higher cognitive activities make use of the same structures as those involved in sensorimotor activity. She gives a good overview of those in the twentieth century who have held this theory.[12] Newton points out that the theory explains the use of bodily and spatial reference in nonphysical and abstract fields. She also notes that it accords with a view of human experience which goes back to phenomenology and which holds that intentionality is a human activity rooted in embodiment and hence any account of intentionality should be connected to our bodily existence.[13] Neither Johnson's theory of intentionality and consciousness nor Newton's restricts its discussion to the brain. It is the active body, moving in the world, which underlies all cognitive activity.

If Sartre is to take seriously his claim that the body is the subject of consciousness, then he needs to follow out the consequences of a theory of consciousness rooted in the body. One such consequence relates to the self-consciousness of consciousness. It has been made abundantly clear in earlier chapters that for Sartre all consciousness, even at the pre-reflective level, must be present to itself. Now if consciousness just is the body's presence to the world, as Sartre argues, then the body must be present to itself in being present to the world. So there must be a kind of consciousness of the body, what I will call bodily self-consciousness, and this must form part of our awareness of the world. The most basic form of self-consciousness must be bodily awareness. It is this level of self-consciousness that I intend to explicate in this chapter, and it is this level of self-consciousness that I contend is the one most capable of grounding the deep-rooted intuition that all consciousness is self-consciousness. Sartre, of course, makes reference to this type of self-awareness in his discussion of the body in part 3 of *Being and Nothingness*, but he undercuts his own discussion and fails to explore fully enough the meaning and significance of the body's presence to itself. If he had done so, he would have been able, I think, to provide firmer support for many of the claims of *Being and Nothingness*, although ultimately there are obvious reasons why he shunned doing so. In this chapter I will examine Sartre's analysis of bodily self-consciousness and propose a more radical position with regard to this fundamental level of self-consciousness. In Chapter 6 I will consider the multiple ways in which such a theory of bodily self-awareness can strengthen certain of Sartre's primary positions in *Being and Nothingness* while undermining others.

SARTRE ON BODILY SELF-CONSCIOUSNESS

Although the facticity of the for-itself, which Sartre discusses in part 2 of *Being and Nothingness*, is a consequence of the embodiment of consciousness, Sartre never directly discusses the body until part 3 of the work. One of the main points he makes is that there is a distinction between the body-for-me (that is, the lived body) and the body-for-others. The distinction is that between the body as subject and the body as object. This distinction at the level of the body parallels in certain respects Sartre's more general ontological distinction between the for-itself and the in-itself. Self-consciousness is involved in both my body's existence for me and in its existence for others. The body as it is for itself, as subject, is part of the structure of non-thetic self-consciousness, Sartre claims. It is only in my body's existence for others that I am conscious of my body as an object, as a being-in-itself. This discovery of my body as an object is a revelation of my being, according to Sartre, and involves self-presence, but "I am present to it [that is, to my body] without its *being me* and without my *being it*" (BN, p. 304). I am present to myself in my existence for others only in an alienated fashion. The more fundamental and primary form of self-presence is the self-presence involved in my body's existence for itself. At the end of this section on the body, Sartre says that my body can appear to me as the body of the other—that is, as an object—but that is not essential to its existence. There could be bodies, he says, that could not take a point of view on themselves. So Sartre does not think we should start with our existence as objects as a foundation for the study of corporeality. It is to our body as it exists for itself that we should look first. Following Sartre's lead I will examine in this section the self-presence involved in the body's existence as subject of consciousness, as a being that exists for itself.

Sartre characterizes the body as it is for itself as a point of view on the world, as a center of reference and action. It is "the instrument which I am and which can not be utilized by any instrument" (BN, p. 352). The body as it exists for itself is "the factual condition for all possible action on the world" (BN, p. 327). Sartre follows a kind of Cartesian line that leads him to the body's consciousness of itself. "Since I can be nothing without being the consciousness of what I am, the body must necessarily be in some way given to my consciousness" (BN, p. 329). But because my body as it exists for itself is a point of view on which no point of view can be taken, the body cannot be given to consciousness as an object. The relationship between consciousness and the body is not an *objective* but an *existential* one, Sartre says. It is to stress this point that he speaks in such disfigured prose of consciousness 'existing' its body. But "consciousness can exist its body only as consciousness. Therefore *my* body is a conscious structure of my consciousness" (BN,

p. 329). This self-awareness on the part of the body exists on the level of unreflective consciousness. Sartre says that "the body belongs . . . to the structures of the non-thetic self-consciousness" (BN, p. 330). Exactly how Sartre thinks the body belongs to these structures is complicated. He says that the body cannot be identified purely and simply with non-thetic self-consciousness. The reason it cannot is because the body must be surmounted and nihilated for consciousness of the world to be possible. "Consciousness (of) the body is lateral and retrospective; the body is the *neglected*, the '*passed by in silence*'. And yet the body is what this consciousness *is*; it is not even anything except body" (BN, p. 330). Consciousness of the body is like consciousness of a sign, Sartre says. You have to be conscious of the sign for its meaning to exist, but you must surpass the sign toward its meaning. The sign, Sartre notes, must be neglected and never apprehended for itself in order for the meaning to be apprehended (BN, p. 330). So also with the body: it is the means by which we are conscious of the world, but as such it must be surpassed and nihilated. There is a strange kind of presence/absence structure to the body's consciousness of itself. Although Sartre never speaks of it in these words, I think it fits his characterization of the body as that which is neglected and passed over in silence and yet is absolutely necessary for consciousness of the world. I have to "lose myself in the world in order for the world to exist" (BN, p. 318). The body's presence to itself must also be a kind of absence. In an analogous way I must be conscious of the sign to understand the meaning that the sign conveys, yet the sign must be present as a kind of absence. Sartre says that "absence is a structure of *being-there*" (BN, p. 342). This kind of presence/absence structure might be made clear by considering the duck/rabbit drawing.

One can alternately see this drawing as a duck or a rabbit, but not both at once. To be aware of the rabbit, for example, the duck must be absent in one sense and yet still present in another. If there is no duck "in the picture," it is not the duck/rabbit drawing. When one is conscious of the rabbit, the duck exhibits a kind of presence that manifests itself as absence.[14] The same is true in our awareness of the world; without bodily self-consciousness, consciousness of the world is impossible. Yet such self-consciousness must manifest itself as a kind of absence in order for consciousness of the world to be possible.

For Sartre, the world and the body are always present to consciousness but in different ways (BN, p. 334). If I am reading, I am positionally conscious of the words on the page but against the ground of the world. The world as ground indicates my body as corporal totality. But when I focus on a particular *this* against the ground of the world, that figure points toward "a functional specification of the corporal totality" (BN, p. 334). Sartre uses the example of reading. In reading the eyes appear as figure on the ground of the corporal totality just as the words appear as figure on the ground of the world. So both the specific organ, the eyes in the case of reading, and the body as a totality are present to consciousness when consciousness is present to the world. My awareness of my own body "forms a part of that distance-less existence of positional consciousness for itself" (BN, p. 334).

It is important to note that for Sartre the only bodily self-awareness that is part of the structure of non-thetic self-consciousness is the awareness of one's body as subject. It is only the body as it exists for-itself that is integral to the most basic level of self-consciousness for Sartre. The self-consciousness involved in the body's existence for others is a consciousness of the self as a being from whom I am alienated. When Sartre returns in part 4 of *Being and Nothingness* to a discussion of the consciousness of self that is involved in consciousness of the world, he focuses on the self as existing for itself. "The value of things, their instrumental role, their proximity and real distance (which has no relation to their [objective] spatial proximity and distance) do nothing more than outline my image—that is, my choice" (BN, p. 463). For Sartre, what a person wears, how she furnishes her home, the city in which she lives, and the books she reads all reveal the person as a being that exists for itself. In apprehending the objects and places of the world as well as in apprehending my past and present, I apprehend myself as freedom, as a being that exists for itself. Perception also involves consciousness of oneself as a being that exists for itself. All perception involves consciousness of self not only because perceiving consciousness is consciousness of perceiving, a point which Sartre made in the introduction to *Being and*

Nothingness and which I examined in Chapter 4, but also because what I perceive is determined by my goals and ends, that is, by my choices. To the perceiver, the in-itself reflects back the perceiver as giver of meaning, as choice, as fundamental project and freedom. Even the states of my body (Sartre's example is the fatigue I feel on a hike) are revealed to be what they are relative to my project. Consciousness of these states is thus consciousness of my body as lived—as subject, not object (BN, pp. 454–55). Consciousness of my surroundings also involves consciousness of my body as subject.

> To the extent that I apprehend this countryside with my eyes which unfold distances, my legs which climb the hills and consequently cause new sights and new obstacles to appear and disappear, with my back which carries the knapsack—to this extent I have a non-positional consciousness (of) this body which rules my relations with the world and which signifies my engagement in the world. (BN, p. 454)

For Sartre, there can be no communication between one's body as subject and one's body as object. "Since these two aspects of the body are on different and incommunicable levels of being, they can not be reduced to one another" (BN, p. 305). Sartre appears to think the only choices are either the reduction of one aspect of the body to the other or their total separation.

> It is impossible for a determined process [physiological, neurological, and so forth] to act upon a spontaneity [consciousness], exactly as it is impossible for objects to act upon consciousness. Thus any synthesis of two types of existents is impossible; they are not homogeneous; they will remain each one in its incommunicable solitude. (BN, p. 442)

I think it is, at least in part, because Sartre maintains such a rigid distinction between the body as subject and the body as object and because he believes that only consciousness of the body as subject is involved in one's unalienated consciousness of oneself that he refuses to consider hard scientific evidence as contributing anything to our understanding of subjectivity. As Peter Caws points out in his book on Sartre, Sartre does not dwell at all on the physical aspects of the body.[15]

Sartre might reply to all this that his use of the phenomenological method excludes consideration of evidence not derived from reflection on conscious experience. Even his description of our existence as objects, our existence for others, is done within the context of an experience that is accessible to reflection, our conscious experience of shame. Phyllis Morris, in criticizing Sartre for his failure to give a full enough account of bodily agency, suggests a similar response open to Sartre. She faults him for equating purposive activity with conscious activity and consequently not accounting for nonconscious purposive activity. She notes that a possible, although not adequate, response to her criticism might be that Sartre's use of the phenomenological method excludes any consideration of nonconscious activity.[16] Caws mentions a similar Sartrean response to his criticism of Sartre's failure to explore "the complex foundations of our own physical, biological, or psychological nature."[17] Sartre, he says, would dismiss this criticism as irrelevant because his phenomenological enterprise allows him to bracket such concerns. Caws's reply to this response is that "our freedom might be more complete in light of a fuller knowledge of its material setting and limitations."[18] Owen Flanagan, in *Consciousness Reconsidered*, makes a similar point. Flanagan argues that we ought to use what he calls "the natural method" in studying consciousness. This method treats with respect the findings not only of phenomenology but of psychology and neuroscience as well. It does not privilege one over the others. He argues that none of these approaches alone can fully elucidate the nature of consciousness.[19] We need to rely on all the available sources that study human consciousness. Phenomenology can both give direction to a scientific study of the mind and help substantiate the findings of science. Flanagan argues that we ought to "listen carefully to what the neuroscientists say about how conscious mental events of different sorts are realized [in the brain], and examine the fit between their stories and the phenomenological and psychological stories."[20] This would require us to give up the Cartesian view that consciousness is infallible about itself. Flanagan is quite willing to give up that view. As we saw in Chapter 3 with regard to pure reflection, Sartre, of course, in certain ways is not.

I think another reason for Sartre's refusal to acknowledge that scientific evidence might play a role in our understanding of consciousness is his belief that consciousness cannot be an effect of the unconscious or the physiological (BN, pp. lv–lvi). His argument for this belief is that to the degree that consciousness is an effect of the unconscious, it would be unconscious (of) itself. He thinks a consciousness unconscious (of) itself is a logical absurdity. In Chapter 4 I criticized his failure to ground this claim. But there is an additional problem. Why does Sartre believe that if consciousness is caused by the physiological, it would be unconscious of itself? Perhaps he is assuming that consciousness of an effect requires consciousness of all the causes of that effect. But he offers no argument for such an unstated assumption, and it is certainly not immediately obvious how one would defend such a claim. In addition to excluding the consideration of certain sources of evidence about the nature of consciousness, a reliance on the phenomenological method alone leaves Sartre without any support for his claim that the body is the subject of consciousness. Reflection alone will not reveal the material basis of consciousness or even that it has a material basis.[21] Most important with regard to my project in this book, Sartre's persistent adhesion to the absolute division between the for-itself as subject and the for-itself as object, as well as his refusal to utilize the results of investigations into the nature of consciousness unless they rely on the method of phenomenology, bars him from data that might be useful in supporting his thesis about the self-consciousness of consciousness. Although Sartre maintains that the body is the subject of consciousness, there is still a residue of dualism in his ontology. So he remains adamant in his position that physical processes can have nothing to do with consciousness, and consciousness must be nothing. But if the *body* is the subject of consciousness, then the functions and the phenomenology of consciousness must have a basis in biology, and understanding that basis ought to help ground and support the results of the phenomenology.[22] That does not mean that it makes the phenomenology unnecessary or that the phenomenology does not capture something that an objective, scientific account may miss or be unable by its very nature to capture. In fact, as Flanagan points out, an objective description can explain why no objective description can completely capture lived experience. It cannot do so because of the way each person is hooked up to her own nervous system. Acknowledging the limitations of an objective, scientific viewpoint is one thing. But refusing to allow biology and neuroscience to have anything to contribute to the ongoing attempt to understand the nature of consciousness is to forget that it is the body that is the subject of consciousness. It is to forget, in Sartre's case, that his ontology, while distinguishing the for-itself and the in-itself, also reunites them in the human being when it declares that the for-itself is a body, that it is *in* the world.[23]

BODILY INTENTIONALITY

The fact that self-consciousness must first be the body's presence to itself is clearest, I think, at the most fundamental level of intentionality—the bodily intentionality present in motor activity and in perception.[24] Many of the points Sartre makes in his characterization of the body's existence for itself and the self-presence that entails can be strengthened and clarified by an examination of this most basic level of intentionality. It is in the continual flow of the sensorimotor body as it interacts with the world that we find the most foundational level of the body as a self-conscious subject of consciousness. This is a form of intentionality that underlies the intentionality of the mental and of language. I intend to examine this level of intentionality utilizing the work of both philosophers and scientists to establish the plausibility, at least, of thinking that even at this most primordial level of intentionality there is a self-presence necessary for consciousness of the world. The discussions I will consider bring the body back as central to discussions of intentionality and consciousness, just as Sartre's analysis does. They extend Sartre's view that action is at the root of intentionality by focusing on a level of action that Sartre rarely addresses: the sensorimotor activity of the pre-personal intentional system that is the body. I have no interest, in this context, in defending any of the theories I will outline below. My point in examining them is to highlight the importance, indeed the very existence, of this most basic level of intentionality. I do this to see whether at this most basic level of our interaction with the world there is a consciousness that is self-consciousness.

A growing body of evidence and argument supports the view that the body's most fundamental form of presence to the world is as a sensorimotor system acting with intentionality but below the level of personal existence. On this view it is the activity of the pre-personal intentional system that is the body that is the foundation on which personal conscious existence and cognitive functions, including language, rest.[25] If there is sufficient evidence that this level of bodily intentionality and consciousness requires self-consciousness, then that fact may be used both to support the view that all consciousness is self-consciousness and to explain the intuitive appeal of the view.

Even on the most primitive levels of conscious life, simply to survive an organism must be able to distinguish its biological self from that which is not itself. There must be an ability to make a me/not-me distinction. Dennett, in *Consciousness Explained*, remarks on this me/not-me distinction: "As soon as something gets into the business of self-preservation, boundaries become important. . . . [T]his distinction between everything on the inside of a closed boundary and everything in the external world—is at the heart of all biological processes."[26] Of course, the body's ability to make this distinction does not, at every level, require consciousness, much less self-consciousness. As Dennett notes, the immune system, for example, can distinguish between self and nonself by means of antibodies that are essentially shape detectors. "It is important to recognize [Dennett quite colorfully points out] that this army of antibodies has no generals, no GHQ with a battle plan, or even a description of the enemy: the antibodies represent their enemies only in the way a million locks represent the keys that open them."[27] But this ability to distinguish self from nonself also functions on the level of the conscious organism as a whole, and that is where the possibility of self-consciousness arises. When Flanagan discusses the nature of *self*-consciousness in *Consciousness Reconsidered*, he describes it as a continuum that begins "with the dim and inchoate self/nonself distinction, the awareness of what is me and mine and what is not me and not mine. Such awareness requires virtually nothing in the way of knowledge or awareness of my nature: birds, cats, and dogs are aware of the self/nonself distinction."[28]

Edelman argues that one of the elements that is necessary for the appearance of even the most primary level of consciousness is a "*self-nonself discrimination* by the nervous system as a function that is *biologically based or structurally inherent*."[29] Edelman won the Nobel Prize for his work in immunology, so he is acutely aware of the body's need to be able to distinguish that which is itself from that which is not. In *The Remembered Present* he argues that two different neural orders are needed for a conscious organism to be able to make the self/nonself distinction, although the two orders must, of course, be in communication with each other. There must be one neural order to deal with interoceptive signals (that is, input from within the organism) and one to deal with exteroceptive signals (input from the world). This accords well with Sartre's point that consciousness requires a withdrawal from that of which it is conscious. There must be a difference between consciousness and the world, between the for-itself and the in-itself, for consciousness to be possible, on Sartre's view. This requires that consciousness be nothingness for Sartre. But Edelman roots this self/nonself distinction in biology and in the body. He proposes a way for a conscious organism to make this distinction without relying on the ambiguous claim that consciousness is nothingness. At the same time, Edelman's theory remains consistent with Sartre's view that negation is necessary for consciousness. On Edelman's view the nervous system of a conscious creature must be such that a difference can be drawn between what is me and what is not me and each domain is defined, in a sense, as *not being* the other domain.[30]

Considerations thus far leave open the question of whether a conscious organism's ability to make the self/nonself distinction means that for all conscious creatures there is a kind of primitive, biologically assured self-awareness. Flanagan seems to think it does. Edelman suggests otherwise when he remarks that interoceptive input is processed nonconsciously. An examination of how this distinction works at the level of action and perception might deepen our intuitions that self-consciousness is present, albeit in a primitive form, from the very first appearance of consciousness.

Although much of the recent discussion of intentionality, especially among analytic philosophers, has centered on the intentionality of language and of higher cognitive functioning in general, I agree with those who claim there is a more basic level of intentionality on which these forms rest. I have been calling this level bodily intentionality or the intentionality exhibited by the sensorimotor body in perception and action. In his book entitled *Intentionality*, Searle argues that "the biologically primary forms of Intentionality [are] perception and action. . . . Beliefs and desires are not the primary forms, rather they are etiolated forms of more primordial experiences in perceiving and doing."[31] Searle notes that visual experiences, for example, have intentionality because they, like beliefs and desires, are directed toward objects and states of affairs in the world. In the more recent *Rediscovery of the Mind*, Searle reiterates his view that "intentionality occurs in a coordinated flow of action and perception."[32] For Searle, the intentional content of perceptual experience is propositional in nature. This is so with visual experience because "from the point of view of Intentionality, all seeing is seeing *that*: whenever it is true to say that *x* sees *y* it must also be true that *x* sees that such and such is the case."[33] According to Searle, "There are perceptual experiences; they have Intentionality; [and] their Intentional content is propositional in form."[34] Likewise, all actions, although not all bodily movements, involve intentionality.[35] The intentional content of actions is also propositional for Searle: "In the Intentional explanation of actions, the propositional content in the explanation must be identical with a propositional content of an Intentional state that functioned causally, via Intentional causation, in the production of the behavior."[36]

Searle's view of intentionality, with its emphasis on the propositional content of all intentional states, although it acknowledges the intentionality of perception and action, still clings to a primarily mental notion of intentionality. It is only in what Searle calls the *preintentional* background that the embeddedness of intentionality in the body becomes very evident. For Searle, the roles of bodily skills, practices, and know-how function as a ground for intentionality but are not themselves intentional, because they have no representational (that is, for Searle, propositional) content. Intentionality, for Searle, is rooted in the preintentional capacities of the body. But these bodily capacities function below the level of intentionality.

In *The Body in the Mind*, Johnson develops a theory of meaning that is akin in important respects to Searle's work on intentionality, but he acknowledges more fully the kind of bodily intentionality I want to argue is foundational to consciousness. Johnson sees meaning and intentionality as embedded in the human body and its interactions with the world. Unlike Searle, Johnson believes that there is a primary level of meaning and understanding which is nonpropositional and that it is this level which grounds higher, more abstract levels of cognition. For him "there is no aspect of our understanding that is independent of the nature of the human organism." What creates meaning in the first place and also ties together the concrete and abstract levels of meaning for Johnson are image schemata. He argues:

> In order for us to have meaningful, connected experiences that we can comprehend and reason about, there must be pattern and order to our actions, perceptions, and conceptions. *A schema is a recurrent pattern, shape, and regularity in, or of, these ongoing ordering activities.* These patterns emerge as meaningful structures for us chiefly at the level of our bodily movements through space, our manipulation of objects, and our perceptual interactions.

The meaning and use of such concepts as force and balance, for example, which come to be used in such abstract contexts as the force of a moral obligation or the balance involved in justice, are, on Johnson's view, learned first at the level of the body as it interacts with its environment.

These meanings are then extended by metaphor to the level of the mental and the abstract. One of the concepts that Johnson explores in depth is balance. He contends that we come to understand the meaning of balance "in the most immediate, preconceptual fashion through our bodily experience." On Johnson's account of meaning, the recurring experience of bodily equilibrium and its loss gives rise to image-schematic structures that pull together and make sense of these experiences. We go on to use metaphorical elaborations of these image schemata to understand more abstract cases of balance (balancing a checkbook or balancing work and love, for example). This theory of meaning ties together the physical and the mental. Physical experiences provide us structures by which we order our psychological experience, for example. To illustrate how this works in the psychological realm, Johnson uses the example of our concept of emotional balance. Physical experience also underlies our understanding of mental operations such as the reasoning used in logic and mathematics. The metaphors of force and balance, among other metaphors used in these domains, are extensions of the image schemata developed out of our bodily experience of physical force and balance. Intentionality, on this view, is seen as arising from bodily experience in the first place and as applying to the mental only by extension. Understanding, Johnson argues, in language that at times echoes very directly that of the phenomenologists, "*is the way we 'have a world.'*" It is not only a set of beliefs: "These beliefs are merely the surface of our embodied understanding . . . [and] our understanding is our bodily, [as well as] cultural, linguistic, historical situatedness in, and toward, our world."[37]

For Johnson, these image schemata are part of what Searle calls the "background." Yet they are not distinct from meaning and intentionality but part of their very fabric. Johnson argues, against Searle, that there is more to be said about physical skills and their role in meaning than Searle thinks: "The image-schematic structures of our skillful actions do not exist only as preintentional gestalts. They can be cognitively extended and elaborated so that they come to play a role in our understanding of abstract, nonphysical, or nonspatial situations." Johnson disagrees with Searle's view of the background because he thinks that you cannot draw a clear-cut line between intentional mental states, on the one hand, and preintentional mental and bodily capacities, on the other. Going from one to the other, we find "a continuum rather than a dichotomous gap." For Johnson, at least part of Searle's background, with its emphasis on bodily (as well as social) capacities and practices, must be included in the realm of meaning and intentionality.[38]

BODILY INTENTIONALITY AND SELF-CONSCIOUSNESS

We have finally arrived at the main point of this chapter. I contend that there are good reasons to think that at the level of bodily intentionality—that is, at the level of perception and action as the most basic modes of the body's presence to the world—there is a consciousness of self, and that consciousness is a bodily self-consciousness. A variety of authors argue this point. As I mentioned early in the chapter, I will not attempt to defend any of these theories, offering them as an exploration of this point and as evidence for the plausibility of this view. It is this view that could serve to shore up the belief that all consciousness is self-consciousness.

Gareth Evans was a British philosopher who died quite young in 1980. His work, most of it published posthumously, has influenced a great many British and American philosophers. In *The Varieties of Reference* he argues that the content of perceptual experience is *nonconceptual* as well as conceptual. It is because of the relationship of action to perception that this is so. In explicating this relationship, Evans argues that perception and action require self-awareness. Perception involves having a sense of objective space and having a sense of objects or sounds, for example, as in space or as coming from a certain place in space. But to have that sense, one must have a sense of egocentric space, according to Evans. That is, one must have a sense of space in relation to one's own body. It is within the framework of egocentric space that what Evans calls 'here'-thoughts function. The only way to establish a sense of something's being 'here' rather than elsewhere is in terms of space that is oriented to one's own body. But 'here'-thoughts cannot get a grip, Evans argues, "where there is no *possibility* of action and perception." One might think, he says, that one could have a sense of here even if one were a brain in a vat with no possibility of perception or action by arguing that 'here'- is simply 'the place I occupy' or 'where I am'. But Evans rightly points out that this gives a primacy to 'I' over 'here' which cannot be sustained. If "I identify *here* as *where I am* . . . [then] 'How do I identify myself, and make sense of my being located somewhere?' " Such self-identification requires the use of 'here'-thoughts.

> The subject conceives himself to be in the centre of a space (as its point of origin), with its co-ordinates given by the concepts 'up' and 'down', 'left' and 'right', and 'in front' and 'behind'. We may call this 'egocentric space', and we may call thinking about spatial positions in this framework

centring on the subject's body 'thinking egocentrically about space'. A subject's 'here'-thoughts belong to this system: 'here' will denote a more or less extensive area which centres on the subject.

Egocentric space is intimately connected to perception and action because it is in its terms that the contents of our experiences in space take shape and our present plans for action are formulated. When we perceive sounds, for example, we perceive them as coming from a certain direction. That aspect of the content of an auditory experience is grasped not by the application of such concepts as 'from in front of the chapel' or 'from behind the schoolhouse' but rather in terms of bodily action. The direction of the sound can be specified only in relation to the perceiver's own body. The egocentric terms we use to specify the direction from which the sounds come, from right or left or in front of or behind, for example, "derive their meaning in part from their complicated connections with the subject's *actions.*" Evans quotes Charles Taylor on the connection between the orientational structure of the perceptual field and action. Because this quote sums up this connection so well, I repeat it in its entirety.

> Our perceptual field has an orientational structure, a foreground and a background, an up and down . . . This orientational structure marks our field as essentially that of an embodied agent. It is not just that the field's perspective centres on where I am bodily—this by itself doesn't show that I am essentially agent. But take the up-down directionality of the field. What is it based on? Up and down are not simply related to my body—up is not just where my head is and down where my feet are. For I can be lying down, or bending over, or upside down; and in all these cases 'up' in my field is not the direction of my head. Nor are up and down defined by certain paradigm objects in the field, such as the earth or sky; the earth can slope for instance . . . Rather, up and down are related to how one would move and act in the field.

Evans argues that the spatial information that is present in perception can be referred to only with terms that derive their meaning in part by being connected to bodily actions.[39]

To be able to think about an objective spatial world at all, Evans argues, the subject must use a "cognitive map," which Evans defines as "a representation in which the spatial relations of several distinct things are simultaneously represented."[40] To have such a representation means the subject has to be able to make sense of the idea that he himself might be at some point on the map. But to envision himself at some point in egocentric space, he has to be able to think of the relations that hold between himself and objects as of the same kind as those which hold between two objects. "This means that he must be able to impose the objective way of thinking upon egocentric space."[41] Thus, on Evans's view, the relationship between egocentric space and objective space is a two-way one. The subject must possess a sense of both objective and egocentric space to have perceptual experiences, and these senses are intimately connected to the subject as an actor in the world. Evans sums up this point most clearly in the following quote:

> Any thinker who has an idea of an objective spatial world—an idea of a world of objects and phenomena which can be perceived but which are not dependent on being perceived for their existence—must be able to think of his perception of the world as being simultaneously due to his position in the world, and to the condition of the world in that position. The very idea of a perceivable, objective, spatial world brings with it the idea of the subject as being *in* the world, with the course of his perceptions due to his changing position in the world and to the more or less stable way the world is.[42]

On Evans's view, perception involves the subject's awareness of himself as a sensorimotor organism acting in the world. There can be no perceptual consciousness of the world without consciousness of oneself as embodied. It is this bodily self-awareness that perception and action require which provides the nonconceptual components that Evans thinks are necessary, along with the conceptual components, for perception and action.[43]

Christopher Peacocke is an analytic philosopher who has been influenced by Evans's work. Peacocke argues, like Evans, that part of the representational content of perceptual experience is nonconceptual. The conceptual content is anchored in the nonconceptual, and the nonconceptual includes spatial types, one of which he calls a 'scenario'. A scenario involves "a way of locating surfaces, features and the rest in relation to . . . a labelled origin and family of axes." The origin in perceptual experience is the body of the perceiver, and the axes are determined relative to that body. Peacocke contends that perception involves not simply a representation of events or objects in the world but also a representation of them in space relative to the perceiver's body. "Scenario content [Peacocke says] is spatial representational content." He argues that we could not attribute spatial contents to the states of an organism "unless the subject were on occasion to employ states with these contents in identifying places over time." But to make such identifications, one must construct a cognitive map of the world around oneself and use spatial representational content to do so. To do this the subject has to be able to use some form of the first-person concept. In explicating what all this comes to, Peacocke says that "to identify places over time requires the subject to be able to integrate the representational contents of his successive perceptions into an integrated representation of the world around him, both near and far, past and present." He calls this ability 'spatial reasoning' and claims such reasoning is used to construct a cognitive map, a representation of the world around the subject. Such a map requires that the subject represent not only the world but her location in it. Peacocke reasserts the point made by Evans. Perceptual consciousness requires self-consciousness, and such self-consciousness is consciousness of oneself as a body in space.[44]

Both Evans's notion of egocentric space and Peacocke's notion of the scenario content of experience recall Sartre's use of the concept of hodological space. Sartre borrowed this concept from the psychologist Kurt Lewin.[45] Hodological space, like Evans's egocentric space, refers to the subject because it is created by the subject's goals and needs. As Adrian Mirvish points out in his article "Sartre, Hodological Space, and the Existence of Others," hodological space involves no fixed set of coordinates independent of any particular subject. There is, rather, a constantly varying field of force of the experiencing subject. This field of force is space structured relative to the subject's body and to her goals. "It refers to a map or spatial organization of our environment in terms of our acts and needs" (BN, p. 279, translator's n. 20). Unfortunately, Sartre did not develop this notion to any great extent in *Being and Nothingness*. For Sartre our experience is of a spatially ordered world, and that space is structured relative to myself both as subject and as object. Sartre is cognizant of this when he discusses hodological space as a human space. We are situated in a space structured not only by our own needs and goals but by the projects of others as well. Within this space the other as object appears, but I also appear as another to other subjects. Mirvish argues that Sartre's notion of our relation to others, if interpreted in the light of his use of the concept of hodological space, along with his use of Gestalt mechanisms, "allows us to see . . . that positive . . . human relations, although they may be extremely difficult to realize and sustain, are not at all precluded by Sartre."[46] Our existence as subject and object, as lived body and body looked at, is woven together in the human space in which we are located. It is also within his few remarks on hodological space that Sartre most clearly brings together perception and action and how it is as a perceiving agent that I exist in the world.

> The space which is originally revealed to me is hodological space; it is furrowed with paths and highways; it is instrumental and it is the *location* of tools. Thus the world from the moment of the upsurge of my For-itself is revealed as the indication of acts to be performed. . . . [F]rom this point of view perception and action are indistinguishable . . . [although] perception is naturally surpassed toward action. (BN, p. 322)

The concept of hodological space focuses on the subject as a perceiving, acting, bodily agent. It is this self to which the for-itself as consciousness is present in being present to the world. But Sartre's development of this bodily self-presence as a prereflexive presence to oneself as subject as well as object is minimal and inadequate. This is because of his adherence to a division between the lived body and the body as an object in space, in the world, open to the look of another. In an appendix to a chapter in Evans's *Varieties of Reference*, the editor notes Evans's response to Sartre's belief that if I begin with the body as it exists for others, the objective body, "my body *in the midst of the world*" (BN, p. 303), I can never unite it with my consciousness. Evans thought Sartre was right in one way, that is, "I can identify myself with a bit of matter only if I know that bit of matter 'from the inside'."[47] But Evans thought this sense of oneself from the inside provided the foundation for "an ability to identify myself with an element of the objective order—a body of others, if you like—unreservedly."[48] My sense of myself as subject and as a body in the world are not split and at odds with each other on Evans's view as they are, for the most part, on Sartre's. With the notion of hodological space, Sartre approaches a notion of the lived body moving in a space that involves the self as object as well as subject. But the union between the two aspects of the self that could have been developed with reference to this concept of space is rejected in *Being and Nothingness*. Sartre does say that "of course our human-reality must of necessity be simultaneously for-itself and for-others" (BN, p. 282). But although these two aspects are simultaneous for Sartre, they are also distinct and separate, as he makes clear in his discussion of the body.

Although Evans's account of perception and action brings together the subjective and objective aspects of one's bodily experience (Sartre's being-for-itself and being-in-itself), he still maintains that there is a distinction between the two. But Adrian Cussins, in more recent work on the embodied nature of cognition, while acknowledging that Evans's work has both influenced and inspired his own, argues that there is a level of perceptual experience and action in which no such distinction is made. Cussins contends that the nonconceptual content of experience is basic and that the conceptual content (including objectivity and subjectivity) is built up out of the nonconceptual. For both Evans and Peacocke, experience always involves a mix of both conceptual and nonconceptual content.[49] Cussins disagrees. He maintains that the nonconceptual content of experience is prior to the conceptual. His view has a kinship with the view espoused by Merleau-Ponty in the *Phenomenology of Perception*. Merleau-Ponty argues that there is primary perceptual consciousness which lacks conceptual content and in which the distinction between objective and subjective plays no role. For both Cussins and Merleau-Ponty, there is a pre-predicative and pre-objective realm of experience out of which the objective arises. I wish to examine both Cussins's and Merleau-Ponty's analyses of this level of basic perception, not to defend their claim that there is such primary perception, although I think they are right about that. Rather, I wish to argue that even if there is a kind of basic perceptual consciousness on which other, more complex forms of consciousness rest, a consciousness in which a distinction between subjective and objective does not exist, a kind of self-consciousness is still present at even this most basic level of perception. The self-consciousness present at this level is the body's presence to itself.

Cussins approaches issues of cognition and intentionality from an analytic perspective and stresses the role of embodiment in intentionality. He is one of a growing number of analytic philosophers, many of whom have been influenced by Evans, who are beginning to remember the body as it moves and acts in the world. He is dealing, he says, with " 'the problem of embodied cognition.' "[50] Although he argues for a solution to this problem that is computational as well as psychological in character, he does not, like the functionalists, neglect the material basis for cognition. He argues against those who believe "that the only kind of representational content is propositional or conceptual content."[51] He wants a theory of nonconceptual meaning and content because he believes that perception, as well as other intentional states, involves nonconceptual as well as conceptual content. Cussins contends that the content of experience, its cognitive significance, is specified not just by that to which the experience refers but by what Cussins calls the "realm of embodiment." This realm encompasses bodily skills, abilities, and activities. Content, Cussins says, involves carving the world up in certain ways. The nonconceptual content of perceptual experience carves the world up not by the application of such concepts as that of objects or properties or states of affairs but by relying on ways of moving in the world (and the set of bodily skills and activities which underlie or just are that movement). Cussins discusses the example of a perceptual experience of a coffee mug that is full (and the attendant thought that it is full). The content of the experience is specified not solely in terms of that to which the experience refers—the cup of coffee—but also in terms of one's ability to grasp the mug, track its movements, and adjust one's judgments and actions relative to perceived changes in the mug's appearance. "These abilities are not available to the subject as the content's referent, but they *are* available to the subject as the subject's experience-based knowledge of how to act on the object, and respond to it."[52]

Although most human perceptual experience involves both conceptual and nonconceptual content, Cussins maintains that it is the nonconceptual content that is explanatorily basic. He argues for the possibility of a theory of representation that does not bring in notions of truth or reference. His theory of cognitive trails explicates how representation is possible without concepts and how representation that does involve the conceptual arises out of this logically prior kind of representation. To go into detail about Cussins's theory of representation would take us too far afield, but suffice it to say that the theory explains how there could be representation and hence intentional states whose content is specified solely in terms of the realm of embodiment. Cussins argues that it is possible to conceive of experience as representational, cognitively significant, without conceiving of it in terms of reference and truth and even without conceiving of it as involving a mind/world distinction. Such experience would also lack any conception of the subject of experience as an object in the world. Yet the subject as a bodily subject of experience would still enter into the cognitive significance of this kind of experience, because the content of experience would be specified in terms of the subject's bodily skills and activities. Cussins thinks that experience for Evans is possible only if the nonconceptual content, which is fixed by the realm of embodiment, is transformed by exercising one's conceptual abilities. Cussins disagrees. Cussins never says whether experience that lacks conceptual content is ever experienced by humans. He is interested in the possibility of its conception. But the implication is that such experience is possible and perhaps at times actual. Whether Cussins thinks such experience is conscious is unclear from his discussion of it. He does say that it would not be experience *within a consciousness*, because that would require the subject/object distinction.[53] But the subject/object distinction that Cussins thinks such experience lacks is the distinction between the subject of experience as an *object* in the world and other objects in the world. That would rule out the possibility of such experience being self-conscious in one sense of the word. But it doesn't follow from that fact that the experience is not a conscious one. If it is, I would argue it would still involve self-consciousness of a certain type. If the content of such experience is specified partly in terms of one's bodily movements and skills, then the content of the experience includes one's bodily self along with elements of the world, even if the subject of experience cannot draw a distinction between the two (now or ever). If such experience is not conscious experience, then we have no need to argue that even on this level of consciousness all consciousness is self-consciousness.

Although Cussins implies the possibility of a kind of primary, nonconceptual perceptual experience, his focus is on a theory of representation that can account for the representational content of such experience. Merleau-Ponty, however, focuses directly on such experience itself, providing a phenomenological description of it.

In the *Phenomenology of Perception*, long before Evans and others began to pay attention to the embodied nature of the subject of consciousness, Merleau-Ponty argued that there is bodily experience prior to thought. There is, Merleau-Ponty says in his discussion of primary perception, "a communication with the world more ancient than thought." Merleau-Ponty anticipates Cussins by claiming that this level of experience is prior to any questions of truth or knowledge. It is an experience of a pre-objective world in which the distinction between subject and object is not yet present. "The ante-predicative life of consciousness," he calls it in the preface to the *Phenomenology of Perception*. Merleau-Ponty argues that there is a pre-personal life playing below my personal life. This pre-personal life is the life of the organism. There is, he says, in an often quoted passage from the *Phenomenology of Perception*, "another subject beneath me, for whom a world exists before I am here, and who marks out my place in it. This captive or natural spirit is my body." It is my body as a sensorimotor organism perceiving and acting in the world that first expresses intentionality. There is a bodily intentionality, on Merleau-Ponty's view, on which all other forms of intentionality rest. He argues that meaning, indeed consciousness itself, begins not with intellectual representation and cognition but with sensorimotor activity. The most primary form of consciousness is not reflectively aware of itself. The 'I think' is not what is fundamental. "Consciousness is in the first place not a matter of 'I think that' but of 'I can'." He accepts Sartre's rejection of Descartes's starting point (on the traditional reading of Descartes)—the reflective cogito. But he goes beyond Sartre's rejection of reflective self-consciousness as primary. What characterizes the most fundamental level of consciousness, for Merleau-Ponty, is neither the actual ascription of experience to oneself (the actual use of the 'I think') nor even the latent capacity for such ascriptions. Rather, the 'I can perceive and act' is what characterizes it. The use of the first-person pronoun, however, does not mean that Merleau-Ponty believes an ego inhabits consciousness. He, like Sartre before him, claims there is a pre-personal consciousness that rests beneath the life of the historicized 'I'. What Merleau-Ponty calls the habitual body is a body conscious in an anonymous and pre-personal sense.[54]

In his analysis of bodily intentionality, Merleau-Ponty emphasizes, as Evans does, the intimate relation between perception and movement. They are not separate from each other but function together. These functions of the body occur within a system formed by bodily and external space. But Merleau-Ponty does not think that either of these senses of space are objectified at this level, as they are for Evans. He contends that at the level of primary perception and action, neither movement nor bodily space are conceptualized or represented.[55] Bodily space is brought into existence only in action. The goals of actions, as well as actions themselves, are brought out against the backdrop of bodily space. This analysis of the body's motility—a motility that Merleau-Ponty argues forms basic intentionality—brings us "to the recognition of something between movement as a third person process and thought as a representation of movement—something which is an anticipation of, or arrival at, the objective and is ensured by the body itself as a motor power, a 'motor project' (*Bewegungsentwurf*), a 'motor intentionality'."[56] Motor intentionality is preconceptual and functions without the positing of objects. Like Cussins, Merleau-Ponty argues that intentionality is first related to actions, skills, and goals rather than to thoughts and concepts. Thus both authors contend that there is a level of meaning that is constituted not within the realm of ideas and mental representations but within the realm of motor activity.

For Merleau-Ponty, then, there is a pre-objective and pre-predicative perceptual consciousness that is more primary than experience of both an objective world and the body as an object in that world. At this level of experience, the perceiving subject is revealed to us, Merleau-Ponty says, as the perceived world.[57] He argues, as Sartre does, that reflective self-awareness rests on unreflective experience. But although primary perceptual consciousness is unreflective, it is not unselfconscious. For Merleau-Ponty, unreflective experience reveals a "world which is given to the subject, because the subject is given to himself."[58] The subject is given to himself as pre-personal and bodily. In primary perception the self exists as immediately present to the world and to the body.[59] For Merleau-Ponty self-consciousness in its most fundamental form is bodily self-consciousness. The body is present to itself even before a conceptual distinction arises between subject and object, self and world. It is in one act of perception that the body and the world are given. "External perception and perception of one's own body . . . are the two facets of one and the same act."[60]

Merleau-Ponty does say that reflection refers to unreflective experience that is "a past which has never been a present." This might be taken to imply either that unreflective experience is not *conscious* experience or that it is not *self-conscious* (conscious) experience. He does, in places, refer to such experience as *preconscious*. This might appear inconsistent with his frequent references to primary perception as perceptual consciousness. But he makes it clear in the following passage that when he refers to such experience as preconscious, he means only that it lacks reflective self-consciousness. "The consciousness of the world is not *based* on self-consciousness: they are strictly contemporary. There is a world for me because I am not unaware of myself; and I am not concealed from myself because I have a world. This pre-conscious possession of the world remains to be analyzed in the pre-reflective *cogito*." Such preconscious experience is unreflective and yet still self-conscious. In primary perception the bodily subject of experience is conscious both of itself as body and of the world. Behind the Cartesian cogito there is, on Merleau-Ponty's view, a tacit cogito, "myself experiencing myself." Merleau-Ponty's belief in the union of the self and the world and the self-presence that primary perception involves is clearly articulated in his discussion of the cogito in part 3 of the *Phenomenology of Perception*. Although he agrees with Sartre that there is a type of self-consciousness that is more fundamental than the self-consciousness created by reflection, his discussion of unreflective experience reveals that he remembers more clearly than Sartre does that it is the body which is the subject of consciousness. Hence Merleau-Ponty stresses that the self to which the subject is present in being present to the world is not consciousness as a negation of the world but the sensorimotor body as it moves and acts in the world. Although some Merleau-Ponty scholars go too far in criticizing Sartre for having forgotten the body altogether, it is true that Sartre failed to track far enough the consequences of his belief that the body is the subject of consciousness.[61]

It is his following out the implication of a belief in the embodied nature of consciousness that leads Merleau-Ponty to focus on the intentionality of the body and the bodily self-consciousness entailed by that. This focus and the phenomenology that flows from it allow Merleau-Ponty to overcome the separation between the in-itself and the for-itself that is built into Sartre's ontology. The for-itself for Sartre is a negation of the in-itself. But for Merleau-Ponty in the *Phenomenology of Perception*, the for-itself is *first of all* body. "The 'They' of prepersonal life is not a personal subject . . . but is a subject interwoven with the natural world, because it lives only through its body. Natural life, in Merleau-Ponty's sense, is indeed a life that is '*bodily*' through and through."[62]

For Merleau-Ponty the self-apprehension on the pre-reflective level is not consciousness grasping itself as nothingness but rather the body's presence to itself as an organism engaged in perceptual and motor activity. It is a self-consciousness that functions at the sensorimotor level and not at the conceptual level. Although Sartre acknowledges that pre-reflective self-consciousness must involve consciousness of the body as the subject of experience, his analysis of the self-consciousness of consciousness emphasizes the nonsubstantiality of consciousness far more than it does its embodied nature. For Merleau-Ponty it is the body, the subject of consciousness, as a being-in-the-world that is the middle term that unites the psychic and the physiological, the for-itself and the in-itself. "It is because it is a preobjective view that being-in-the-world can be distinguished from every third person process, from every modality of the *res extensa*, as from every *cogitatio*, from every first person form of knowledge—and that it can effect the union of the 'psychic' and 'physiological'."[63] Merleau-Ponty says that the psychic and the physiological are linked and in unreflective experience are no longer even distinguishable as for-itself and in-itself.[64] It is the body's presence to itself that unites consciousness and the world. Consciousness and matter are not separated by the fact that the former is intentional and reflexive and the latter is not. The most basic form of intentionality and reflexivity is bodily in nature, according to Merleau-Ponty. It is his "discovery of corporeal reflexivity . . . [that is] the means to overcome ontological dualism."[65] At the outset, he says, "neither subject nor object are *posited*."[66] In primary perception there is no irreparable rupture between the for-itself and the in-itself.[67]

There are important differences between the *Phenomenology of Perception* and Merleau-Ponty's last work, *The Visible and the Invisible*. Nevertheless, he continues to maintain that the most primary level of self-consciousness is the body's presence to itself. In addition he addresses once again, in his discussion of flesh, the union of the for-itself and the in-itself. He rejects as he did in the earlier work the Sartrean split between the for-itself and the in-itself and reemphasizes the bodily nature of the subject of consciousness and its immediate presence to itself. Merleau-Ponty believes that "since the seer is caught up in what he sees, it is still himself he sees." He says that "my body is a *Gestalt* and it is co-present in every *Gestalt*." At the most fundamental level of Being, there is no distinction between subject and object. This applies to the body as well. For Merleau-Ponty the body which looks and the body which is looked at overlap. There is an intertwining between the flesh of the world and myself as flesh. It is precisely because both seer and seen are flesh that communication between them is possible. He once again emphasizes the bodily nature of the self and the bodily self-presence that is fundamental to our nature. The body, aware of itself in being aware of the world, stands in a relation "of embrace" with the world, not in a relation of negation. Each morning I awake to "that blending with the world that recommences for me . . . as soon as I open my eyes."[68]

INPUT FROM SELF AND WORLD

To shore up my contention that even on the most basic level of bodily intentionality there is self-consciousness, I will examine the mounting evidence that strengthens the plausibility of the hypothesis that there is a form of bodily self-consciousness which is part of the very nature of consciousness. First I will consider a sampling of the philosophical arguments and empirical evidence that support the belief that all consciousness involves bodily input. I will then review the conflicting views about whether it is always possible for the subject of experience to make such bodily data reflectively conscious. Finally, I will argue that even if such bodily data are not always accessible to reflective consciousness, that fact does not undermine the claim that all consciousness is, in some sense, bodily self-consciousness. I think the plausibility of this interpretation of the self-consciousness of consciousness goes some way toward overcoming the problems created both by Sartre's distinction between the self as subject and the self as object as well as by his more general ontological distinction between being-for-itself and being-in-itself, on which the former distinction rests.

Bodily Data

A growing number of theories lend support and specification to the view that consciousness requires input from the body as well as from the world. What makes the intuition that all consciousness is self-consciousness so strong and deep rooted, I think, is precisely the fact that consciousness of the world requires a processing of bodily data as well as a processing of stimuli from the external world.

Edelman, within the context of his theory of neural Darwinism, makes a plausible case for the view that input from both self and world is necessary for consciousness. I have already referred to Edelman's claim that consciousness requires both a self/nonself distinction and two different neural orders to allow the conscious organism to realize this distinction. Such a distinction is necessary for primary consciousness to appear. Edelman defines primary consciousness as that form of consciousness which is basic to all other higher forms of consciousness. It includes perceptual awareness as well as more complex states in humans. It is not personal and does not require language. Self at this level "refers to autonomic activities that sustain the survival of an [biologically defined] individual. Self is fundamentally determined by the signaling activity of areas mediating homeostatic—autonomic, hedonic, neuro-endocrine—brain functions." Edelman argues that primary consciousness requires that the organism discriminate between present perceptual categorizations and past perceptual categorizations that form what he calls 'self patterns'. The need for this kind of discrimination is what necessitates the self/nonself distinction at the level of primary consciousness. Primary consciousness "is based on the *difference* in the nature of internal and external categorizations." Given this characterization of primary consciousness, it follows that such consciousness is generated not by external stimuli alone but by interoceptive stimuli as well. It requires input from both self and world. But, on Edelman's view, human consciousness involves a level of consciousness that goes beyond primary consciousness. Edelman calls this level "higher-order consciousness." It requires more than just the input from self and the self/nonself discrimination that operate at the level of primary consciousness. Higher-order consciousness also requires a *concept* of the self. Edelman argues that language and social interaction are necessary for the development of such a concept. The self-consciousness of higher-order consciousness is built on and includes but goes beyond the processing of bodily data. Unlike primary consciousness, higher-order consciousness is personal and involves not only consciousness of the world but consciousness of consciousness. It involves a direct, noninferential awareness of our own perceptions, thoughts, and mental states. Such self-awareness requires the ability to form a model of the self in relation to a model of the world. The notion of a self that functions at this level is not just that of a biological individual, Edelman claims, but of a social individual. The conscious organism must utilize thought and language to develop such a sense of self. According to Edelman, it is image schemata that help organize thought and language. It is the need for such schemata that brings the body back into central focus. "Image schemata involve concepts connected to positions and states of the body as it relates to objects or events—for example, 'obstacle', 'resistance', 'object', 'motion', 'containment', and 'blockage'." This aspect of the use of bodily data echoes both Sartre's notion of hodological space and Evans's and Peacocke's notions of egocentric space. It appears that for Edelman, although the self-consciousness of higher-order consciousness goes beyond the self- (that is, bodily) input involved at the level of primary consciousness, it does build on such bodily input. On Edelman's account, higher-order consciousness makes use of image schemata of the body in its development of a conceptual model of the self. Because of that, bodily data are required for the development of higher-order consciousness.[69]

In his discussion of image schemata, Edelman mentions the work of Johnson that I noted earlier in the chapter, as well as the pioneering work of British psychologist Sir Henry Head on the existence and use of a schema of the body. The schema, on Head's account, is a kind of postural model of oneself, and it records and keeps track of the postural changes of the body. The schema is a constantly changing model of one's body in time and space. One of the primary functions of this schema is the presentation to consciousness of data relating to the position of the body in space. Whether or not Head's idea of a schema of the body is correct, it at least points to the necessity for a conscious organism to process input from its body as well as from the external world as it moves and acts in the world.[70]

In the article "The Representing Brain: Neural Correlates of Motor Intention and Imagery," French neurophysiologist, Marc Jeannerod argues that the empirical data suggest that motor imagery and motor preparation are not merely related but are functionally equivalent. He thinks they share the same neural substrate and differ only in degree, not in kind. Jeannerod reviews a whole array of empirical data to support his hypothesis. Whether the evidence he reviews actually does support his hypothesis is debatable. But such evidence does suggest that both perceiving and imaging consciousness involve a (not necessarily visual) representation of the body. Within the context of his argument, he extends Head's 'schema' theory. He argues that motor images are kinesthetic representations of the self in action. On Jeannerod's view, one does not form a *visual* image of oneself acting but *feels* oneself executing an action. "Representing the self in movement . . . requires a representation of the body as the generator of acting forces." The important point for my argument is that on Jeannerod's account motor imagery (if there exists such imagery) would involve a representation of what Sartre calls the lived body. It would be an image of oneself from a first-person, not a third-person, point of view. And it would be an image of oneself as a body in action. Such bodily schema, Jeannerod argues, must encode the goal of the action. "The goal of an action includes an internal representation of both the external object toward which it is directed, and the final state of the organism when that object has been reached." The body is represented not only as in action but also in terms of the final goal of the action. Once again we see the possibility of a neurophysiological explanation of one of Sartre's claims about consciousness: that consciousness anticipates and projects itself into the future. For Sartre, it is a not yet existent state of affairs that propels the subject forward toward the future and hence it is nothingness—that is, a lack in being—that produces action. On Jeannerod's account it is something, not nothing, that propels the subject into action. This something is a representation of that which is not yet. "The notion of the representation of a goal therefore implies that the organism is looking ahead toward a new state, the representation of which steers the transformation until its completion." My argument is not that this particular neurophysiological account is correct. The position I am defending is that if the body is the subject of consciousness, then some such account must correlate with and support the phenomenological data.[71]

Natika Newton is yet another theorist who highlights the importance of somatic data to consciousness. In "Consciousness, Qualia, and Reentrant Signalling" she argues:

> In any perceptual experience there is a constant background of bodily input which provides a framework for perceived objects. I perceive the orientation of my eyes and the edges of my eye sockets framing the visual field, my posture and the position of my limbs, visceral states, etc. I also perceive a correlation between bodily motions and alterations in the appearance of objects.[72]

Newton thinks the self-awareness that accompanies perceptual awareness—that is, the awareness not just of the object of perception but of the perceiving itself—is simply an awareness of this bodily data. She points to William James, who thought that in a certain sense of self-awareness, awareness of self is awareness of bodily behavior. In additon she uses the fact that perceptual objects appear as external to the perceiver as support for her claim about the nature of the self-awareness involved in perception. When I perceive physical objects, for example, I perceive them as external to my body. That could not be the case, Newton argues, unless I were aware of my body.

One of the most obvious sources of bodily data used for the creation of cognitive maps and body schemata is proprioception. Oliver Sacks is probably most responsible for popularizing the importance of proprioception for our sense of ourselves. He highlights the importance of what

C. S. Sherrington called our 'sixth sense' by discussing a person who has lost that 'sense'. As Sacks notes, it is by means of proprioception that the position, tone, and motion of our muscles, tendons, and joints are monitored and adjusted. Proprioception allows a person to be aware of the position of her limbs, for example, without having to look to find them. But Christina, the individual that Sacks discusses in "The Disembodied Lady," had lost all proprioception. The neurological damage Christina suffered destroyed her "position-sense," as Sacks calls it. Because the sense of the body is given not only by proprioception but by vision and the vestibular system as well, Christina had to learn to rely on these latter two alone to be able to move in the world. This was a long and painstaking process and one that never allowed her to regain the fluidity and grace of movement she had before the neurological damage occurred. Christina described her situation phenomenologically as a state of disembodiment. She said she could no longer feel her body. She felt that her body was blind. Sacks describes her situation several years after the initial damage: "She continues to feel, with a continuing loss of proprioception, that her body is dead, not-real, not-hers—she cannot appropriate it to herself."[73] She experiences this loss of her connection with her body as a profound loss of self.

Is the Subject Conscious of Bodily Data?

I think there is convincing and growing evidence that consciousness and our sense of ourselves require the processing of bodily data. The question remains, however, whether the existence and the necessity of such bodily input support the contention that all consciousness involves at least bodily self-awareness. That is, must the subject of consciousness be aware of such bodily data to be aware of the world? Does the sensorimotor body have to be conscious of itself, or can it simply process input from itself nonconsciously?

Does proprioception, for example, provide a kind of basic bodily self-awareness? Are the results of proprioception conscious? Oliver Sacks thinks not. Sacks believes proprioception provides a "continuous but unconscious sensory flow from the movable parts of our body."[74] Perhaps one could argue, against Sacks, that we are conscious of the results of proprioception, but on the level of pre-reflective rather than reflective consciousness. Drew Leder, in *The Absent Body*, notes that although the results of proprioception are usually unnoticed, "I can . . . proprioceptively hone in on the position, the level of tension or relaxation, in any region of the muscular body."[75] If I pay attention, I can feel the strain of my muscles as I push pen against paper; I can feel the weight of my arm against the table as I write and the cross of my legs as I sit at the desk. I can tell you without thought or hesitation the position of the little finger on my left hand or the spot in space that my big toe now occupies. One can acknowledge that such bodily self-awareness remains peripheral or in the background of our awareness, but it doesn't follow from that fact that bodily self-awareness is altogether lacking. It remains in the background most of the time precisely because of the presence/absence structure of bodily self-consciousness that I discussed earlier in the chapter.

G. E. M. Anscombe, however, discusses a case of sensory deprivation in which she claims bodily self-awareness is absent but consciousness and indeed self-conscious thought are still possible. Anscombe imagines herself in a state of severe sensory deprivation: "Sight is cut off, and I am locally anaesthetized everywhere, perhaps floated in a tank of tepid water; I am unable to speak, or to touch any part of my body with any other."[76] My body, she contends, is not present to my senses and hence not present to me at all. But I can still think about myself and my situation. She uses this case as partial evidence that 'I' is not a referring expression.[77] Evans argues against Anscombe's position by claiming that a person cannot have self-conscious thoughts ('I'-thoughts, as he calls them) without having a notion of herself as an object situated in time and space. But his argument is with regard to self-consciousness on the level of reflection. The question that is more basic to my argument is whether *pre-reflective* consciousness would be possible without at least a minimal level of bodily self-awareness.

Edelman discusses sensory deprivation in *The Remembered Present*, arguing that without both external stimuli and proprioceptive input, primary consciousness could not arise. But although he thinks existing consciousness under these conditions might be severely affected, he is not sure it would disappear altogether.[78] However, he points out that sensory deprivation experiments, although they can reduce world input to a level almost never experienced by a waking animal, cannot remove all proprioceptive data. Even if all such data could be removed, the sustaining of some degree of awareness would utilize, according to Edelman, already conceptualized input from self and world in conjunction with the slight amount of present external stimuli still available in such cases.

But even if the presence and use of bodily data in cases of sensory deprivation could be established, that would not prove that such data are available to the conscious subject. Edelman argues that the self-input he claims is necessary for consciousness and the distinction between self and nonself which that involves is nonconscious at the level of primary consciousness. And some of it—that which arises from the autonomic, hedonic, and neuroendocrine systems—is nonconscious at the level of higher-order consciousness as well. But he does think higher-order consciousness is self-conscious. However, there can be consciousness, Edelman's primary consciousness, that is not self-conscious. It is not clear whether Edelman thinks humans with normal brain structure can ever experience primary consciousness. He certainly makes it clear that if humans could—possibly split-brain patients actually do, he thinks—they would have no intuition of its nature because such experience would lack self-consciousness. So there does seem to be a kind of consciousness, on Edelman's account, where the bodily data are nonconscious. For Head the bodily schemata are physiological conditions that have "an automatic influence . . . directly upon the highest efferent centres without the intermediation of consciousness."[79] Postural schemata are not images in consciousness on Head's theory, although they do present to consciousness data relating to the position of the body in space. Jeannerod believes that motor preparation is entirely nonconscious. But he does think the motor images at play in imagining action are accessible to consciousness. He even thinks "if motor preparation (normally very brief) could be prolonged [by inhibiting the actual performance of the action], the intention to act would become progressively a motor image of the same action," and then it too would be accessible to consciousness.[80]

Although I think the present evidence goes a long way toward supporting the belief that all consciousness involves bodily input, I do not think there is sufficient empirical evidence to prove that all consciousness involves a pre-reflective bodily self-awareness *that could be made reflective*. In *most* cases of *human* consciousness it is probably true that at least some of the somatic data involved in consciousness are accessible to reflective consciousness. But I think neither the present empirical evidence nor the kind of logical arguments Sartre constructs to defend his thesis about the self-consciousness of consciousness are sufficient to establish that *all* consciousness involves an awareness of the body that can be focused on and separated from the rest of the content of a conscious state. But that fact does not undermine my attempt to establish that all consciousness is in some sense a consciousness of the body.

The Blending of Input from Self and World

If we go back to Edelman's theory of neural Darwinism and his argument that consciousness requires input from both self and world, I think we can find at least a plausible basis from which to construct support for the Sartrean belief in the self-consciousness of consciousness. Newton does a good job of showing how Edelman's notion of reentrant signaling can be used to support her claim that "perhaps the most striking thing about conscious awareness of objects is the *immediate experiential apprehension* of oneself aware of them. Even when our attention is not on ourselves but on what we perceive, conscious perceptual awareness includes awareness of our own perceiving."[81] This is so because the internal and the external inputs necessary for consciousness are blended in such a way that the final result is an awareness of both self and world. "Common to all these processes is the blending, by what Edelman calls 'reentrant signalling,' of the results of parallel perceptual processes into a unified representation."[82] According to Edelman's theory, groups of neurons processing both external input and internal input exchange the results of this processing with each other by means of reentrant signaling. "Reentry is a process of temporally ongoing parallel signaling between separate [neural] maps along ordered anatomical connections."[83] The sensorimotor activity of a moving organism produces local maps (visual maps as well as those of other modalities), and through reentrant signaling global maps are constructed.[84] These maps and the reentrant signaling between them are necessary, Edelman speculates, for conscious perceptual awareness as well as for nonconscious perceptual categorization.[85] Although Edelman never directly connects this aspect of his theory with the question of the self-consciousness of consciousness, Newton does. She uses these aspects of his theory, along with the results of other, current neuroscientific work, to explain the self-awareness she claims is awareness of bodily input. Self-consciousness at the level of reflection "is due simply to the spotlighting of bodily input."[86] Although there are two neural orders on Edelman's theory that ground the distinction between self and nonself at the biological level, consciousness of the external world does not necessarily involve making such a distinction conscious. In most cases of human consciousness, however, the person who is the subject of consciousness can become reflectively aware of herself as perceiving, for example. She simply focuses on the bodily input involved in a conscious state.[87] When I am drinking, for example, rather than being aware of the taste and feel of the fluid as it slides past my tongue and down my throat, I shift my focus instead to such things as the muscular sensations in my tongue and throat and to the weight and coolness of the glass against my hand. There may be higher levels of reflective self-awareness, indeed there no doubt are, but I propose that the fundamental self-awareness upon which all reflective consciousness rests is bodily self-awareness, which may not always be easily distinguishable from awareness of the world. There could be cases of consciousness that, although self-conscious, could not be made reflectively so. But in most cases of human consciousness, such pre-reflective self-consciousness is available to reflective consciousness. Whether it is or not, however, consciousness is self-consciousness.[88]

I am indeed, as Sartre would have it, in the presence of myself as well as of the world, and that presence does not necessarily require consciousness of the distinction between self and world. My consciousness of the world is a result of the blending of input from both self and world. Because of this the self is in a sense simply consciousness of the world. In pre-reflective consciousness the self is absent as a separate focus of attention because I do not call forth bodily responses to the external environment and focus on those alone. We return once again to the presence/absence structure of bodily self-consciousness.[89] It is also the case, as Newton points out, that "if the self is simply part of the content of experience, then awareness is non-relational. The apparent duality is conceptual, not experiential."[90] Unlike perceptual consciousness of an object, consciousness of self at the pre-reflective level does not require a subject/object dichotomy. I think that is the point toward which Sartre is driving when he contends that nothing separates consciousness from itself at the level of pre-reflective consciousness. Yet Sartre wants a separation, which can be accounted for on the kind of analysis of fundamental self-consciousness that I am proposing. Self-input and world input are separate because they are received and processed initially by separate neural orders. However, given the resultant blending (possibly by means of reentrant signaling), it is really nothing that separates them. The duality of self and world and hence the duality of consciousness of self and consciousness of the world are unified by being contents of one and the same object of consciousness. Even when I can pay attention to the body's presence and place the world in the background, the body's presence is always given within the context of my presence to the world. It is always given in hodological or egocentric space, just as the world is always given within the context of the body. In most cases I can shift focus from external input to internal, but like the duck/rabbit drawing, that shift does not make two what is one.

Biology and Phenomenology

I n Chapter 5 I argued that the most fundamental level of self-consciousness is the body's awareness of itself in sensorimotor activity. I suggested that an examination of that level of self-consciousness might provide support for some of the analysis of consciousness that Sartre offers in *Being and Nothingness*. In this chapter I wish to extend that discussion. By way of conclusion, I will sketch some ways in which a biological theory of consciousness and a sense of bodily self-consciousness as the most fundamental level of self-consciousness might possibly provide support for Sartre's phenomenology-based analysis of consciousness. I am aware, of course, that Sartre would resist any objectivist accounts of consciousness. But my contention is that phenomenology and biology can both be useful in trying to understand consciousness. Exploring the connections between science-based and phenomenology-based accounts of consciousness brings to light the way in which phenomenology anticipates and can help direct biological research on the nature of consciousness.[1] In addition it reveals how biological findings can account for some of the phenomenological descriptions of consciousness offered by philosophers. If it is the body that is the subject of consciousness, then neither phenomenology nor biology should be disowned.

For Sartre the reason that the Law of Identity fails to apply to the for-itself is because all consciousness is self-consciousness. In Chapter 2 I explored the relation between these two claims and showed how pivotal they are within the context of the major claims of *Being and Nothingness*. In this chapter I will argue that a notion of primary self-consciousness as bodily awareness can also be used to support Sartre's belief that the Law of Identity does not apply to the for-itself. In Chapter 3 I explored Sartre's belief that there are three types of self-consciousness in our existence for ourselves—the self-consciousness of the pre-reflective cogito, of pure reflection, and of impure reflection—arguing that he fails to offer a characterization of each type that keeps the three distinct. Here I will examine ways in which a theory of bodily self-consciousness can provide more sense and substance to these distinctions. In Chapter 4 I offered counterexamples to Sartre's claims about the self-consciousness of consciousness. In this chapter I intend to reconsider those counterexamples in light of the idea of bodily self-consciousness to see if that notion can provide ways to overcome these counterexamples.

The hardest problem, however, remains. Sartre uses the self-consciousness of consciousness and the nothingness to which it gives rise to ground his belief in human freedom. Can the idea of bodily self-consciousness do the same, or does it inevitably undermine the basic substance of Sartre's position in *Being and Nothingness*? I will suggest that there may be ways to make my claim about the nature of the primary level of self-consciousness compatible at least with a belief in human freedom. Whether my analysis of self-consciousness can ground the kind of radical freedom Sartre is after is, however, doubtful. That might be one reason why Sartre did not follow out the implications of his belief in the embodied nature of consciousness as far as he might have.

THE LAW OF IDENTITY

I made clear in Chapter 2 that for Sartre it is because all consciousness is self-conscious that the Law of Identity does not apply to the for-itself. The grounding of the self-consciousness of consciousness in bodily self-awareness does not undermine Sartre's belief that the reason the for-itself fails to coincide with itself is because it is self-conscious. *Bodily* self-consciousness also gives rise to a failure of coincidence between consciousness and itself. I wish to examine two of the most important reasons why the for-itself fails to coincide with itself for Sartre: (1) because the for-itself exists always as presence to itself, and (2) because consciousness is and is not its past (and future) self. Some support for both claims can be provided by an appeal to the notion of bodily self-consciousness.

The For-Itself as Presence to Itself

Given his belief in the self-conscious nature of all forms of consciousness, it follows that for Sartre even pre-reflective consciousness is self-conscious. Since for Sartre consciousness requires a withdrawal from or nihilation of that to which consciousness is present, pre-reflective consciousness must involve a nihilation not only of the object of consciousness but of the self as well. Because of this double nihilation, the for-itself does not coincide with itself. If we return to Edelman's biological theory of consciousness and in particular to his notion of reentrant signaling introduced in Chapter 5, we find a theory that accounts for consciousness's failure to coincide with itself and for how such a failure arises from the bodily self-awareness that all consciousness requires. Edelman, quite plausibly I think, contends that consciousness requires a processing of bodily input and world input. These two inputs must be constantly updated as well as blended, and his theory of reentrant signaling is offered to explain how such updating and blending are achieved. Reentrant signaling is, as I mentioned in Chapter 5, the parallel signaling between separate neural maps that are created by the processing of input from self and world. Such signaling is the means by which input from these two neural orders is blended. This process is not a simple one, however. The already processed and blended neural input from self and world is continually *reprocessed* along with new input from both self and world. "Recursive synthesis allows signals from higher-order perceptual constructs to be used as inputs for lower-order maps through repeated reentrant signals."[2] This is how the brain constantly updates its representation of the world and the subject's place in the world. If anything like the story Edelman tells is true, one can see how something similar to a double nihilation of self and object of awareness is possible and indeed necessary for the body to be conscious of the world. The blending of input from both self and world means that consciousness of the object of awareness just is, in a sense, consciousness of oneself. Because of the constant updating and reprocessing of such input, the for-itself is continually nihilating and withdrawing from itself in withdrawing from and nihilating its object of awareness.

Of course, a good chance exists that Edelman's highly speculative theory of reentrant signaling will be replaced by some more accurate biological theory. It still stands to reason, however, that bodily input as well as input from the external world must be received, united, and constantly updated in some manner for consciousness of the world to be possible. Whether this process is best explained by reference to cognitive maps or neural maps or to some combination of the two I leave for others to determine. My point here is that there is good reason to think that by appeal to a biological theory of consciousness, we can move toward accounting for what Sartre's phenomenological analysis of consciousness reveals—that the Law of Identity fails to apply to the for-itself.[3] There is always a slight fracture between the self and itself. This point becomes clearer when we examine a second reason Sartre gives for the noncoincidence of the for-itself with itself.

The For-Itself and Its Past

Although Sartre maintains that the Law of Identity fails to apply to the for-itself because the for-itself is and is not its past and is and is not its future, I intend to limit my discussion to his claim about consciousness and its past. Sartre says the for-itself is related to its past by means of nihilation. I do not suggest that I can support all Sartre means by this claim by reference to a biological theory of consciousness or the bodily nature of primary self-consciousness. What follows is an appeal to biological theories of consciousness to give sense to Sartre's enigmatic claim that the for-itself both is and is not its past. But the sense I think can be given to this claim by means of such theories does not line up in any exact way with the sense Sartre gives to it.

There are numerous neurobiologists and cognitive scientists who maintain that memory is necessary for consciousness and in particular for perceptual awareness. In *The Astonishing Hypothesis: The Scientific Search for the Soul*, Francis Crick argues, as he did in an earlier article written with Christof Koch, that short-term memory is necessary for consciousness.[4] Crick states, "It seems as if the brain needs to impose some global unity on certain activities in its different parts so that the attributes of a single object . . . are in some way brought together."[5] That global process requires, on Crick's theory, an attention mechanism and short-term memory. He discusses three cognitive scientists—Ray Jackendoff, Philip Johnson-Laird, and Bernard J. Baars—who also believe short-term memory is necessary for consciousness.[6] Owen Flanagan, in *Consciousness Reconsidered*, claims that "short-term memory may be the sole necessary and sufficient condition for having a minimal streamlike consciousness." He also refers to others who agree with his claim.[7] Edelman is another who contends that memory is necessary for consciousness: short-term in the case of primary consciousness, and short-term and long-term in the case of higher-order consciousness. If memory is indeed necessary for consciousness, then I think one can argue that Sartre is right, in a certain sense at least, that consciousness both is and is not its past.

To explain how consciousness's need for memory would cause the for-itself both to be and not to be its past, I will refer once again to Edelman's theory of neural Darwinism. I do so because his theory is worked out in enough detail to give us a very specific sense of the role of memory in conscious experience. Even if the details of the theory are inaccurate, I think an examination of it will give us some idea of how memory's role in conscious experience creates a union and a separation between present consciousness and its past. Edelman argues in chapter 5 of *The Remembered Present* that memory is involved even with primary consciousness, because the conscious animal needs to match present value–free perceptual input and categorization with past value–ladened categorization. Objects and events are categorized and valued according to how well they serve the animal's survival needs. Value-category matches are stored in memory and then used to discriminate which present patterns of perceptual input have value for the organism. Reentrant connections are needed to link the special memory system that contains past value-category matches with the cortical systems processing present perceptual input. So value is connected to present perceptual categorizations by means of reentry signaling. The determination of the value of present perceptual input then affects what goals are selected by the organism and hence what behavior it engages in. The categorization, the matching of categories with values, and the memory storage of such matches are accomplished by special neural structures. Edelman concludes, "If our viewpoint is correct, consciousness could not exist without memory."[8] With human consciousness (higher-order consciousness, in Edelman's terminology), the memory systems and the categorizations they hold are more complex. Higher-order consciousness involves the "ability to relate various systems of memory to a *symbolic* representation of the self acting on the environment and vice-versa."[9] Consciousness results from the interaction of previous memories and current brain activity and hence Edelman's title, *The Remembered Present*.

If it is true that current consciousness involves both the use of past perceptual categorization and value-category matches as well as the continual reprocessing of internal and external input, present consciousness would both be and not be its past. It would be its past in the sense that the immediate and more distant past would be part of the present experience. Recently processed input from both self and world is, on Edelman's account, reprocessed and blended with current input to update continually one's representation of oneself and the world. Such reprocessing and blending would mean that present consciousness is, in a sense, its immediate past. In addition the use of either or both short-term and long-term memory to create present consciousness would link present consciousness again to its past. It is the fact that the past is constantly being utilized to create present consciousness that unites the past to present consciousness. Present consciousness, however, would not be identical to its past, on Edelman's view at any rate, because new data are continually being added to earlier, already processed data as well as to earlier perceptual categorization. The constant addition of new input separates present consciousness from its past. On this account bodily self-consciousness both unites and separates consciousness from its past. It is the body's awareness of itself (its past input and categorizations) that makes consciousness its past, and it is also the body's self-awareness (awareness of its present input) that separates consciousness from its past.[10]

THE TRIPARTITE DISTINCTION

In Chapter 3 I raised problems with Sartre's account of the distinction between the self-consciousness of pre-reflective consciousness and the self-consciousness of pure reflection and of impure reflection. An appeal to the notion of bodily self-consciousness I developed in Chapter 5 can help overcome these problems.

Sensorimotor Activity and Self-Consciousness

In Chapter 5 I proposed that it was because all consciousness required the processing of bodily input that all consciousness, even pre-reflectively, is self-consciousness. On this view the pre-reflective self-consciousness present in sensorimotor activity would be a *pre-attentive* processing of bodily data. *Paying attention* to such data would constitute the most fundamental type of self-consciousness on the level of reflective consciousness. William James points out that it may well be that the most fundamental form of self-awareness is awareness of bodily feelings and sensations.[11] The difference between pre-reflective and reflective self-consciousness on the most fundamental level of self-awareness would, on this interpretation, consist of simply a shift in focus. The shift would be from the object of consciousness, a result of the blending of input from both self and world, to a focus on the self-input alone. Self-consciousness would be present in pre-reflective consciousness because consciousness is aware of the somatic data in being aware of the world. This interpretation would preserve Sartre's belief that consciousness of self at the pre-reflective level just is consciousness of the world. Nothing would divide consciousness from itself. Reflective self-consciousness would not divide consciousness from itself either. It would simply involve this shift in focus. Likewise, nothing would divide consciousness from what it reflects on, because as Sartre says, consciousness is the body (BN, p. 330), and reflective self-consciousness is the body's reflective awareness of itself. This interpretation of self-consciousness also allows us to distinguish pure from impure reflection. The most basic level of pure reflection would be the attending to bodily input as lived, not objectified. In hammering a nail in a plank, for example, I shift my attention from the nail and wood to the weight of the hammer in my hand or the muscular tension in my arm. Impure reflection would be the attempt to objectify the somatic data, to grasp the bodily input from a third-person point of view. It would be, in a way, like the attempt to touch one's hand touching, which Sartre thinks fails (BN, p. 304). It would be the attempt to think of oneself on the bodily level as other, as an object. But since nothing separates me from my body, this attempt would fail, as Sartre says it must.

Thinking of the most fundamental level of self-consciousness as the body's awareness of itself provides a way to distinguish, at the level of sensorimotor intentionality, three levels of self-consciousness without any of the three collapsing into any one of the others. If the move from pre-reflective to reflective self-consciousness is simply a shift in focus, then nothing divides consciousness as body from itself, and the relation of consciousness to itself remains noncognitive, just as Sartre claims it is.

More Sophisticated Levels of Self-Consciousness

Perhaps it is our ability in sensorimotor activity to shift our attention from the blend of self and world input to the self-input alone that is the foundation for more sophisticated levels of pre-reflective and reflective self-consciousness. Remembering that bodily self-consciousness is the most fundamental form of self-consciousness, we can look at the role both pre-reflective and reflective self-consciousness play in existential psychoanalysis to see how a 'shift in focus' model of these distinctions might be used to explain more sophisticated levels of self-consciousness. Sartre says in his discussion of existential psychoanalysis that one is always pre-reflectively *conscious* of the fundamental project that one is. Existential psychoanalysis attempts to turn that consciousness into knowledge. Pure reflection, Sartre claims, provides the material for existential psychoanalysis but is not its basis. As I explained in Chapter 3, this is so, for Sartre, because reflection grasps only one's behavior, not the fundamental project that the behavior symbolizes, and because reflection cannot fix the fundamental project by means of concepts as existential psychoanalysis does. Existential psychoanalysis, like impure reflection, requires taking a third-person point of view on oneself. Sartre says it is not something unconscious that we are grasping in reflection and existential psychoanalysis. We are not apprehending something that was previously unconscious. What reflection and existential psychoanalysis (along with impure reflection) allow us to apprehend is the body—the behavior of the body, the patterns that behavior creates, and the fundamental choice those patterns reflect.

On my interpretation, pre-reflective consciousness would still involve consciousness of the fundamental project or choice as Sartre says it does. This is so because pre-reflective consciousness would be consciousness of the behavior of the for-itself and such behavior constitutes the fundamental choice one is. The human being is "an organized unity of conduct patterns or of 'behaviors'. To be ambitious, cowardly, or irritable is simply to conduct oneself in this or that matter in this or that circumstance. . . . [F]or human reality, to be is to act" (BN, p. 476). But on the pre-reflective level no attention would be paid to one's behavior. Reflection would involve a shift in focus away from awareness of the world that all behavior involves and toward one's behavior itself and the patterns it makes. This does not mean the person is aware of something she was unaware of before. Rather, what was always present to consciousness would be paid attention to, and the behavior and especially the patterns that constitute the for-itself's character would suddenly jump out as a figure from a background or as the duck does from a duck/rabbit drawing. The person would suddenly "see" these patterns with the same kind of suddenness that accompanies "seeing" the duck for the first time in the duck/rabbit drawing. Once the duck is seen, it is clear as day. So too with reflection. It is, as Sartre maintains, a lightning intuition. One suddenly sees an arrangement or pattern to one's behavior. That pattern was always before one's eyes, but it is only with a shift in the focus of one's attention that the pattern becomes clear. What one is focusing on does not change in one sense (it is the same drawing one sees both before and after one sees it as a duck, for example); but what one sees after the shift does change (one sees the drawing as a drawing of a duck for the first time). In pre-reflective consciousness, consciousness as the body in action is absorbed in the world. In reflection, consciousness takes a step back, as it were, so one can see one's behavior forming a pattern and hence creating one's character.

Existential psychoanalysis also involves a change in one's focus. If it is successful it allows one to take several steps back from what one is. One takes an actual viewpoint on oneself by grasping the meaning these patterns of behavior symbolize, which involves conceptualizing this meaning. Thus through existential psychoanalysis one begins to be able to tell a story about one's own life and the patterns one's actions create. It is akin to impure reflection, which also, I think, involves putting what one sees about oneself into language and thus telling oneself (and others) a story about who one is and what one's life means. Although impure reflection and existential psychoanalysis both objectify one's behavior and the meaning of one's behavior, involving one in the attempt to take a third-person point of view on oneself, existential psychoanalysis should help one tell a story that is more honest and accurate and does a better job of "fitting the facts," so to speak. But in either case as soon as one begins to tell a story about oneself, a certain distance sets in between oneself and the person the story is about. And yet one knows it is oneself to whom the story refers. It is a shift in point of view that creates this sense of distance. One is trying to see oneself from the point of view of the other. With this shift in point of view comes a change in focus. The same is true with visual perception. If the perceiver changes her point of view on an object by stepping back from the object of perception, even if the object on which she is concentrating remains the same, certain details fade and others come into view. The distance created in existential psychoanalysis and impure reflection, a distance created by a shift in point of view and focus, feels like a loss of self at the same time as it feels as though one is somehow grasping oneself more firmly. On Sartre's view, the distance that both existential psychoanalysis and impure reflection create between the for-itself and itself—a distance that comes to nothing for Sartre—is, I think, caused by this shift in point of view and focus that gives one the paradoxical feeling of having simultaneously both captured and fled the self.

Grounding higher forms of self-consciousness and self-knowledge in the bodily self-awareness present in sensorimotor activity and interpreting these higher forms in terms of an apprehension of one's behavior and its meaning reinforces Sartre's belief that our essence as well as our freedom is rooted in action. This interpretation also accords well with what Sartre says about the relation between the for-itself as fundamental choice and the for-itself as body. Sartre identifies both the body and fundamental choice with consciousness. He states, for example, "The body is what this consciousness is; it is not even anything except body" (BN, p. 330), and, "Our being is precisely our original choice, the consciousness (of) the choice is identical with the self-consciousness which we have. . . . Choice and consciousness are one and the same thing" (BN, p. 462). It follows from Sartre's identifying both choice and the body with consciousness that choice and the body are, in some sense, one. Sartre never explicitly spells out that implication of his claims, but I think it is present in his identification of choice with action/behavior. Sartre says that the "fundamental project which I am is a project concerning not my relations with this or that particular object in the world, but my total being-in-the-world" (BN, p. 480). But what else is my being-in-the-world but my being as body? And what else is it that creates behavior and its patterns but the body in action? So both consciousness and knowledge of oneself are in some fundamental sense an apprehension of the body. Those who think I am pushing Sartre much too close to a classical behaviorism are those who make the Cartesian mistake of thinking that apprehending the mind is distinct from apprehending the body. But I think one can argue that apprehending one's beliefs, desires, and thoughts, for example, just is a certain way of apprehending one's body. Indeed if consciousness is the body, awareness of one's mental states would have to be awareness of one's body. Such an interpretation accords well with Sartre's account of anger in *Being and Nothingness*. Anger, for Sartre, is the body acting within the context of the world and the other (BN, p. 294).

Problems Overcome

Distinguishing pre-reflective and reflective self-consciousness by appeal to bodily self-consciousness overcomes some of the problems I raised with Sartre's way of distinguishing these types of self-consciousness in *Being and Nothingness*. As I argued in Chapter 3, Sartre's account of self-consciousness at the level of reflection fails because he does not have a way of distinguishing it from pre-reflective self-consciousness without causing the collapse of the distinction between pure and impure reflection. Given my interpretation of the three types of self-consciousness, we do have a way to distinguish pre-reflective and reflective self-consciousness without causing the distinction between pure and impure reflection to collapse. I examined two ways Sartre might distinguish pre-reflective from reflective self-consciousness, raising objections to each. Let us reexamine those two ways in light of my discussion of self-consciousness above.

The Latency Account. I argued in Chapter 3 that if we attempt to distinguish pure reflection from pre-reflective self-consciousness by thinking of reflective self-consciousness as the realization of a latent capacity for self-consciousness at the pre-reflective level, we run into trouble. On the one hand, we might think of consciousness at the pre-reflective level as having the *potential* for self-consciousness, which can be realized only in reflection. But this goes against Sartre's explicit and often repeated belief that pre-reflective consciousness is *actually* self-conscious. To avoid this problem, we might think of pre-reflective consciousness as conscious of itself, but without the attribution of consciousness to an owner of experience (an 'I' or an ego). On this view pre-reflective consciousness is actually self-conscious in one way and potentially self-conscious in another. But if pure reflection is a realization of pre-reflective consciousness's latent capacity for the attribution of experience to an ego, then the characterization of pure reflection will coincide with Sartre's characterization of impure reflection. But if we utilize my interpretation of the distinction between the three types of self-consciousness, we can maintain a latency account without collapsing the distinction between the three types. Pre-reflective self-consciousness would be the body's pre-attentive awareness of itself as a conscious entity acting in the world with the latent capacity to shift attention to the behavior and patterns of behavior created by (and indeed one with) the body in action. Pure reflection would be a realization of that latent capacity but without attributing these behaviors and patterns to a self. Only with impure reflection or existential psychoanalysis would what one is attentively aware of be conceptualized both as a pattern and within the context of the fundamental choice that the pattern reveals.

The Epistemological Elements Account. Utilizing this same interpretation of the three types of self-consciousness, we can strengthen and clarify Sartre's confused attempt to distinguish the three by means of the presence or absence of epistemological elements. In Chapter 3 I examined whether Sartre could distinguish pre-reflective and reflective self-consciousness by claiming the latter is knowledge and the former is not. He tries this route but quickly realizes that characterizing pure reflection as knowledge will destroy both the distinction between pure and impure reflection and the unity Sartre thinks reflective consciousness must maintain to insure its infallibility. To overcome these problems, Sartre backs off from his original claim and says pure reflection is only a quasi knowledge of a quasi object (BN, pp. 162, 155). It is an intuition of the self that does not involve taking a point of view on the self. But given that characterization of pure reflection, Sartre has trouble distinguishing it from pre-reflective self-consciousness. What he needs is an explanation of this noncognitive intuition of self that would keep reflective consciousness from collapsing into pre-reflective consciousness or impure reflection.

At one point Sartre tries to explain the lightning intuition pure reflection provides by maintaining that in pure reflection nothing divides consciousness from itself. There is insufficient distance between the reflective consciousness and the consciousness reflected on to make the latter an object and the former knowledge. Because this characterization also fits pre-reflective self-consciousness, Sartre goes on to distinguish the two by claiming that a deeper nothingness divides consciousness from itself in pure reflection than in pre-reflective self-consciousness. To try to make sense of this claim, I looked at the distinction Sartre draws between a consciousness of oneself that involves conceptualization and one that does not, noting that Sartre ties this distinction to the one between consciousness and knowledge. For Sartre, consciousness lacks conceptualization, whereas knowledge does not. I suggested that it might be possible for Sartre to use these dual distinctions to characterize and keep separate pre-reflective self-consciousness and pure and impure reflection. On this interpretation the distinction between pre-reflective self-consciousness and the self-consciousness present in pure reflection would become the distinction between a consciousness that is a nonconceptualized consciousness of itself and one that involves conceptualization but not full-bodied knowledge. Impure reflection and the self-awareness gained in existential psychoanalysis would be a fuller conceptualization of self and would constitute knowledge. But I have raised problems with distinguishing the three types of self-consciousness as well as with distinguishing consciousness and knowledge by appeal to the presence or absence of concepts. I think the interpretation of these three levels of self-consciousness as grounded in a notion of self-consciousness as bodily self-awareness offers some promising ways to overcome these concerns.

The first problem with distinguishing the three types of self-consciousness as well as with distinguishing consciousness and knowledge by appeal to the presence or absence of concepts is whether consciousness without conceptualization is possible. I maintained that Sartre offers no argument that it is. In Chapter 5 I discussed, within the context of developing a notion of bodily self-consciousness, the theories of Cussins and Merleau-Ponty, which give some plausibility and sense to the idea of nonconceptual consciousness and yet allow us to hold on to Sartre's position that all consciousness is self-consciousness. If such nonconceptual consciousness is possible, then we could give an account of pre-reflective self-consciousness in terms of nonconceptual consciousness, which would keep pre-reflective self-consciousness distinct from reflection that involves conceptualization. But the second problem I raised in Chapter 3 would still remain.

If pure reflection is characterized as a self-consciousness that uses concepts, can it be kept distinct from impure reflection and the self-knowledge aimed for in existential psychoanalysis? This really devolves into the question of whether there can be a self-consciousness which uses concepts but which does not objectify or take a point of view on the self. My interpretation of the three types of self-consciousness offers two possible solutions to this problem. On the one hand, we could avoid this second problem by simply denying that pure reflection uses concepts and yet leave intact the distinction Sartre wishes to maintain between pre-reflective and reflective self-consciousness. We could distinguish pre-reflective self-consciousness from pure reflection by appeal to the distinction between pre-attentive apprehension of one's actions and the patterns they make and an attentive apprehension of these same things. As I argued above, this distinction could be explicated by reference to the distinction between pre-attentive and attentive apprehension of the bodily input necessary for all perception and action. An account could be given of the attentive but nonconceptual apprehension of bodily data, and then that account could be used as a model for understanding more sophisticated levels of reflective self-awareness. On the other hand, we could accept Sartre's claim that pure reflection involves conceptualization, but conceptualization of one's behavior only, not of the fundamental project the behavior reveals. That would allow us to keep pure and impure reflection distinct without causing the collapse of the distinction between pure reflection and pre-reflective self-consciousness. But we would still be left with the following question: Why does the conceptualizing of one's behavior without conceptualizing the fundamental project that the behavior reveals (and in fact is) constitute only a quasi knowledge of a quasi object? I think Sartre would answer this question by claiming the conceptualization involved in pure reflection lacks the distance necessary for knowledge. For Sartre, a certain distance between consciousness and its object is required for consciousness's apprehension of its object to constitute a point of view, and taking a point of view is necessary (although not sufficient) for real knowledge.

Perhaps we can make sense of this notion of distance (or its absence) by thinking of it in terms of our bodily existence. If we talk about point of view in the most literal sense, one could contend that taking a point of view on something requires either temporal or spatial distance. One could argue, appealing to a theory of metaphor such as the one Mark Johnson defends in *The Body in the Mind*, that any notion of psychological or emotional distance is just a metaphorical extension of these primary forms of distance that are rooted in our bodily existence. A self-consciousness that involves taking a point of view and hence objectifying the self would require temporal or spatial distance (in either a literal or metaphorical sense), and no such distance is present in pure reflection. This is so because for reflective consciousness to form a unity with the consciousness on which it reflects, a unity Sartre insists is present in pure reflection, the behavior and even the patterns it forms over time have to be conceptualized as one with (present) reflective consciousness. Pure reflection, Sartre says, apprehends the past, but "the past as that which haunts the present in non-thematic form" (BN, p. 157). On Sartre's account, all consciousness is historicized. It drags its past behind it and is pointed toward its future. Pure reflection apprehends consciousness, and hence as consciousness "reflection . . . apprehends [and is itself] temporality" (BN, p. 158). But this creates no temporal distance between reflective consciousness and the consciousness reflected on because reflection grasps the past *as present* and as one with itself. That is why Sartre believes pure reflection is apodictic. If I grasp my past *as past*, with the help of memory, then error is possible, Sartre says, because I no longer am my past. The unity is broken. It is only because he believes there is a sense in which I am (now) my past that Sartre can compare pure reflection to a man who *while he's writing* feels himself observed (BN, p. 152). Pure reflection is an apprehension of consciousness in the present, but as historicized, as all consciousness is. In pure reflection no temporal distance separates the reflective consciousness from the consciousness on which it reflects. Since consciousness is reflecting on itself, there is no spatial distance either between the consciousness that reflects and the consciousness on which the reflection is directed.

With existential psychoanalysis there is both temporal and spatial distance. Existential psychoanalysis attempts to bring the subject to *knowledge* of the fundamental choice of which she has always been *conscious*. Knowledge, for Sartre, requires a separation between knower and object known. To achieve this separation, the subject as well as the analyst must adopt a third-person point of view and attempt to objectify the person the subject is. Because one *is* one's fundamental choice, it might appear that no temporal distance is involved in existential psychoanalysis and impure reflection. But I think the third-person point of view, which Sartre maintains characterizes existential psychoanalysis and impure reflection, as well as the separation between subject and object that knowledge requires, breaks the unity of present consciousness with its past and creates temporal distance. The analyst certainly has spatial distance from the subject and attempts to allow the patient to experience such distance from herself at least metaphorically. The introduction of a third-person point of view creates temporal and spatial distance from oneself and changes one's focus. Such a change in viewpoint and hence focus creates a distinction between pure and impure reflection.

An appeal to a notion of our bodily existence and in particular to bodily self-consciousness as the most fundamental form of self-consciousness offers the possibility of clarifying the distinction Sartre draws between three types of self-consciousness. Each move to a different mode of self-consciousness is produced by a change in focus. In moving from pre-reflective self-consciousness to pure reflection, one shifts one's focus from the world to oneself as a being conscious of and acting in the world. With impure reflection and existential psychoanalysis, one changes one's focus by changing one's point of view from first to third person. I suggest that these more sophisticated levels of self-awareness are grounded in and can be understood by reference to bodily self-consciousness.

THE LONG DISTANCE TRUCK DRIVER AND
PEOPLE WITH BLINDSIGHT

In Chapter 4 I argued that the ways open to Sartre for diffusing the long-distance truck driver and individuals with blindsight as counterexamples to his claim about the self-conscious nature of consciousness were both problematic. On the one hand, it is difficult to see how, relying on his notion of pre-reflective self-consciousness as the primary mode of self-consciousness, he can assimilate these cases to his characterization of consciousness as presence to being and to the self, especially with regard to people with blindsight. On the other hand, if he simply denies they are cases of consciousness at all, he undermines the very thesis he wants to defend: that all consciousness is self-consciousness. For if Sartre allows for cases of nonconscious perceptual processing affecting behavior of which the subject is unaware, he leaves open the possibility of such processing affecting behavior that is accompanied by consciousness of itself. Consciousness would then be, in certain ways, caused by and dependent on the nonconscious. But, for Sartre, if consciousness is dependent on the nonconscious, then consciousness is, to a certain degree, unconscious of itself. So the second possible avenue for diffusing the counterexample I raised against Sartre in Chapter 4 undermines his central thesis. For this reason I would contend that the least problematic way to diffuse these counterexamples is the first way: assimilation of these cases to his characterization of consciousness as self-consciousness. Using the notion of bodily self-consciousness, I think we can at least approximate such an assimilation.

We first need to offer some justification for treating these cases as cases of *conscious* cognitive activity, including but not limited to conscious perception.[12] Although at this time there seems to be no way to establish with certainty that these are cases of conscious cognitive activity, I do think there is some evidence that lends plausibility to interpreting them as such. It is easier to do this with the case of the long-distance truck driver than with the case of the individuals with blindsight, but I will offer some support for interpreting both as cases of consciousness.

These cases have to be categorized as either cases of conscious cognitive activity or as cases of nonconscious cognitive activity. I attempt to support categorizing them as cases of conscious cognitive activity in two ways: first, by undermining the very possibility of nonconscious cognitive activity, and second, by offering evidence for the possibility of consciousness of a type that might reasonably be attributed to the truck driver and to those with blindsight. Having established the plausibility of treating these cases as cases of conscious cognitive activity, I offer a way to assimilate these cases to Sartre's characterization of consciousness by appealing to the notion of bodily self-consciousness.

The Evidence for Nonconscious Cognitive Activity

For the last three decades or more, there has been intense debate among cognitive scientists over the possibility of nonconscious cognitive activity. Max Velmans, a psychologist at the University of London, whose work I referred to in Chapter 4, argues that consciousness does not enter into any form of human information processing. He contends that consciousness is unnecessary for such cognitive activities as choice, learning and memory, and the organization of complex, novel responses, especially those that need planning, reflection, or creativity.[13] To support his thesis he appeals to experimental studies purportedly showing nonconscious cognitive functioning. As I noted, he thinks blindsight is an example of nonconscious processing and identification of visual stimuli. His arguments allow for the possibility (indeed, the actuality) of nonconscious visual processing in the case of the long-distance truck driver as well.

However, many of the commentators on Velmans's target article criticize his thesis as well as his interpretation of the experimental studies that he believes support his thesis. In commenting on the studies that Velmans uses, Kenneth S. Bowers notes that "whether a manipulated variable was (un)consciously processed is very much a matter of interpretation. Such interpretations are undermined by data, and subject to interpretative biases of the investigator."[14] Richard A. Carlson criticizes Velmans for failing to give an explicit description of the term *consciousness*. Carlson points out that because of this failure it is difficult to know what hypothesis about consciousness Velmans is rejecting. He also raises problems with Velmans's claim that the phenomenon of implicit learning (learning to recognize a pattern without any awareness of past occurrences of the pattern) is an example of cognitive functioning without consciousness.[15] Fred Dretske thinks Velmans has confused the *act* of awareness with the *object* of awareness. A state is conscious, Dretske argues, not because it is an object of awareness but because it is an act of awareness. Thus, Dretske contends, a subject's lack of awareness of an act of awareness is not evidence that the act is unconscious.[16] Dan Lloyd contends that Velmans's argument for cerebral functioning without consciousness rests on two doubtful assumptions: first, Velmans assumes that consciousness can be identified with introspection, and second, he assumes that a mental process is conscious only if there exists "the ability to report or signal the correct identity of a stimulus, often some time after its presentation."[17] There is also a basic ambiguity in Velmans's discussion of masked-priming studies and dichotic listening studies. Certain remarks he makes about the absence of *reportable* consciousness in subjects in these studies suggest, as Jeffrey A. Gray points out, that there is such a thing as *nonreportable* consciousness. If that is so, Velmans's arguments become much weaker, as Gray contends.[18] Velmans makes other remarks, however, that indicate he believes the absence of reportable consciousness is the absence of consciousness altogether. This ambiguity undermines his use of this evidence to support his belief in nonconscious cognitive activity.[19]

Psychologist Daniel Holender, in a 1986 article in *Behavioral and Brain Sciences*, raises methodological problems with studies in dichotic listening, parafoveal vision, and visual masking.[20] These studies have been used by both philosophers and psychologists to prove the existence of nonconscious cognitive activity and purportedly show the existence of semantic activation (of representations of meaning stored in memory) without conscious identification of the stimuli responsible for such activation. Holender refers to such supposed situations as SA/CI (semantic activation without conscious identification), contending that most, if not all, claims for SA/CI in dichotic listening, parafoveal vision, and visual masking are based on flawed experimental methods used in these studies.

These methods are flawed because they fail "to reveal whether or not the meaning of the critical stimulus was available to consciousness at the time of presentation."[21] In fact, he thinks that "on the basis of the current evidence it is most likely that these stimuli were indeed *consciously* identified."[22] Although he thinks pattern-masking investigations are the most likely to prove the existence of SA/CI (if SA/CI is possible at all), Holender believes it is premature to consider the results of these studies as evidence of semantic activation without conscious identification. Many, if not most, of the commentators on Holender's article agree with Ira Fischler, who believes that "at the methodological level, Holender has provided a thorough and sobering demonstration of both the insufficiency of presently available evidence for SA/CI and the frequent overwillingness to accept this evidence."[23]

Consciousness-Plus-Quick-Forgetting

Of course, none of the criticism of Velmans's position or the arguments of Holender prove the nonexistence of nonconscious cognitive activity; but they do cast doubt on the alleged evidence for its existence. To add support for the plausibility of treating the case of the long-distance truck driver as a case of conscious cognitive activity, I refer to my discussion of short-term memory in this chapter. If Crick and Koch as well as Edelman and others are correct in maintaining that only short-term memory is necessary for consciousness (at least of the most basic type), then it is possible that a person could be conscious and yet lack the ability to report on her experiences after they had occurred.[24] As mentioned in Chapter 4, Mary Potter and her colleagues offer experimental evidence that consciousness-plus-quick-forgetting is possible. They found that subjects who could recognize and identify pictures at the time of viewing were unable to report that experience later if the time needed to store an event in long-term memory was unavailable to them. Unlike the individuals with blindsight, the subjects in these studies reported what they saw without being forced to do so, thus the attribution of conscious awareness to these subjects appears warranted. Such studies show that a person may be conscious of an event and yet, under certain circumstances, be unable to report it even a short time later. Inability to report one's experiences after they have occurred would be an insufficient criterion for establishing lack of consciousness, although Velmans and many others use this as the main criterion for establishing an absence of consciousness. In the case of the long-distance truck driver, his inability to report *after* he 'came to' the experiences he had during the time *before* he 'came to' would fail to prove that his cognitive activity during that period was nonconscious. The long-distance truck driver could be a case of consciousness-plus-quick-forgetting.

It is more difficult to argue that the case of the individuals with blindsight is one of consciousness-plus-quick-forgetting because the subjects are asked to report on the events in the blind portion of their visual field at the time these events are occurring. We could still attribute consciousness to these people if we are willing to countenance the possibility of a consciousness that is unaware of itself. I have discussed several authors—Dretske, McGinn, and Armstrong among them—who claim that such consciousness is possible. But wouldn't the acceptance of such a consciousness undermine Sartre's claim that all consciousness is self-consciousness? Not altogether. Even a consciousness that is unaware of itself as consciousness would be self-conscious in the bodily sense I discussed in the previous chapter.

Bodily Self-Consciousness

If the long-distance truck driver and people with blindsight can be construed as cases of conscious awareness, then I think we can build support for attributing at least bodily self-awareness to the truck driver and to those with blindsight. In Chapter 5 I tried to establish that consciousness of the world requires consciousness of one's body. If this is so, then the truck driver and the people with blindsight would be present, in one sense, to themselves if they are present to the world. This is most obvious in the case of the long-distance truck driver. How could the truck driver have continued driving without an accident if he lacked somatic data? He must have been conscious, for example, of where his hands and feet were relative to the steering wheel and to the gas and brake pedals. If he were conscious during the time before he 'came to', he would have had to have been as conscious of those details as he must have been of such things as the direction of the road and the position of other vehicles relative to his truck. There must have been self-consciousness in the sense of bodily awareness if consciousness existed at all.

But the type of self-consciousness that I am claiming characterizes these cases, if they are cases of consciousness, differs from the kind Sartre claims must characterize all occurrences of consciousness. For Sartre, pre-reflective consciousness is self-conscious because it is aware of itself *as* awareness of an object. It is conscious of itself as consciousness of an object, and as such, it is conscious of itself *as* perceiving consciousness. In developing the notion of bodily self-consciousness, however, I argued that consciousness is conscious of itself *in* being conscious of any object, because the object is the result of the blending of input from both self and world. Although in the case of the truck driver there may well have been consciousness of the perceiving as well as of the world and the body, it seems unlikely that such self-consciousness was present in the case of the individuals with blindsight, who deny that they are perceiving. It is easier, I think, to diffuse the case of the long-distance truck driver as a counterexample to Sartre's thesis about the nature of consciousness by claiming that the truck driver was conscious and hence self-conscious than it is to use this same route to diffuse the case of those with blind-sight.

Part of the reason why a notion of bodily self-consciousness cannot satisfy Sartre's demand for self-consciousness in all occurrences of consciousness is that the acceptance of *bodily* awareness as *self*-awareness requires a rejection of Cartesian dualism that goes deeper than Sartre's. It requires as well a more fundamental acceptance of the body as the subject of consciousness than Sartre is willing to give. For all Sartre's efforts to identify consciousness with the body, he wants to maintain their distinction as well. As Hazel Barnes points out in her essay "Sartre's Concept of the Self," Sartre refuses to reduce consciousness to the body.[25] He refuses to identify consciousness with the body because he wants to ensure the existence of human freedom. He wants to reject Descartes's dualism and at the same time maintain a belief in human freedom: a belief that Descartes defended by means of his dualism. It is not clear that it is possible to hold both that the body is the subject of consciousness and that human freedom is as radical in its nature as Sartre claims it is.

FREEDOM

I have been arguing throughout this chapter that the notion of bodily self-consciousness can be used to make sense of some of Sartre's phenomenology-based claims about the nature of human consciousness.

But what remains the hardest question is whether such a notion of self-consciousness is strong enough to support the edifice Sartre builds upon his claim that all consciousness is self-consciousness. Sartre grounds his belief in human freedom in the self-conscious nature of consciousness. Can the existence of bodily self-consciousness ground the notion of radical human freedom that Sartre defends?

For Sartre, self-consciousness grounds human freedom because it ensures that the Law of Identity fails to apply to the for-itself and hence that the for-itself is nothing. It is identical to nothing, not even itself. This is so, on Sartre's view, because presence requires a withdrawal from that to which consciousness is present, which includes consciousness's presence to itself. Such withdrawal removes consciousness from the realm of being and hence from the causal order of the world. Because of that, human beings are free. On Sartre's account, then, it is because consciousness is self-consciousness that freedom characterizes human reality.

Can the bodily self-consciousness I argue is the most primary form of self-consciousness perform this same function? I do not think it can in any direct sense. But it does so indirectly because it is a necessary condition for our existence as bodies in the world capable of perception and action. And it is our bodily existence that is the most fundamental ground of our existence as free beings. I think what it means to make this claim becomes clear when one contrasts Merleau-Ponty's discussion of freedom in the *Phenomenology of Perception* with Sartre's discussion of freedom in *Being and Nothingness*. Sartre attempts to ground human freedom in the nothingness of consciousness. In contrast, Merleau-Ponty grounds it in our existence as bodies and in the bodily self-consciousness that accompanies the body as the subject of consciousness. For Merleau-Ponty it is precisely because the for-itself is a being immersed in the world rather than a negation of it that a human being can be conscious and free: "Thus it is by giving up part of his spontaneity, by becoming involved in the world through stable organs and pre-established circuits that man can acquire the mental and practical space which will theoretically free him from his environment and allow him to *see* it." Merleau-Ponty argues that it is our bodily (as well as our social) existence that both allows us to be free and sets limits on that freedom. For Merleau-Ponty "the pre-objective present, in which we find our bodily being, our social being, and the pre-existence of the world . . . [is] the basis of our freedom." It is precisely because of this basis that our freedom is limited. That is why for Merleau-Ponty "the anonymity of our body is inseparably both freedom and servitude." We are born into the world with a certain kind of body (a human body) and in the midst of a world already constituted in many ways by nature and society. But within that context, an infinite number of possibilities are open to us. Because of that, Merleau-Ponty thinks that "there is, therefore, never determinism and never absolute choice."[26] This is very different from Sartre's view that human freedom is an all-or-nothing affair and humans are either wholly determined or wholly free (BN, p. 442). For Merleau Ponty our being-in-the-world—that is, our existence as bodies—unites the psychic and the physiological and in doing so is the basis, at one and the same time, of our freedom and of the limits of our freedom. Choice is always based, according to Merleau-Ponty, on a certain givenness.

Sartre acknowledges, at times, this interconnection between freedom and facticity; but there is a deep ambiguity in his discussion of the relation between the two. Sartre, of course, acknowledges that to be a point of view on the world (that is, to be a conscious being, a for-itself), one must be in the world. Hence, for Sartre, the body is the subject of consciousness. So he acknowledges this intimate relation in human existence between the for-itself and the in-itself. But he also believes that unless consciousness is nothingness, outside the causal order completely, it cannot be free. Consequently, he wishes to distance consciousness even from its bodily existence.

In his discussion of freedom and facticity, he does indeed note that freedom would not make any sense without the given. It is thanks to being-in-itself "that freedom arises as freedom" (BN, p. 482). A person is free, Sartre claims, only if she can realize her projects. If a simple wish or conception were enough for an end to be realized, there would be no way to distinguish the possible from the real. "If the object appears as soon as it is simply conceived, it will no longer be chosen. . . . Once the distinction between the simple *wish* . . . and the *choice* is abolished, freedom disappears too" (BN, p. 483). This is one reason why Sartre claims that "the co-efficient of adversity in things is no argument against our freedom" (BN, p. 482). Without the resistance of things, there would be no freedom. But this coefficient of adversity in things arises only by means of us, only in light of the ends we posit. Sartre acknowledges, however, that any situation is a product of the in-itself as well as the for-itself. We are not free to qualify the brute given in any way we please. If I see a crag as not scalable, for example, that is in light of my project of climbing the mountain. But my freedom, he says, cannot determine whether the rock will or will not lend itself to scaling. That is determined by the brute being of the rock. Merleau-Ponty discusses this example of Sartre's and agrees with him that it is because of the presence of humans that attributes in general exist. But he also agrees with Sartre that I am not free to attribute any property at all to the rock. "Whether or not I have decided to climb them, these mountains appear high to me, because they exceed my body's power to take them in its stride. . . . Underlying myself as a thinking subject [one with ends] . . . there is, therefore, as it were a natural self which does not budge from its terrestrial situation and which constantly adumbrates absolute valuations."[27] The difference between their two analyses of this same situation may be subtle, but it hinges on the emphasis each one gives to the role of the body as a limit as well as a basis of freedom. Merleau-Ponty stresses the importance of my bodily existence to my valuations of the world. Sartre mentions the body in his list of the given, along with my place, my past, my position, and my relations with others. However, he goes on to devote a separate section to a discussion of each of the items in this list *except* the body. His final emphasis is on the role of freedom and the ends that the for-itself posits in constituting the meaning of the world. Merleau-Ponty lays equal stress on the contribution of our bodily existence to the constitution of the world's meaning.

But this is simply a difference in emphasis. The real ambiguity in Sartre's view of the relation between the for-itself and the in-itself is evident in his discussion of the need for consciousness to withdraw from being in order to be present to being. It is this withdrawal from being, including its own being as a bodily presence to the world, that places consciousness outside the causal order and separates it even from its bodily existence. This is where the real foundation of human freedom rests for Sartre. It rests in consciousness's existence as non-being. In part 1 of *Being and Nothingness*, Sartre argues that presence to being requires a withdrawal from being. Because consciousness is always self-conscious and hence present to itself, it must withdraw from itself as well. That is why he contends that it is the self-consciousness of consciousness that makes a human being a being that is its own nothingness. It is in the spelling out of what this withdrawal from being comes to that the deep ambiguity in Sartre's view of the relation between the for-itself and the in-itself (and hence between consciousness and the body) surfaces. In the section "Transcendence" *in Being and Nothingness*, Sartre says that consciousness as a presence to being must nihilate not only the particular object of which it is conscious but also being in general, the totality of being. It is because of this latter nihilation that consciousness is nothingness.[28] But in the conclusion of *Being and Nothingness*, he weakens his position and claims that the for-itself is not a nihilation of being-in-itself in general but only of a particular in-itself. The for-itself

> is the nihilation of an individual and particular In-itself and not of a being in general. The For-itself is not nothingness in general but a particular privation; it constitutes itself as the privation of *this being*. Therefore we have no business asking about the way in which the for-itself can be united with the in-itself since the for-itself is in no way an autonomous substance. (BN, p. 618)

I think the ambiguity in Sartre's position arises from his desire to maintain that consciousness is both embodied and free. The view expressed in the conclusion of *Being and Nothingness* accords well with his belief in the embodiment of consciousness. But I think at least one reason Sartre argues in the section on transcendence that consciousness nihilates the totality of being and hence is nothing in a more radical sense is because of his adherence to Descartes's avenue for establishing human freedom. By completely removing consciousness from the realm of being, he removes it from the causal laws that govern that realm. He seems to think, at least throughout much of *Being and Nothingness*, that it is necessary to do so to secure the freedom of the for-itself.[29]

At least two reasons exist for this ambiguity in Sartre's position as well as for his refusal to follow out the consequences of his view that the body is the subject of consciousness. First, a full acceptance of the implication of the belief that the body is the subject of consciousness will undermine Sartre's arguments for human freedom. Second, for Sartre the body's presence is experienced as nausea. In my non-thetic consciousness of my body, I exist my body, Sartre says, as a taste—as nausea (BN, p. 344). It is this negative attitude toward the body, in addition to Sartre's founding human freedom on the existence of consciousness as nothingness, that drives him at times toward a refusal of the for-itself's existence as body. It is what motivates, I think, his ambivalent attitude toward the body and what bars him from using bodily self-awareness as the ultimate ground for the self-consciousness of consciousness. Because Merleau-

Ponty does not share this ambivalent attitude, he can treat bodily self-consciousness as primary, and he can accept without reservation the body's role in grounding (and at the same time limiting) human freedom.

The reason the body is the fundamental ground of our freedom is because our most basic freedom is freedom of movement. Such freedom requires a body and indeed is that which defines us as bodies. Our bodily existence gives us the kind of existence in the world that allows for freedom. Plants are in the world in a certain sense, but we think of them as neither bodies nor as free. At the most basic level, freedom involves the control of movement from within the organism. Although plants (or parts of them) move, the control of such motion comes from sources external to them: wind, sun, and water, for example. With animals some of the control comes from within the organism itself, and consequently we think of animals (of a certain size anyway) as *bodies*. We think of animals as being in the world in a way that is qualitatively different from how plants (and certain inanimate objects) are in the world. Animals do not just occupy space. They propel themselves in and through space. I suggest that it is this capacity for self-movement that is the basis on which all other freedoms rest.[30] Such freedom makes sense only in the context of a bodily existence. It is the existence of this freedom that brings us back to bodily self-consciousness. Such self-consciousness, I argued in Chapter 5, is a necessary condition for movement. The sensorimotor body must be aware of itself to navigate in the world. So although bodily self-consciousness does not ground freedom in any direct way, it is a necessary condition for the body's movement in the world. Such freedom of movement is, I think, the ground for more sophisticated forms of intentional action.

Although this notion of bodily self-consciousness can illuminate and strengthen many of the points Sartre makes in his analysis of consciousness in *Being and Nothingness*, it should be obvious by now that it cannot do all the work Sartre wishes it to do. This is most obvious when it comes to the question of whether bodily self-consciousness can ground Sartre's belief in the radical nature of human freedom. It cannot. I doubt whether any analysis that keeps the bodily nature of the subject of consciousness steadily in mind could do so.

Notes

INTRODUCTION

1. I discuss the positions of these philosophers in Chapter 4.

2. John R. Searle, *Intentionality: An Essay in the Philosophy of Mind* (Cambridge: Cambridge University Press, 1983), p. 90.

3. Because my central point in the book is that it is only in remembering the body that the belief in the self-conscious nature of consciousness can be saved, I do not appeal to functionalist or computational accounts of the mind, which largely ignore the bodily basis of consciousness.

4. I am thinking of writers such as Hegel, Husserl, Heidegger, and Freud, for example. I do, at the beginning of Chapter 2, discuss Sartre's use and transformation of Husserl's phenomenological method.

5. There has been no end of work on consciousness in the last decade or two. I am, of course, appealing to only a portion of that work.

6. It is Thomas Nagel's critique of purely objective accounts of consciousness that is best known among analytic philosophers. Nagel's critique is in great part an echo of Sartre's. Although he occasionally acknowledges his debt to Sartre, I think the extent to which Nagel repeats the criticisms raised years earlier by Sartre is unknown to most of Nagel's readers. See both Nagel's classic essay "What Is It Like to Be a Bat?" in *Mortal Questions* (New York: Cambridge University Press, 1979), and his *The View from Nowhere* (New York: Oxford University Press, 1986).

7. I am thinking of philosophers such as Hegel and Husserl, for example.

8. Readers familiar with *Being and Nothingness* can skim this material to glean my main point about the absolutely crucial importance of this claim about consciousness to Sartre's analysis.

9. Because of the purpose of my analysis in Chapter 2, I make little use in this chapter of the secondary literature on Sartre.

10. John R. Searle, "The Mystery of Consciousness," *New York Review of Books*, 2 November 1995, p. 63, makes clear his commitment to this belief when he remarks that "the term 'qualia' is misleading because it suggests that the qualia of a state of consciousness might be carved off from the rest of consciousness and set on one side, as if you could talk about the rest of the problem of consciousness while ignoring the subjective, qualitative feel of consciousness. But you can't set qualia on one side, because if you do there is no consciousness left over." Nagel's claim in "What Is It Like to Be a Bat?" p. 166, that "an organism has conscious mental states if and only if there is something that it is like to *be* that organism—something it is like *for* the organism" indicates his commitment to the same belief.

THE TRADITION

1. Gilbert Ryle, *The Concept of Mind* (New York: Barnes and Noble, 1949), p. 14.

2. René Descartes, "Objections and Replies to *Meditations on First Philosophy*," in *The Philosophical Writings of Descartes*, 2 vols., trans. John Cottingham, Robert Stoothoff, and Dugald Murdoch (Cambridge: Cambridge University Press, 1984), II, 77. I will refer to the Cottingham, Stoothoff, and Murdoch translations of Descartes's works as CSM I or II. I follow convention and cite as well *The Philosophical Works of Descartes*, 2 vols., trans. Elizabeth Haldane and G. R. T. Ross (1911; reprinted, Cambridge: Cambridge University Press, 1969), II, 13 (henceforth abbreviated HR), and *Oeuvres de Descartes*, 12 vols., ed. Charles Adam and Paul Tannery (Paris: Cerf, 1897–1913; rev., Paris: Vrin/C.N.R.S., 1964–76), VII, 107 (henceforth abbreviated AT).

3. Descartes, "Objections and Replies," CSM II, 171; HR II, 115; AT VII, 246.

4. Ibid., CSM II, 113; HR II, 52; AT VII, 160.

5. Descartes, *The Passions of the Soul,* CSM I, 335; HR I, 340; AT XI, 343. Haldane and Ross translate this passage as, "For it is certain that we cannot desire anything without perceiving by the same means that we desire it."

6. René Descartes, *Descartes: Philosophical Letters*, trans. and ed. Anthony Kenny (Minneapolis: University of Minnesota Press, 1970), p. 93; AT III, 295. The letters are not included in CSM or HR.

7. I follow the Haldane and Ross translation here because it brings out more clearly than CSM that for Descartes one cannot understand without being aware that one understands. Descartes, "Objections and Replies," HR II, 73; CSM II, 132; AT VII, 188.

8. Because, as Jonathan Bennett points out in *Locke, Berkeley, Hume: Central Themes* (Oxford: Clarendon, 1971), Descartes uses " 'thought' etc. to sprawl over the

whole range of the mental" (p. 224), whatever claim Descartes is making here is even stronger than it might first appear.

9. Robert McRae, " 'Idea' as a Philosophical Term in the Seventeenth Century," *Journal of the History of Ideas* 26 (April–June 1965): 182–83. In the introduction to *Being and Nothingness* Sartre could not sound more Cartesian, given this rendition of Descartes's position.

10. Bernard Williams, *Descartes: The Project of Pure Enquiry* (Atlantic Highlands, N.J.: Humanities Press, 1978). It is this confusion in Descartes that leads him, Williams argues, to deny incorrectly that animals are conscious. For Williams there can be consciousness that is not self-consciousness.

11. Ibid., p. 286.

12. Ibid., p. 226.

13. Richard E. Aquila, "The Cartesian and a Certain 'Poetic' Notion of Consciousness," *Journal of the History of Ideas* 49 (October–December 1988): 547.

14. To support his reading of Descartes, Aquila (ibid., n. 21) gives a more complete excerpt from Descartes's letter to Mersenne, 28 January 1641, which I quoted above. In the letter, Descartes claims not only that "we cannot will anything without knowing that we will it" but also that we could not "know this without an idea; but I do not claim that the idea is different from the action itself."

15. Ibid., p. 561. Aquila argues that for Descartes, perception, for example, and consciousness of perception are one. Sartre makes just such a claim in the introduction to *Being and Nothingness*.

16. In "Thoughtless Brutes," *Proceedings and Addresses of the American Philosophical Association* 46 (November 1973): 5–20, Norman Malcolm contends as Williams does that Descartes's analysis of consciousness is mistaken because it does not allow for animals to be conscious. He claims Descartes fails to distinguish between thinking and having thoughts. I think the implicit presence in Descartes of a distinction between implicit and explicit knowledge and consciousness approaches this distinction Malcolm argues for, although Malcolm wants an even stronger distinction such that animals can be said to think. Although I claim Descartes's analysis of the self-conscious nature of consciousness is more subtle than that attributed to him by Williams and Malcolm, I certainly don't intend to argue that it follows from anything implicitly or explicitly present in Descartes's work that animals could think.

17. Descartes never makes clear the exact nature of the relationship between consciousness and knowledge. What he does say on the matter I will discuss later in this chapter. Sartre states quite clearly in the introduction to *Being and Nothingness* that pre-reflective consciousness is not a knowledge.

18. René Descartes, *Principles of Philosophy*, CSM I, 195–96; HR I, 222; AT IX, 29. Robert McRae, "Innate Ideas," in *Cartesian Studies*, ed. R. J. Butler (New York: Barnes and Noble, 1972), pp. 37–39.

19. McRae, "Innate," p. 40, quoting Descartes, "Objections and Replies," HR II, 241; AT IX, 225; and p. 41.

20. McRae, "Descartes' Definition of Thought," in *Cartesian Studies*, pp. 66, 67, 68.

21. Margaret Dauler Wilson, *Descartes* (New York: Routledge and Kegan Paul, 1978), pp. 164, 153. On p. 156 she quotes passages in which Descartes seems to equate consciousness and knowledge.

22. McRae, "Descartes' Definition," p. 57.

23. Wilson, *Descartes*, p. 160.

24. The presence of this distinction in Descartes is also defended by Daisie Radner, "Thought and Consciousness in Descartes," *Journal of the History of Philosophy* 26 (July 1988): 439–52. On Radner's reading of Descartes, however, pre-reflective consciousness is noncognitive.

25. I use the term *levels* in referring to these types of consciousness because for Sartre pre-reflective consciousness is a necessary condition for reflective consciousness. At the level of reflective consciousness, Sartre draws a further distinction between pure and impure reflection. This distinction is not present in Descartes's analysis of consciousness. In addition, Sartre's characterization of reflection differs from that of Descartes. For Descartes (on McRae's and Wilson's views, at any rate), reflection is paying attention to what is in our mind. That kind of analysis would fail to capture the subtlety and depth of Sartre's discussion of reflection. In Chapter 3 I will discuss in detail Sartre's analysis in *Being and Nothingness* of the distinction between pre-reflective and reflective consciousness and the self-consciousness present in both.

26. See Edwin McCann, "Cartesian Selves and Lockean Substances," *Monist* 69 (July 1986): 458–82, for a defense of the view that for Descartes the self is known not by a direct intuition but by its attributes.

27. There are many other differences between Sartre and Descartes. Sartre, for example, rejects the instantaneity of the Cartesian cogito. He sees consciousness as temporal. In addition Descartes uses the self-consciousness of consciousness as a basis for his epistemology, whereas Sartre uses it as a basis for his analysis of human consciousness as freedom.

28. John Locke, *An Essay concerning Human Understanding* (1689), ed. Peter H. Nidditch (Oxford: Clarendon, 1975). All quotations from the *Essay* are from this edition and are noted in the standard way by book, chapter, and section number: II.i.10, II.i.12, II.i.19, II.i.19, II.xxvii.9. Like Descartes, Locke talks of this self-consciousness in cognitive terms, and for Sartre, as I noted above, self-consciousness is not knowledge. I leave aside the issue of personal identity which Locke ties so closely to this consciousness that he says must accompany all thinking. Although I use the female pronoun as generic throughout most of the text, I use the male pronoun here because Locke uses it in his discussion of the sleeping person.

29. Ibid., II.i.19.

30. Ibid., II.xix.3, II.xix.4. I leave open the question of whether it is possible to make sense of a theory of *degrees* of attention.

31. See Aquila, "The Cartesian and a Certain 'Poetic' Notion of Consciousness," for a good discussion of the inner directedness of Lockean self-consciousness as

opposed to Descartes's characterization of the most fundamental mode of self-consciousness, which is for Descartes, as it is for Sartre, outer directed, toward the world at large.

32. D. J. O'Connor, *John Locke: A Critical Introduction* (Baltimore: Penguin, 1952), p. 98, makes this point clear.

33. The different uses to which Locke puts the term *idea* have been much discussed. See especially Gilbert Ryle, "John Locke on the Human Understanding," in *Locke and Berkeley: A Collection of Critical Essays*, ed. C. B. Martin and D. M. Armstrong (Notre Dame, Ind.: University of Notre Dame Press, 1968).

34. Locke, *Essay*, II.xxvii.9, II.xxvii.13, II.i.4. D. M. Armstrong argues in several of his writings for an analysis of self-consciousness that is similar to Locke's, although Armstrong identifies himself more closely with Kant than with Locke.

35. Ibid., IV.ix.3.

36. Whether this consciousness of oneself is a direct grasp of oneself or is mediated by an idea is a subject of dispute. See Robert J. Roth, "Locke on Ideas and the Intuition of the Self," *International Philosophical Quarterly* 28 (June 1988): 163–69, and Thomas Heyd, "Reply to Roth: Locke Is Not a Cartesian with Respect to Knowledge of Our Own Existence," *International Philosophical Quarterly* 29 (December 1989): 463–67.

37. Locke, *Essay*, II.iv.20.

38. Ibid., II.xix.4.

39. Kantian scholarship is notorious for the difficulties it encounters in interpreting Kant's frequently dense and obscure texts. The fact that statements within one text often contradict one another and that Kant attaches several meanings to some of his key terms are just two examples of the problems faced by Kantian commentators. My aim in this section is to present Kant's discussion of self-consciousness, particularly of transcendental self-consciousness, in a manner clear and concise enough so that its similarity to and difference from the Sartrean analysis of the pre-reflective cogito are clear. I am not examining the role of self-consciousness in the actual argument of the Transcendental Deduction. I will also be drawing on material from the Paralogisms to help elucidate Kant's notion of self-consciousness.

40. Our existence for others is ignored by Kant in the *Critique of Pure Reason*. He sees it only in terms of his ethics. Hence he has no notion of self-consciousness that involves the social nature of the self. Sartre, however, sees our existence for others in ontological and epistemological terms and highlights a dimension of self-consciousness that arises out of our existence for others.

41. Immanuel Kant, *Critique of Pure Reason* (1st ed. 1781; 2d ed. 1787), trans. Norman Kemp Smith (New York: St. Martin's, 1965). All references to this work will be from this translation and will be noted in the text in the standard way by reference to the first (A) and second (B) original editions. Any reference to Kant's *Critique* refers to this work.

42. Kant usually refers to inner sense in this way, although at A107 he identifies it with empirical apperception rather than simply seeing it as a means to empirical apperception.

43. The relation between inner sense and outer sense and between self-affection and affection by things other than the self is complicated. It is in the "Refutation of Idealism" section of the *Critique of Pure Reason* that this relation takes on the most force, at least in terms of Kant's argument against skepticism. I am interested in empirical apperception here only as it contrasts with transcendental apperception. It is clear, however, that for Kant we can affect ourselves only through our apprehending "the representations of things that affect us, i.e., those of outer things" (Kant, "The Leningrad Reflexion on Inner Sense," trans. Hoke Robinson, *International Philosophical Quarterly* 29 [September 1989]: 257).

44. In Chapter 3 I will examine Sartre's claim that self-consciousness at the level of reflection would be impossible if consciousness were not self-conscious pre-reflectively.

45. The exact nature of the relationship between synthesis and transcendental apperception will be explored later in this section.

46. Norman Kemp Smith, *Commentary to Kant's "Critique of Pure Reason,"* 2d ed., rev. (Atlantic Highlands, N.J.: Humanities Press International, 1992), p. 250.

47. P. F. Strawson, *The Bounds of Sense* (London: Methuen, 1966), p. 94. Although Strawson thinks transcendental self-consciousness involves the ability to self-ascribe experiences, we will see later that he does not think that is all there is to transcendental self-consciousness.

48. Kant notes that in raising the question of how I can be an object to myself, that is, how empirical self-consciousness is possible, another question is raised: "How the 'I' that thinks can be distinct from the 'I' that intuits itself . . . and yet, as being the same subject, can be identical with the latter; and how, therefore, I can say: 'I, as intelligence and *thinking* subject, know myself as an object that is *thought*'" (*Critique*, B155). Sartre addresses a similar point in his discussion of reflective consciousness. He believes that although reflective consciousness introduces a duality into consciousness, it does so without destroying the unity of consciousness. In Chapter 3 I will examine what this claim comes to for Sartre.

49. Sydney Shoemaker, "Commentary: Self-Consciousness and Synthesis," in *Self and Nature in Kant's Philosophy*, ed. Allen W. Wood (Ithaca, N.Y.: Cornell University Press, 1984), p. 151; Patricia Kitcher, "Kant's Real Self," in *Self and Nature in Kant's Philosophy*.

50. See Kemp Smith, *Commentary*, pp. 246–51, for a discussion of these points.

51. Strawson, *Bounds of Sense*, p. 98.

52. Ibid. Dieter Henrich, "The Identity of the Subject in the Transcendental Deduction," in *Reading Kant: New Perspectives on Transcendental Arguments and Critical Philosophy*, ed. Eva Schaper and Wilhelm Vossenkuhl (New York: Basil Blackwell, 1989), p. 268, takes a position akin to Strawson's in arguing that for Kant consciousness does not require actual self-consciousness, empirical or transcendental. It requires only the possibility of these two modes of self-consciousness.

53. C. Thomas Powell, *Kant's Theory of Self-Consciousness* (Oxford: Clarendon, 1990), especially his introduction.

54. Paul Guyer, "Kant on Apperception and *A Priori* Synthesis," *American Phil-*

osophical Quarterly 17 (July 1980): 205–12. Guyer's main point is that Kant has no argument for his claim that all consciousness involves self-consciousness. Although Guyer reads self-consciousness as transcendental, he appears to have conflated Kant's notion of empirical and transcendental self-consciousness. Terence Wilkerson, "Kant on Self-Consciousness," *Philosophical Quarterly* 30 (January 1980): 47–60. Although he too implies that the self-consciousness involved is transcendental, he seems not to have even taken into account, in any serious way, Kant's distinction between the two types of self-consciousness.

55. Wilfred Sellars, ". . . This I or He or It (the Thing) Which Thinks," presidential address to the Eastern Division of the American Philosophical Association, 1970, *Essays in Philosophy and Its History* (Boston: D. Reidel, 1974).

56. Patricia Kitcher, *Kant's Transcendental Psychology* (New York: Oxford University Press, 1990), p. 92 n. 5. This reverses the position she held in her earlier paper "Kant's Real Self."

57. Jonathan Bennett, *Kant's Analytic* (Cambridge: Cambridge University Press, 1966). Since Bennett is more interested in discussing the issues with which Kant was wrestling than in doing an exegesis of the Kantian text, it is not always clear whether he believes Kant thought all consciousness involves self-consciousness.

58. See, for example, Kant, *Critique*, A363.

59. The representation of the self includes its representation as simple and substantial as well.

60. It is impossible to offer a reading of Kant's notion of transcendental apperception that is consistent with all he says on this topic, but I am claiming that the one I defend here does the best job of making sense of the various and often contradictory remarks made by Kant on this subject.

61. See Stephen Priest, "Descartes, Kant, and Self-Consciousness," *Philosophical Quarterly* 31 (October 1981): 348–51, for an example of a commentator who takes this view. Kitcher in *Kant's Transcendental Psychology* and Richard E. Aquila in *Matter in Mind: A Study of Kant's Transcendental Deduction* (Bloomington: Indiana University Press, 1989) interpret Strawson in this way, but Strawson clearly thinks transcendental apperception is more than simply the possibility of the self-ascription of experience. Although transcendental self-consciousness involves the capacity for the self-ascription of experience and indeed grounds that capacity, Strawson says it "is not to be *identified* with the possibility of empirical self-ascription of experiences" (*Bounds of Sense,* p. 108).

62. See, for example, Kant, *Critique*, A383.

63. Aquila and Kemp Smith, in addition to Strawson, are examples of commentators who argue that such a characterization of consciousness is incomplete. These commentators claim that although transcendental self-consciousness grounds empirical self-consciousness, it is not reducible to the mere possibility of such self-consciousness.

64. Guyer distinguishes several senses of *apperception* ("Kant on Apperception," p. 207 n. 7).

65. Kemp Smith, *Commentary,* pp. 247, li, 285, 262; see also p. 252.

66. Jay F. Rosenberg, *The Thinking Self* (Philadelphia: Temple University Press, 1986).

67. The question arises whether there could be any other kind of consciousness for Kant. If nonintentional consciousness is possible for Kant, then the claim that all consciousness is self-conscious would have to be weakened somewhat to attribute it to Kant. Rosenberg identifies intentional consciousness with the "conceptual representation of an objective world" (ibid., p. 10). Can there be consciousness without concept application for Kant? Rosenberg certainly thinks there can be such consciousness, what he calls "pure positional consciousness." Such consciousness lacks self-consciousness. He seems to imply that this is a Kantian position, an implication he fails to support. At most he argues that the claim that there is such consciousness does not contradict Kant's mutuality thesis. Hubert Schwyzer in *The Unity of Understanding: A Study in Kantian Problems* (Oxford: Clarendon, 1990) contends that Kant does not claim that all consciousness involves self-consciousness but that he defends a weaker claim: that all *intentional* consciousness requires self-consciousness. Schwyzer does have an argument for his position, the details of which I will not rehearse here. Suffice it to say that for Schwyzer and possibly for Rosenberg, Kant believes there can be consciousness without concept application. This is so, on Schwyzer's view, because Kant distinguishes between a conscious state and an object of consciousness and because he thinks the former can exist without the latter. Hence Schwyzer thinks that nonintentional consciousness is a possibility for Kant. Whether he is right in his interpretation hinges on the answers to two questions: (1) Does Kant believe that there could be nonconceptual representations, and (2) Would such representations amount to conscious experience? There is conflicting textual evidence about Kant's answer to the first question. Attributing an affirmative answer to Kant for the second question commits Kant to the possibility of consciousness without an object. And yet Kant says that synthesis, which is necessary for conscious experience, must in the first instance involve the application of the concept of an object in general. One might think that Kant's account of aesthetic experience could provide an example of nonintentional consciousness. Aesthetic experience does not require, on Kant's view, the actual application of concepts. It does, however, involve their imminent application and knowledge by the subject of that imminent application. Because of this, aesthetic experience cannot be used as a counterexample to the claim that consciousness is always intentional for Kant.

Even if it could be established that for Kant there could be consciousness which was nonintentional and which did not require the use of concepts, to do so would fail to undermine the kinship between Kant and Sartre. Because Sartre thinks all consciousness is intentional, even the weaker version of Kant's claim about the self-consciousness of consciousness would link Sartre to Kant.

68. Rosenberg, *The Thinking Self*, pp. 5–6.

69. Aquila, *Matter in Mind*, pp. 149, 160, 160, 172. Kant does argue in the "Refutation of Idealism" section of the *Critique* that consciousness of objects in space is required for *empirical* self-consciousness. However, since my interest here lies in the points of contact between Sartre's notion of pre-reflective self-consciousness and

Kant's transcendental self-consciousness, I discuss only the connection between *transcendental* self-consciousness and consciousness of objects.

70. Aquila, *Matter in Mind*, p. 172.

71. At B130 of the *Critique*, Kant says synthesis may or may not be conscious. At B133 he says transcendental apperception requires that synthesis be conscious.

72. Aquila's interpretation of Kant shares this problem with Kitcher's account even though Aquila rejects Kitcher's functionalist account of Kant (see Aquila, *Matter in Mind*, p. 240 n. 46) and even though Aquila is interested in Kant's notion of self-consciousness, whereas Kitcher is interested in Kant's notion of the self.

73. Strawson, *Bounds of Sense*, p. 94, says, "Our consciousness of the identity of ourselves is fundamentally nothing but our consciousness of this power of synthesis, or combination, and of its exercise."

74. Kitcher, *Kant's Transcendental Psychology*, p. 122. Kitcher does say on page 123 that for Kant, "thinking selves are not merely systems of cognitive states, because some faculty must always be present to synthesize states." She never makes it clear how she would reconcile this remark with her position that thinking selves are nothing more than sets of cognitive states for Kant. It is only the latter view that plays a role in her argument.

75. Kitcher is guilty of doing exactly what she criticizes Strawson and others for doing: sanitizing Kant in a way. In chapter 1 of *Kant's Transcendental Psychology*, she accuses other scholars of cleansing Kant of all trace of transcendental psychology. Although she doesn't do that, she does try to eliminate the thinking subject as anything other than a system of mental states connected in certain ways. She tries to cleanse Kant's account of any elements that conflict with a functionalist account of the self.

76. Powell, *Kant's Theory of Self-Consciousness*, p. 32.

77. Ibid., p. 7.

78. Richard E. Aquila discusses the relation between *empirical* self-consciousness and consciousness of objects in *Representational Mind: A Study of Kant's Theory of Knowledge* (Bloomington: Indiana University Press, 1983).

79. Aquila, *Matter in Mind*, p. xii, argues that Kant's analysis of consciousness is much more Sartrean than is usually acknowledged.

80. This point is complicated in Sartre. Consciousness is nothing but consciousness of objects, and yet it is not identical to any particular consciousness of an object because it is not identical to itself. What this puzzling claim means will become clearer in the next two chapters.

81. See especially the First Paralogism; Kant, "The Leningrad Reflexion on Inner Sense," p. 253; and Henrich, "Identity of the Subject," p. 267, for support for this reading of Kant.

82. Jean-Paul Sartre, *Being and Nothingness* [*L'Etre et le Néant*, 1943], trans. Hazel E. Barnes (New York: Philosophical Library, 1956), p. lii. All future references to this work will be noted in the text with BN and the page number.

83. For Sartre and Kant it is not an object at the level of reflective consciousness either. The self as subject is unknowable for both.

84. Jean-Paul Sartre, *The Transcendence of the Ego* [*La Transcendance de l'ego*, 1936], trans. Forrest Williams and Robert Kirkpatrick (New York: Farrar, Straus and Giroux, 1957), p. 33. All future references to this work will be noted in the text with TE and the page number.

85. Strawson, Henrich, and Karl Ameriks, *Kant's Theory of Mind: An Analysis of the Paralogisms of Pure Reason* (Oxford: Clarendon, 1982), all argue this point with regard to Kant.

86. Another difference in their analyses of the unity of consciousness is that for Sartre the intentional object unifies consciousness (TE, p. 38), whereas for Kant it is the constitution of the object through the use of concepts that provides the unity of consciousness.

87. Rosenberg, *The Thinking Self*, especially chapter 2 and p. 70. Rosenberg (p. 70) points out that Kant sees transcendental self-consciousness as part of the structure of intentional consciousness, but he seems not to have understood that for Sartre pre-reflective self-consciousness is also part of the structure of intentional consciousness. Rosenberg finds Sartre's notion of pre-reflective or non-positional self-awareness puzzling and mysterious. I will argue in Chapter 3 that Sartre's attempt to give a coherent account of self-consciousness at the pre-reflective level fails.

88. There are other differences between Sartre's and Kant's accounts of self-consciousness as well. For Kant self-consciousness, whether transcendental or empirical, is not direct but is mediated by representations. In the former case it is mediated by the representation of the 'I' as identical through time. In the latter case it is mediated by representations in inner sense. For Sartre, consciousness, whether of the self or of the world, is unmediated by mental representations. It is direct and immediate. Another difference is that for Kant the self-consciousness of consciousness grounds the unity of consciousness and the identity of the self. For Sartre, however, the self-consciousness of consciousness is the basis, as I explain in Chapter 2, for the duality that is somehow inherent in the unity of consciousness and for the lack of self-identity that characterizes the for-itself.

THE FORCE OF THE CLAIM

1. Sartre is not interested in whether there are or can be other beings besides humans who are or can be conscious and hence self-conscious. Nonhuman animals, for example, are simply left out of Sartre's account.

2. The reason Sartre talks about 'consciousness' or 'the for-itself' rather than an 'I' or a 'self' is because self-consciousness is originally a consciousness of consciousness, not a consciousness of an ego or empirical self. For a good discussion of why Sartre uses the terminology of being-for-itself and being-in-itself, see Joseph S. Catalano, *A Commentary on Jean-Paul Sartre's "Being and Nothingness"* (New York: Harper and Row, 1974), pp. 43–44.

3. For a good discussion of positional and non-positional and pre-reflective and reflective consciousness, see Phyllis Sutton Morris, "Sartre on the Self-Deceiver's

Translucent Consciousness," *Journal of the British Society for Phenomenology* 23 (May 1992): 103–19.

4. Given the briefness of this discussion of Husserl's phenomenological method, I cannot help but oversimplify. Husserl discusses this method in such works as *Ideas: General Introduction to Pure Phenomenology* [*Ideen zu einer reinen Phänomenologie und phänomenologischen Philosophie*, 1913], trans. W. R. Boyce Gibson (London: George Allen and Unwin, 1931), and *Cartesian Meditations: An Introduction to Phenomenology* [*Méditations cartésiennes*, 1931], trans. Dorian Cairns (The Hague: Martinus Nijhoff, 1960).

5. Of course, there are other differences between Husserl and Sartre. For example, Husserl used the phenomenological method to achieve the epistemological certainty that Descartes was after. That is not the goal Sartre is pursuing. Husserl also believed one must engage in phenomenological description from an assumptionless point, a point without a point of view, so to speak—Nagel's "view from nowhere." Sartre denies we could achieve such a point.

6. What the phenomenological reduction comes to for Sartre is the rejection of the transcendental ego (TE, p. 53). That is very different from what the phenomenological reduction was for Husserl, which explains the controversy over whether Sartre rejects the phenomenological reduction. See, for example, Thomas W. Busch, *The Power of Consciousness and the Force of Circumstances in Sartre's Philosophy* (Bloomington: Indiana University Press, 1990), pp. 10–11, and Maurice Natanson, "Phenomenology and Existentialism: Husserl and Sartre on Intentionality," in *Phenomenology*, ed. Joseph J. Kockelmans (Garden City, N.Y.: Doubleday, 1967), p. 346.

7. I do not mean to imply that there are no philosophical arguments offered in *Being and Nothingness*. But the descriptions stand out more clearly. The arguments advanced by Sartre must sometimes be reconstructed from various remarks made throughout the text. I attempt such reconstructions in later chapters.

8. Of course, Sartre maintained this claim in works written earlier than *Being and Nothingness*, but I will focus on its use in this work alone.

9. We have seen in Chapter 1 that Descartes's view has more subtlety to it than the standard view implies.

10. Sartre takes himself to have refuted a certain form of realism as well, given his discussion of the nature of consciousness. A realism which holds that consciousness and its objects are two separate entities must be false given the intentionality of consciousness and given the fact that for Sartre consciousness, although it is absolute, is not a substance.

11. In note 21 to this chapter, I discuss in detail how these two features are connected.

12. Sartre claims that a human being must *be freedom* rather than simply claiming a human being must be *free* because he thinks that freedom is not just one characteristic among others that humans possess but is the very being of human reality (BN, p. 25).

13. Sartre points out that in this early section of *Being and Nothingness*, he is

dealing with freedom only in connection with the problem of nothingness. He returns to the question of human freedom in much more detail toward the end of the book.

14. Sartre uses parentheses around the 'of' in "consciousness (of) believing," for example, to indicate that he is referring to the self-consciousness of belief at the pre-reflective level. For Sartre, consciousness is non-thetically conscious of itself at this level.

15. In later chapters I will examine views that run counter to this one.

16. There is not, for Sartre, a universal past that is particularized in concrete pasts. It is the other way around. There are particular pasts first, and we unite these to form *the past*.

17. Of course, the for-itself *is* its past in the mode of not being it. The for-itself both is and is not its past in the sense that although the past defines a person in the present, a person is always free to transcend the past and the self-definition one's past imposes on oneself. This point was made in the earlier section on human freedom and becomes even clearer in the later section of the book where Sartre returns once again to the issue of human freedom.

18. Just as the for-itself is and is not its past, so too, for Sartre, it is and is not its future. I am my (future) possibilities in the sense that they give meaning to my present actions. But I also may not realize those possibilities, and in that sense I am not my future. It is because the for-itself transcends both its past and future that it is freedom.

19. In the last section of this chapter on temporality, Sartre discusses reflection, both pure and impure. Reflection, of course, introduces a different level of self-consciousness. Sartre maintains, however, that reflection is possible because consciousness, at the pre-reflective level, is self-consciousness. In Chapter 3, I will discuss these claims at length.

20. Sartre characterizes knowledge alternately as the presence of the in-itself to consciousness and as the presence of consciousness to being. He uses "presence to _____ ." to indicate the intentionality of consciousness.

21. Sartre made clear in the introduction to *Being and Nothingness* that both the intentionality of consciousness and the self-consciousness of consciousness were essential characteristics of consciousness. Within his discussion of what he calls "the circuit of selfness" at the end of the section on the immediate structures of the for-itself and again within his discussion of knowledge in this chapter on transcendence, he elucidates the relationship between the two. To say that consciousness is intentional is to say that it must have an object. Because consciousness just is, on Sartre's view, presence to being, there must be a being to which consciousness is present. But for consciousness to be present to being, it must be conscious of itself as not being the being to which it is present. Hence intentionality is possible only if consciousness is self-consciousness. However, the relationship goes both ways. "In order to be non-thetic self-consciousness, consciousness must be a thetic consciousness *of* something" (BN, p. 172). For Sartre the for-itself makes itself known to itself by means of the in-itself. It is through the in-itself that the for-itself exists, but it is

also through the for-itself that the in-itself exists as a world. For there to be a world, there must be a being whose presence to the world is presence to self, and for a being to be presence (to self and world), there must be objects of consciousness. For there to be presence to _____, consciousness must be conscious *of itself* as (1) consciousness of the object to which it is present, and (2) not being the object to which it is present. Sartre made the first requirement clear in his introduction. In this section on transcendence he discusses the second requirement. Sartre comes close to collapsing the two characteristics of consciousness when he says "the reflected causes itself to be qualified *outside* next to a certain being as *not being* that being. This is precisely what we mean by 'to be consciousness (of) something' " (BN, p. 174). Indeed, the collapsing of the distinction between the intentionality of consciousness and the self-consciousness of consciousness at the pre-reflective level would follow from Sartre's contention that consciousness of an object and consciousness of self as consciousness of an object are one and the same consciousness pre-reflectively. To discuss the intentionality of consciousness and to discuss the self-consciousness of pre-reflective consciousness are two ways of approaching the same thing. Although my focus in this chapter and indeed in the entire book is on the self-consciousness of consciousness, it is not my intention to deny this dual approach to consciousness that is present in Sartre's work.

22. Sartre begins this discussion of motion with the following question: "What must be the being of the moving body in order for its quiddity to remain unchanged while in its being the moving body is distinct from a being at rest?" (BN, p. 210). His answer to this question is more complicated than I've indicated in the text, but my discussion of his answer captures the gist of it.

Sartre considers motion in the context of his discussion of universal time. Without motion, the present would be inapprehensible. It is motion, on Sartre's view, that allows us to distinguish what is from what was. Within this discussion of universal time, Sartre expands the examination of temporality that he began in the previous chapter. He argues once again that the temporality of the world is a reflection of the temporal structure that the for-itself is. In itself, being is atemporal. It is because the for-itself is a being which drags its past with it into the present and which projects itself beyond the present into the future that the objects of consciousness are perceived as having a past and are pointed toward a future. Although I discover temporality outside myself and hence perceive it as objective, Sartre continues to maintain that the time of the world is rooted in the temporal nature of the cogito.

23. Other experiences—fear and anguish, for example—can also have this same effect; but it is on the experience of shame that Sartre focuses.

24. See the second, third, and fourth sections of this chapter for consideration of this point with regard to Sartre's discussion of freedom, lack, possibility, and bad faith.

25. Exactly what Sartre means by one's fundamental project is open to debate. For a good discussion of this concept, see Phyllis Sutton Morris, *Sartre's Concept of a Person: An Analytic Approach* (Amherst: University of Massachusetts Press, 1976).

Sartre discusses Genet's fundamental project in his biography of Genet, *Saint Genet: Actor and Martyr* [*Saint Genet, Comédien et Martyr*, 1952], trans. Bernard Frechtman (New York: New American Library, 1964). Sartre equates consciousness with choice as both are a nihilation of being-in-itself. That is why pre-reflective self-consciousness is characterized earlier as consciousness's awareness of itself as consciousness and here as its awareness of itself as a fundamental choice.

26. The two discussions are connected because, for Sartre, we realize the desire to be through choosing to possess particular objects. It is the role of existential psychoanalysis to figure out why we choose the particular objects we do.

AN INTERNAL CRITIQUE

1. Our consciousness that there exists a dimension of our being which exists for others but which escapes us could perhaps be considered a kind of minimal or degraded form of self-consciousness at the level of our being-for-others. But because we cannot apprehend the self that is created by the look of the other, substantive self-consciousness at this level is beyond our reach.

2. Sartre reiterates these same views when he discusses the two aspects of the body's existence: its existence for itself and its existence for others. It is through the body's existence for others that I discover my body as an object. That is indeed a revelation of its being, Sartre admits, but my body is not revealed as *being me*.

3. Although my experience of the look of the other creates a kind of self-consciousness that escapes me, it is also true for Sartre that pre-reflective self-consciousness is what frees me from the captivity of the other's look (BN, p. 287).

4. The problem Sartre wrestles with here is reflected in a debate between D. M. Armstrong and Sydney Shoemaker on the nature of consciousness and introspection. In Armstrong and Norman Malcolm, *Consciousness and Causality* (Oxford: Basil Blackwell, 1984), Armstrong argues that we should conceive of the introspective awareness that each person has of her own mind on the model of perception. Just as a person can become aware of objects in the world and the states and locations of those objects through perception, so she can become aware of the acts and states of her own mind through a kind of inner perception. This view of introspection rests on a distinction that Armstrong defends most clearly in *A Materialist Theory of the Mind* (London: Routledge and Kegan Paul, 1968). It is a distinction he draws between a state of consciousness and awareness of that state. For Armstrong, pain and awareness of pain, for example, are, in his own words, "distinct existences." He maintains that the "*awareness* (perception) of inner mental states by the person whose states they are . . . is simply a further mental state, a state 'directed' towards the original inner state" (p. 94). What follows from his 'distinct existences' theory is a rejection of the Cartesian position that consciousness is translucent and infallible about its present states. In "Introspection and the Self," in *Midwest Studies in Philosophy*, vol. 10, ed. Peter A. Finch, Theodore E. Uehling Jr., and Howard K. Wettstein (Minneapolis: University of Minnesota Press, 1986), Shoemaker mounts a

sustained attack against the perceptual model of introspection. His criticism of Armstrong's view rests in part on his collapsing, as Sartre does, the distinction between an act or state of consciousness and awareness of that act or state. In the same vein in Shoemaker and Richard Swinburne, *Personal Identity* (Oxford: Basil Blackwell, 1984), Shoemaker argues that the capacity for being conscious of states of consciousness within oneself, such as beliefs and desires, is inseparable from the capacity for having those states. For Shoemaker, as well as for Sartre, being in a mental state (at least of a certain kind, for Shoemaker) and being aware of that state are not logically independent.

5. Later in this chapter I try to make sense of these obscure claims.

6. This attempt by the self to recover the self is really the desire to be God surfacing as reflection: a desire to be a conscious being, a for-itself, a witness to the world and oneself while being the foundation of one's own being and as such coinciding with what one is. This desire, Sartre claims, is a useless passion because the notion of God is self-contradictory.

7. One might think the catharsis-like moment of recognition that can be achieved through existential psychoanalysis might be the catharsis Sartre is referring to here, but Sartre distinguishes the self-knowledge gotten from psychoanalysis from pure reflection, which it may help clarify but to which it is not identical. Every for-itself is capable of the catharsis of pure reflection without the aid of analysis, and consequently the catharsis-like moment in analysis cannot be equated with the catharsis by which the quasi knowledge of reflection is won.

8. Joseph S. Catalano, "Successfully Lying to Oneself: A Sartrean Perspective," *Philosophy and Phenomenological Research* 1 (June 1990): 673–93, considers the use Sartre makes of conceptualization to distinguish consciousness from knowledge in Sartre's discussion of existential psychoanalysis.

9. This distinction might serve as a basis for understanding at least one sense of the difference Sartre sees between non-thetic, thetic, and thematic consciousness. Non-thetic consciousness would be a consciousness that does not involve the use of concepts such as the non-thetic self-consciousness of pre-reflective consciousness. Thetic consciousness would involve the use of concepts, but only as applied to a specific act or behavior. An example of such consciousness would be the self-consciousness of pre-reflective consciousness made thetic at the level of pure reflection. Thematic consciousness would involve the use of concepts as applied to the for-itself as a totality, that is, as a fundamental project. Thematic consciousness is what impure reflection aims at perhaps, but it succeeds in reaching only the unity of the ego and not the deeper unity that one's fundamental project confers on all that one is.

10. What concepts would the for-itself apply to itself that would not amount to its attempting, in bad faith, to transcend itself—an attempt that Sartre says necessarily fails (BN, p. 298)?

11. Sartre does make comments that imply that reflection in general and hence both pure and impure reflection fail. However, the reason he gives for the failure of reflection—that it is an abortive attempt on the part of the for-itself to make

itself an object and identify itself with that object—seems to apply only to his account of impure reflection.

12. Sartre refers to this level of consciousness as non-reflective or unreflective consciousness in *The Transcendence of the Ego*, whereas in *Being and Nothingness* he favors the term pre-reflective consciousness. For the sake of simplicity and because the latter terminology reflects more accurately Sartre's more developed view of consciousness in *Being and Nothingness*, I will refer to this level as pre-reflective.

13. Sartre says later in *Transcendence of the Ego* that the 'I' does appear at the pre-reflective level, but only as an empty I-concept. Sartre also states in *Being and Nothingness* that consciousness at this level is personal, but what makes it personal is not an ego or 'I' within consciousness but the fact that consciousness is always present to itself (BN, p. 103).

14. Sartre argues that if self-consciousness at the pre-reflective level involved one consciousness taking another as its object, an infinite regress would follow because the consciousness that takes the other as its object would, since it too is self-conscious, require another consciousness of which it is the object and so on to infinity. The only way out of this regress is to allow that there can be a consciousness that is not self-conscious. This would be a rejection of Sartre's initial claim that all consciousness is self-consciousness.

15. Sartre explains in his introduction that he uses parentheses around *de* in *conscience de soi* because in speaking of self-consciousness at the pre-reflective level, he does not want the expression *de soi* to indicate knowledge. Yet in this discussion of belief he talks of *knowing* that one believes at the pre-reflective level but still uses the parentheses.

16. See my article "Through the Looking Glass: Sartre on Knowledge and the Pre-Reflective *Cogito*," *Man and World* 22 (1989): 329–43.

17. As I point out in "Through the Looking Glass," the ambiguity of Sartre's analysis of the self-consciousness of pre-reflective consciousness confuses some of his critics. Marjorie Grene, for example, in *Sartre* (New York: New Viewpoints, 1973), attacks Sartre's defense of the claim that all consciousness must be self-consciousness. She reads Sartre as separating consciousness of self from consciousness of the world at the pre-reflective level. But as Sartre points out in the introduction to *Being and Nothingness*, consciousness of the table and consciousness of being conscious of the table, for example, are one and the same. There is only one act of consciousness. It may be that Sartre's illegitimate introduction of epistemological elements in his discussion of pre-reflective consciousness in the sections on bad faith and the immediate structures of the for-itself is responsible for her misreading of Sartre.

18. By way of introducing this analysis of the for-itself's presence to itself, Sartre examines the use of the reflexive pronoun (in French and Latin) used in locutions such as "*il s'ennuie*" (literally, "he bores himself") (BN, p. 76). Sartre's brief remarks here are akin to more recent considerations of what has come to be known as the he-himself problem. Hector-Neri Castañeda first raised this problem in analytic philosophy in a series of articles in the late 1960s, and the discussion has been continued more recently by John Perry and others as well as by philosophers interested in

cognitive science and artificial intelligence research. Issues of self-reference are at the heart of these discussions.

19. Although, for Sartre, the body as it is for itself is part of the structure of non-thetic self-consciousness, I have avoided discussing this dimension of pre-reflective self-consciousness because Sartre claims it cannot be identified with non-thetic self-consciousness (BN, p. 330). I will return to this dimension of pre-reflective self-consciousness in Chapter 5.

AN EXTERNAL CRITIQUE

1. L. Weiskrantz, E. K. Warrington, M. D. Sanders, and J. Marshall, "Visual Capacity in the Hemianopic Field Following a Restricted Occipital Ablation," *Brain* 97 (1974): 709–28.

2. Jean-Paul Sartre, *The Psychology of Imagination* [*L'imaginaire: Psychologie-phénoménologique de l'imagination*, 1940], trans. unknown, 4th paperbound ed. (New York: Citadel, 1966), p. 234. All future references to this work will be given in the text with PI and the page number. I noted in Chapter 3 that in the introduction to *Being and Nothingness*, Sartre uses *consciousness*, not *knowledge*, in speaking of pre-reflective self-consciousness, although in other places in *Being and Nothingness* he slips and describes self-consciousness at the pre-reflective level as knowledge.

3. I am using the male pronoun as generic in discussing the dreamer and the long-distance truck driver because Sartre and Armstrong, respectively, do so.

4. Norman Malcolm, *Dreaming* (London: Routledge and Kegan Paul, 1959; reprinted, New York: Humanities Press, 1962), p. 66.

5. Hilary Putnam, "Dreaming and 'Depth Grammar'," in *Mind, Language, and Reality: Philosophical Papers*, vol. 2 (Cambridge: Cambridge University Press, 1975), pp. 304–24.

6. Daniel Dennett, "Are Dreams Experiences?" *Philosophical Review* 85 (April 1976): 151.

7. D. M. Armstrong, "What Is Consciousness?" in *The Nature of Mind* (Ithaca, N.Y.: Cornell University Press, 1980), p. 60.

8. I have no desire to defend Armstrong's analysis of consciousness, with its reliance on a materialist theory of mind and a perceptual theory of introspection. I am interested in using his example for my own purposes—that is, as a test case for Sartre's claim about the translucency of consciousness.

9. Lawrence Weiskrantz, "Some Contributions of Neuropsychology of Vision and Memory to the Problem of Consciousness," in *Consciousness in Contemporary Science*, ed. A. J. Marcel and Edoardo Bisiach (New York: Oxford University Press, 1988), pp. 186, 187. There have been attacks on this blindsight research, but none would affect the use to which I will be putting this research. Weiskrantz discusses these attacks on pp. 191–92.

10. Although Sartre uses this argument to counter the Freudian view that the drives uncovered by the analyst were unconscious prior to their uncovering, this

argument also works to show that not only must the drives and fundamental choice have been conscious but they must as consciousness have been self-conscious as well. How else could the subject recognize such drives and choices when they are pointed out by the analyst?

11. Alan Allport, "What Concept of Consciousness?" in *Consciousness in Contemporary Science*, ed. Marcel and Bisiach, p. 169.

12. The ability to report one's experiences is debatable even as a positive indicator of consciousness, given the ability of individuals with blindsight to report experiences of which they deny being conscious.

13. Daniel Dennett, *Consciousness Explained* (Boston: Little, Brown, 1991), p. 137.

14. Max Velmans, "Is Human Information Processing Conscious?" *Behavioral and Brain Sciences* 14 (1991): 651–726, including "Open Peer Commentary."

15. Ned Block, "Evidence against Epiphenomenalism," in "Open Peer Commentary" on Velmans, "Human Information Processing," pp. 670–72.

16. Ibid., p. 672 n. 2. See also Mary C. Potter, "Short-Term Conceptual Memory for Pictures," *Journal of Experimental Psychology: Human Learning and Memory* 2 (1976): 509–22.

17. Dennett, *Consciousness Explained*, p. 307.

18. Jeffrey A. Gray, "What Is the Relation between Language and Consciousness?" in "Open Peer Commentary" on Velmans, "Human Information Processing," p. 679.

19. Dan Lloyd, "Consciousness: Only Introspective Hindsight?" in "Open Peer Commentary" on Velmans, "Human Information Processing," p. 686.

20. Graham F. Wagstaff, "No Conscious or Co-Conscious?" in "Open Peer Commentary" on Velmans, "Human Information Processing," p. 700.

21. David M. Rosenthal, "Two Concepts of Consciousness," *Philosophical Studies* 94 (1986): 329–59.

22. Keith Oatley, "On Changing One's Mind: A Possible Function of Consciousness," in *Consciousness in Contemporary Science*, ed. Marcel and Bisiach, pp. 369–89.

23. Robert Van Gulick, "A Functionalist Plea for Self-Consciousness," *Philosophical Review* 97 (April 1988): 149–81. His account, however, splits self-consciousness from introspection and allows even subpersonal symbol-processors to be self-conscious.

24. Roderick Chisholm, *The First Person* (Minneapolis: University of Minnesota Press, 1981).

25. Don Locke, *Myself and Others: A Study in Our Knowledge of Other Minds* (Oxford: Clarendon, 1968).

26. Fred Dretske, "Conscious Experience," *Mind* 102 (April 1993): 263–83.

27. Stephen L. White, "What Is It Like to Be an Homunculus?" *Pacific Philosophical Quarterly* 68 (1987): 148–74, uses this distinction to overcome what he calls "the problem of conscious subsystems" (p. 149), an objection raised against a functionalist account of mind. However, for the purposes of this discussion, I will focus

only on his claim that such a distinction is possible, bypassing the use to which he puts this distinction.

28. Ibid., p. 152.

29. Kathleen V. Wilkes, "_____, Yìshì, Duh, Um, and Consciousness," in *Consciousness in Contemporary Science*, ed. Marcel and Bisiach, p. 35.

30. Thomas Natsoulas, "Conscious Perception and the Paradox of 'Blindsight,' " in *Aspects of Consciousness: Awareness and Self-Awareness*, vol. 3, ed. Geoffrey Underwood (New York: Academic, 1982), pp. 79–109.

31. Marcel Kinsbourne, "Integrated Field Theory of Consciousness," in *Consciousness in Contemporary Science*, ed. Marcel and Bisiach, pp. 239–56.

32. Carlo Umiltà, "The Control Operations of Consciousness," in *Consciousness in Contemporary Science*, ed. Marcel and Bisiach, pp. 334–56.

33. Karl H. Pribram, "Mind, Brain, and Consciousness: The Organization of Competence and Conduct," in *The Psychobiology of Consciousness*, ed. Julian M. Davidson and Richard J. Davidson (New York: Plenum, 1980), pp. 50–51.

34. Wilkes, "_____, Yìshì, Duh, Um, and Consciousness," p. 36.

35. Donald A. Norman and Tim Shallice, "Attention to Action," in *Consciousness and Self-Regulation: Advances in Research and Theory*, vol. 4, ed. Richard J. Davidson, Gary E. Schwartz, and David Shapiro (New York: Plenum, 1986), pp. 1–18.

36. Peter Carruthers, "Brute Experience," *Journal of Philosophy* 86 (May 1989): 258–69.

37. Colin McGinn, *The Problem of Consciousness: Essays toward a Resolution* (Cambridge, Mass.: Blackwell, 1991), pp. 110–13.

38. Natsoulas, "Conscious Perception," p. 98.

39. Ibid., p. 97.

40. The classic cases of blindsight are those in which subjects report that they do not see or even "feel" that anything is present in the blind portion of their visual field. See Weiskrantz, "Contributions of Neuropsychology," p. 189.

41. Velmans, "Human Information Processing," p. 662.

42. Christof Koch and Francis Crick, "Understanding Awareness at the Neuronal Level," in "Open Peer Commentary" on Velmans, "Human Information Processing," p. 683–85.

43. Patricia Smith Churchland, "Consciousness: The Transmutation of a Concept," *Pacific Philosophical Quarterly* 64 (1983): 82. In "Reduction and the Neurobiological Basis of Consciousness," in *Consciousness in Contemporary Science*, ed. Marcel and Bisiach, pp. 273–304, Churchland uses blindsight studies to undermine the obviousness of the belief "that if someone can report on some visual aspect in the environment then he must be consciously aware of it" (p. 288).

44. See Anthony J. Marcel, "Conscious and Unconscious Perception: Experiments on Visual Masking and Word Recognition," *Cognitive Psychology* 15 (1983): 197–237, and "Conscious and Unconscious Perception: An Approach to the Relations between Phenomenal Experience and Perceptual Processes," *Cognitive Psychology* 15 (1983): 238–300.

45. If one wishes to argue that by definition all perception is conscious, then one could simply characterize these cases as involving nonconscious processing of perceptual, or what becomes perceptual, data. The point here is whether it might make sense simply to deny that consciousness is involved in these cases.

46. Indeed, there seems to be mounting evidence to this effect offered, among many other places, in Richard Nisbett and Lee Ross's studies on human inference strategies reported in *Human Inference: Strategies and Shortcomings of Social Judgment* (Englewood, N.J.: Prentice-Hall, 1980). See Churchland, "Consciousness: The Transmutation of a Concept," for a good overview of this kind of evidence.

REMEMBERING THE BODY

1. Sartre has a lot more to say about the body as an object in the world than about its nature as the subject of consciousness. In the section of *Being and Nothingness* entitled "Our Concrete Relations with Others," he does take seriously that we are bodies. However, in that section he deals with our bodily existence in terms of our existence in the world as objects, open to the look of the other.

2. John R. Searle, "Minds, Brains, and Programs," *Behavioral and Brain Sciences* 3 (1980): 417–24. I leave unstated Searle's actual argument against functionalism based on his Chinese room example, of which there is already plenty of discussion. More recently, Searle argues against computational theories of mind in chapter 9 of *The Rediscovery of the Mind* (Cambridge: MIT Press, 1992).

3. Gerald M. Edelman, *Neural Darwinism: The Theory of Neuronal Group Selection* (New York: Basic, 1987). See especially pp. 8 and 24.

4. Gerald M. Edelman, *The Remembered Present: A Biological Theory of Consciousness* (New York: Basic, 1989), p. xx.

5. Ibid., p. 258. These current theories that tie consciousness to the body and in particular to the brain are indebted to William James's account of consciousness. Edelman acknowledges this debt in ibid., pp. 4–5.

6. Although Edelman focuses on brain activity in developing his theory of consciousness, he does agree with Hilary Putnam's point that Edelman puts this way: "the brain and nervous system cannot be considered in isolation from the world and social interactions" (ibid., p. 29). He also brings in language and social interactions when he analyzes a form of consciousness he calls "higher-order consciousness."

7. See, for example, McGinn, *Problem of Consciousness*, p. 14, where he says consciousness is a property of the brain. In contradistinction to this way of speaking, Edelman cautions against directly ascribing "mentalistic terms to the operations of the brain itself rather than the person" *(Remembered Present*, p. 213).

8. For a discussion of the role of the body in consciousness in both Sartre and Wittgenstein, see my article "Hell and the Private Language Argument: Sartre and Wittgenstein on Self-Consciousness, the Body, and Others," *Journal of the British Society for Phenomenology* 18 (May 1987): 120–32.

9. Of course, many other philosophers in both traditions emphasize the role of the body. I am simply giving two examples.

10. Mark Johnson, *The Body in the Mind: The Bodily Basis of Meaning, Imagination, and Reason* (Chicago: University of Chicago Press, 1987), p. xxxvii.

11. Ibid., p. 137. He adds that understanding "is equally a matter of our embeddedness within culture, language, institutions, and historical traditions." I am not, however, dealing with every level and aspect of consciousness and self-consciousness. As mentioned in the introduction to this book, I do not address the issue of the social dimension of consciousness, although it is an extremely important consequence of the fact that consciousness is embodied.

12. Natika Newton, "The Sensorimotor Theory of Cognition," *Pragmatics and Cognition* 1 (1993): 267–68.

13. Ibid., pp. 268–69.

14. In a conversation I had with Newton in 1986, she suggested using the duck/rabbit drawing to illustrate this presence/absence structure. Probably the most famous use of this drawing in philosophical discourse is Wittgenstein's in *Philosophical Investigations*, trans. G. E. M. Anscombe (New York: Macmillan, 1953), pt. 2, sec. 11.

15. Peter Caws, *Sartre* (Boston: Routledge and Kegan Paul, 1979), pp. 106–7.

16. Phyllis Sutton Morris, "Sartre on the Self-Deceiver's Translucent Consciousness," *Journal of the British Society for Phenomenology*, 23 (May 1992): 103–19.

17. Caws, *Sartre*, pp. 96–97.

18. Ibid., p. 97.

19. For Merleau-Ponty as well, neither physiology alone nor psychology alone can explain human consciousness and subjectivity. See Maurice Merleau-Ponty, *Phenomenology of Perception* [*Phénoménologie de la perception*, 1945], trans. Colin Smith (London: Routledge and Kegan Paul, 1962), pp. 76–77, for example.

20. Owen Flanagan, *Consciousness Reconsidered* (Cambridge: MIT Press, 1992), p. 11.

21. Descartes, of course, thinks reflection reveals that the basis of consciousness is immaterial, but Kant, among others, argues against this view.

22. Natika Newton, "Consciousness, Qualia, and Reentrant Signalling," *Behavior and Philosophy* 19 (Spring/Summer 1991): 21–41, is a good example of someone who offers a plausible neuroscientific explanation of some of the most basic phenomenal properties of conscious perceptual experience.

23. Merleau-Ponty, in his later work, recognizes the need to bridge this gap between the self as subject and the self as object. McGinn in *The Problem of Consciousness* argues that this gap cannot be bridged because we can never know how matter produces consciousness. Sartre makes a similar remark at the end of *Being and Nothingness*. For McGinn consciousness will remain a mystery even though it is a natural phenomenon. Flanagan, in chapter 6 of *Consciousness Reconsidered*, does a good job of setting up the structure of McGinn's arguments and then evaluating them.

24. Of course, for Sartre all intentionality is bodily, at least in the sense that the source of intentionality and consciousness is simply the body and its presence to the world.

25. Henrietta C. Leiner, Alan L. Leiner, and Robert S. Dow, "Cognitive and Language Functions of the Human Cerebellum," *Trends in Neurosciences* 16, no. 11 (1993): 444–54, defend the still controversial thesis that cognitive function is an expansion of motor function. They offer evidence that the cerebellum, which until recently most neuroscientists thought was involved in motor functions alone, is actually involved in cognition and language. See also the *New York Times*, 8 November 1994, B5, for new evidence that appears to support this thesis.

26. Dennett, *Consciousness Explained*, p. 174.

27. Ibid.

28. Flanagan, *Consciousness Reconsidered*, p. 199.

29. Edelman, *Remembered Present*, p. 93.

30. In Chapter 6 I will offer an extended discussion of the ways in which biological theories of consciousness, such as Edelman's, can be used to support some of Sartre's phenomenologically based analysis of consciousness.

31. Searle, *Intentionality*, p. 36. Searle capitalizes "Intentionality" and "Intentional" to make clear that he is referring to intentionality as directedness (p. 3).

32. Searle, *Rediscovery of the Mind*, p. 195.

33. Searle, *Intentionality*, p. 40. In addition, the intentional content of perceptual experience is propositional because, like belief and desire, there are conditions of satisfaction for perceptual experiences. See especially *Intentionality*, p. 41.

34. Ibid., p. 45.

35. Sartre defines action in terms of intentionality (BN, p. 433).

36. Searle, *Intentionality*, p. 106.

37. Johnson, *Body in the Mind*, pp. 209, 29, 75, 102, 138.

38. Ibid., pp. 186, 188.

39. Gareth Evans, *The Varieties of Reference*, ed. John McDowell (New York: Oxford University Press, 1982), pp. 153, 153, 153–54, 155, and 156, where Evans quotes Charles Taylor, "The Validity of Transcendental Arguments," *Proceedings of the Aristotelian Society* 79 (1978–79): 154.

40. Ibid., p. 151.

41. Ibid., p. 163.

42. Ibid., p. 222.

43. Adrian Mirvish, "Sartre on Perception and the World," *Journal of the British Society for Phenomenology* 14 (May 1983): 158–74, explains Sartre's adherence to the Gestalt view that we *naturally* individuate objects by drawing them out from their surroundings. Sartre agrees with the Gestaltists that we do not use learning and judgment to organize sensations into particular objects. This individuation, then, goes on at a pre-predicative level on Sartre's view. Mirvish's discussion of this Sartrean position brings out Sartre's commitment to the existence of nonconceptual elements in experience.

44. Christopher Peacocke, "Scenarios, Concepts, and Perceptions," in *The Con-*

tents of Experience: Essays on Perception, ed. Tim Crane (Cambridge: Cambridge University Press, 1992), pp. 107, 127, 127, 128. In the last part of this article, Peacocke shows the role of scenario content—spatial representational content—in action.

45. Adrian Mirvish, "Sartre, Hodological Space, and the Existence of Others," *Research in Phenomenology* 14 (1984): 149–73, does a good job of explaining how Sartre utilizes this notion in *Being and Nothingness*.

46. Ibid., p. 163.

47. Evans, *Varieties of Reference*, p. 266.

48. Ibid.

49. Peacocke, "Scenarios," p. 125, disagrees with Cussins's interpretation of Evans. He claims that for Evans perceptual "experiences are conceived as not having a conceptual content at all." I think this is too strong a reading of Evans. Cussins's reading of Evans is more accurate.

50. Adrian Cussins, "The Connectionist Construction of Concepts," in *The Philosophy of Artificial Intelligence*, ed. Margaret A. Boden (Oxford: Oxford University Press, 1990), p. 368.

51. Adrian Cussins, "Nonconceptual Content and the Elimination of Misconceived Composites!" *Mind and Language* 8 (Summer 1993): 234. Cussins sees his position as in line with Paul Churchland's and Patricia Churchland's eliminative materialism, although on the standard interpretation of the Churchlands' view, they might seem strange bedfellows for Cussins. But Cussins offers an interpretation of their eliminative materialism that makes it more palatable, arguing that they do not claim that there are no such entities as beliefs and desires, for example. Rather, they contend that a certain theory about entities such as beliefs and desires, the propositional attitude theory, is mistaken because it fails to take into account the embodiment of belief and meaning. It is Cussins's belief in the embodiment of meaning and belief that leads him to identify his position, in certain respects, with the Churchlands' view.

52. Adrian Cussins, "Content, Embodiment, and Objectivity: The Theory of Cognitive Trails," *Mind* 101 (October 1992): 655,

53. Ibid., p. 669.

54. Merleau-Ponty, *Phenomenology*, pp. 254, xv, 254, 137.

55. See Ibid., p. 137.

56. Ibid., p. 110.

57. Ibid., p. 72.

58. Ibid., p. x.

59. Ibid., pp. 96–97.

60. Ibid., p. 205.

61. Ibid., pp. 242, 298, 403. Merleau-Ponty scholars who criticize Sartre for forgetting the body are inspired perhaps by remarks like the one Merleau-Ponty made in *The Visible and the Invisible* [*Le visible et l'invisible*, 1964], trans. Alphonso Lingis (Evanston: Northwestern University Press, 1968), p. 77: "The analytic of Being and Nothingness is the seer who forgets that he has a body."

62. Rudolf Bernet, "The Subject in Nature: Reflections on Merleau-Ponty's *Phe-*

nomenology of Perception," trans. R. P. Buckley and S. Spileers, in *Merleau-Ponty in Contemporary Perspective,* ed. Patrick Burke and Jan Van der Veken (Dordrecht, Netherlands: Kluwer Academic Publishers, 1993), p. 58. See also John F. Bannon, *The Philosophy of Merleau-Ponty* (New York: Harcourt, Brace, and World, 1967), for a good discussion of the differences between Sartre and Merleau-Ponty on the relation between the for-itself and the in-itself, especially pp. 134–36.

63. Merleau-Ponty, *Phenomenology,* p. 80.

64. Ibid., p. 87.

65. M. C. Dillon, "The Unconscious: Language and World," in *Merleau-Ponty in Contemporary Perspective,* ed. Burke and Van der Veken, p. 79.

66. Merleau-Ponty, *Phenomenology,* p. 241.

67. Merleau-Ponty's claim that the body is the original source of meaning also allows him to overcome the opposition between the for-itself and the in-itself. Bernet does a good job of showing how this is so. It would require too long a diversion to discuss Merleau-Ponty's view that the body "uses its own parts as a general system of symbols for the world, and through which we can consequently 'be at home in' that world, 'understand' it and find significance in it" (ibid., p. 237).

68. Merleau-Ponty, *Visible,* pp. 139, 205, 271, 35.

69. Edelman, *Remembered Present,* pp. 98, 159, 195.

70. See R. C. Oldfield and O. L. Zangwell, "Head's Concept of the Schema and Its Application in Contemporary British Psychology," *British Journal of Psychology* 32 (1942): 267–86, for a discussion of Head's concept and the empirical data he used to support the existence of such a schema. They point out that on Head's view, when we learn to use a new instrument, it gets added to our schemata.

71. Marc Jeannerod, "The Representing Brain: Neural Correlates of Motor Intention and Imagery," *Behavioral and Brain Sciences* 17 (1994): pp. 189, 197, 197. He relies on a variety of evidence to support his hypothesis, including not only neurological evidence but the introspective reports of subjects as well. He relies on Flanagan's natural method. See the "Open Peer Commentary" for criticisms of Jeannerod's views.

72. Newton, "Consciousness, Qualia," p. 31. It is not clear whether she thinks such perception is conscious in every case.

73. Oliver Sacks, "The Disembodied Lady," in *The Man Who Mistook His Wife for a Hat and Other Clinical Tales* (New York: Harper and Row, 1987), p. 51.

74. Ibid., p. 43.

75. Drew Leder, *The Absent Body* (Chicago: University of Chicago Press, 1990), p. 42.

76. G. E. M. Anscombe, "The First Person," in *Metaphysics and the Philosophy of Mind: Collected Philosophical Papers* (Minneapolis: University of Minnesota Press, 1981), 2:31.

77. There are interesting parallels between Anscombe's position and Sartre's view that consciousness is nothingness.

78. Edelman, *Remembered Present,* pp. 102, 169. He refers the reader to the work of J. P. Zubec, *Sensory Deprivation: Fifteen Years of Research* (New York: Irvington,

1969), and G. F. Reed, "Sensory Deprivation," in *Aspects of Consciousness*, vol. 1, *Psychological Issues*, ed. Geoffrey Underwood and Robin Stevens (New York: Academic, 1979), pp. 155–78.

79. Oldfield and Zangwell, "Head's Concept of the Schema," p. 277.

80. Jeannerod, "The Representing Brain," p. 190.

81. Newton, "Consciousness, Qualia," p. 30.

82. Ibid., p. 24.

83. Edelman, *Remembered Present*, p. 65.

84. Maps are "the ordered arrangement and activity of groups of neurons and large fiber tracts projecting onto laminae and nuclei with defined delimitations of function that are found in organisms with brains having a large variety of functions" (Edelman, *Neural Darwinism*, p. 107).

85. I am greatly oversimplifying Edelman's theory because I want to use it only to illustrate the possibility of a biological theory that would ground Sartre's phenomenologically based intuitions. For more detail on reentrant signaling and neural maps, see *Neural Darwinism*, especially chapters 1 and 5, and *Remembered Present*, especially chapter 4.

86. Newton, "Consciousness, Qualia," p. 33.

87. In such a case the body as subject of consciousness takes its own input as an object of consciousness.

88. Nonhuman animal consciousness—if such exists—would be a case of primary consciousness, to use Edelman's terminology. Because of the blending of self-input and world input, there would be a kind of self-consciousness even with nonhuman animal consciousness. An advantage of a biological theory of consciousness such as Edelman's is that we can develop a theory of the self-consciousness of consciousness that allows for a continuum between human and nonhuman consciousness.

89. Although I have argued in this chapter that a study of bodily intentionality supports Sartre's belief that all consciousness involves a presence to oneself, it is just as true that consciousness also requires an absence of one's bodily self as well. Extending Merleau-Ponty's analysis of the lived body, Leder, in *The Absent Body*, does an admirable job of showing a variety of ways in which consciousness is grounded in and necessitates the disappearance of the body. He notes the focal disappearance of sensory organs when they are the origin of a perceptual field and the more general background disappearance of the body in perception and action. These are forms of absence explored by both Sartre and Merleau-Ponty. I referred earlier in this chapter to these forms of disappearance as part of the presence/absence structure of bodily self-consciousness. But Leder explores even more dramatic forms of bodily disappearance in his discussion of the visceral body. Processes such as digestion, respiration, and circulation of blood are all necessary to the maintenance of the body as a subject of consciousness, yet they are processes unavailable, for the most part, to conscious awareness. In sleep as well the body disappears from consciousness by and large. Yet sleep is absolutely necessary for the maintenance of a body capable of consciousness. Leder says that "the body disappears both as a seat of consciousness

and as a site of an unconscious vitality" (p. 55). He speculates that the bodily absence that consciousness requires might have fueled the Cartesian notion of a disembodied self. It strikes me that it might also contribute to a partial explanation of Sartre's adherence to two apparently inconsistent beliefs: his belief in the embodied nature of consciousness, and his belief that consciousness is nothingness.

90. Newton, "Consciousness, Qualia," p. 37.

BIOLOGY AND PHENOMENOLOGY

1. Edelman, in *Remembered Present*, p. 30, says that his theory of consciousness is one that "takes as its canonical reference human phenomenal experience and the ability to report that experience by language."

2. Ibid, p. 70. Gerald M. Edelman and Vernon B. Mountcastle proposed this idea of reentrant signaling in *The Mindful Brain* (Cambridge: MIT Press, 1978). Newton, "Consciousness, Qualia," pp. 26–27, gives a good overview of several scientists who think feedback loops from higher to lower areas that process sensory input are necessary for consciousness.

3. Of course, my appeal to Edelman's theory of reentrant signaling does not account for all of what Sartre means by his claim that consciousness must nihilate itself and its object to be present to both. Part of what Sartre means by this claim is that the for-itself must be *aware* that it is not *the object of which it is conscious* and that it is not *consciousness of this object* either, although that is all the self comes to for Sartre at the pre-reflective level. Edelman's theory gives us a kind of biologically guaranteed separation *and* union between consciousness, on the one hand, and the self and the world, on the other. But it is not clear that this theory could account for the *awareness* of this odd mixture of separation and union Sartre claims characterizes even pre-reflective consciousness. My contention in this chapter is not that every claim about consciousness that Sartre offers in the course of a phenomenology-based analysis of consciousness can be accounted for or supported by reference to a biological theory of consciousness. I am simply suggesting ways in which biology and phenomenology can reinforce each other. In particular, I am suggesting ways in which the notion of bodily self-consciousness that I introduced in Chapter 5 can shore up and add substance and intelligibility to at least some of the points Sartre makes in his phenomenology-based analysis of consciousness.

4. Francis Crick, *The Astonishing Hypothesis: The Scientific Search for the Soul* (New York: Simon and Schuster, 1994), and Crick and Christof Koch, "Towards a Neurobiological Theory of Consciousness," *Seminars in the Neurosciences* 2 (1990): 263–75.

5. Crick, *Astonishing Hypothesis*, p. 22.

6. Ibid. pp. 16–19. Newton, "Consciousness, Qualia," pp. 35–37, gives a good review of the scientists who support the involvement of memory in conscious experience.

7. Flanagan, *Consciousness Reconsidered*, p. 155. On p. 168, he quotes Crick and

Koch, "Towards a Neurobiological Theory," p. 271: "No person has ever existed who was conscious but lacked short-term memory, this being necessary and possibly sufficient for holding an experience long enough to have it, as it were."

8. Edelman, *Remembered Present*, p. 109.

9. Ibid., p. 187.

10. For Sartre, self-consciousness only *separates* consciousness from its past; it does not serve to unite the two. In Sartre's discussion of anguish in part 1, chapter 1 of *Being and Nothingness*, he maintains that it is consciousness of the past that separates the for-itself from the past that it is. For Sartre, I am my past in the sense that what essence I have is my past, and I cannot understand my present self without reference to the past. Yet the past does not determine what I do now or will do. I am separated from my past by my *consciousness* of my past. Sartre gives the example of the gambler who resolves one day to quit gambling (BN, pp. 32–33). The "gambler" is indeed defined by this resolution, and yet it is precisely his consciousness of this resolution that separates him from it. He transcends the choices that create his essence by his consciousness of those choices. On Sartre's view self-consciousness separates rather than unites consciousness and its past. However, both on the biological theories I am examining and on Sartre's view, self-consciousness establishes a relation between present consciousness and its past.

11. William James, *The Principles of Psychology*, vol. 1 (1890; reprint, New York: Dover, 1950). See, for example, pp. 301–5, 341, 371, 400.

12. In addition to perception, I am thinking of such cognitive activities as discrimination, identification, and decision making, for example.

13. Velmans, "Human Information Processing," p. 651 (abstract).

14. Kenneth S. Bowers, "(Un)conscious Influences in Everyday Life and Cognitive Research," in "Open Peer Commentary" on Velmans, "Human Information Processing," p. 672.

15. Richard A. Carlson, "Consciousness and Content in Learning: Missing or Misconceived?" in "Open Peer Commentary" on Velmans, "Human Information Processing," pp. 673–74.

16. Fred Dretske, "Conscious Acts and Their Objects," in "Open Peer Commentary" on Velmans, "Human Information Processing," pp. 676–77.

17. Lloyd, "Consciousness: Only Introspective Hindsight?" p. 686.

18. Gray, "What Is the Relation between Language and Consciousness?" p. 679.

19. See the remarks of other commentators on Velmans for further criticisms of his position.

20. See Daniel Holender, "Semantic Activation without Conscious Identification in Dichotic Listening, Parafoveal Vision, and Visual Masking: A Survey and Appraisal," *Behavioral and Brain Sciences* 9 (1986): 1–66, including "Open Peer Commentary," p. 2.

21. Holender, "Semantic Activation," p. 3.

22. Ibid., p. 1 (abstract); emphasis mine.

23. Ira Fischler, "Knowing and Knowing You Know: Better Methods or Better Models?" in "Open Peer Commentary" on Holender, "Semantic Activition," p. 33.

Many of the commentators on Velmans's 1991 article continue to support Holender's conclusions.

24. Edelman's primary consciousness would be an example of the most basic type of consciousness.

25. Hazel E. Barnes, "Sartre's Concept of the Self," *Review of Existential Psychology and Psychiatry* 17 (1980/81): 41–65.

26. Merleau-Ponty, *Phenomenology*, pp. 87, 433, 85, 453.

27. Ibid., p. 440.

28. For more on this point, see my discussion in Chapter 2 of the section on transcendence in *Being and Nothingness*.

29. Edelman believes that one can accept a biological theory of consciousness and yet make room for a notion of freedom. This freedom is both guaranteed and limited by the biological roots of consciousness. Edelman describes himself as a compatibilist in *The Remembered Present* (p. 261). Consciousness is a biological phenomenon and hence is within the realm of causation. Yet individuals are free for at least three reasons. First, the unique neuronal structure of an individual's brain is determined by both the selective process of genetic development and the effect of experience on the strengthening of certain synaptic connections and the weakening or loss of others. Second, selective neural systems have recategorical memory. So "if an organism has primary consciousness and a concept system . . . past experiences . . . will lead to storage of changes that alter future behavior. . . . This will change patterns of action so that *local* world events may occur that would *never* have spontaneously arisen in the world in the absence of such organisms" (*Remembered Present*, p. 257). A third reason is present with human beings because once you add the acquisition of higher-order consciousness, causal relations are altered again not only in terms of past memories but also in terms of planned actions. These changes within a person can cause changes in the world. Whether these reasons ensure only variability and unpredictability or whether they actually give rise to a substantive kind of freedom I leave undecided. Certainly Sartre would find such a view of freedom unsatisfactory. I offer it as an example of an attempt to make sense of freedom within the context of a biological theory of consciousness.

30. I offer no argument for this view here. That, I'm afraid, would require another book.

Index

Kathleen Wider is Associate Professor of Philosophy at the
University of Michigan at Dearborn.